IMAGES
of America

EAST BRUNSWICK

IMAGES
of America

EAST BRUNSWICK

Mark Nonestied

ARCADIA
PUBLISHING

ISBN 978-0-7385-6325-1

Published by Arcadia Publishing
Charleston, South Carolina

Printed in the United States of America

Library of Congress Catalog Card Number: 2008927252

For all general information contact Arcadia Publishing at:
Telephone 843-853-2070
Fax 843-853-0044
E-mail sales@arcadiapublishing.com
For customer service and orders:
Toll-Free 1-888-313-2665

Visit us on the Internet at www.arcadiapublishing.com

This book is dedicated to the "glory that was the good old days."

Contents

Acknowledgments

There are many people I would like to thank for making this book possible. Alberta Yuhas was kind enough to open up her entire collection of historic photographs, along with her stories of the good old days. Florence Mount, whose vast collection amazed me, rushed much-needed old photographs to me. Jim Giamerse, from Giamerse Farms, was kind enough to lend the final touch of farming photographs that I needed. Grace Auer shared her photographs and stories of growing up in East Brunswick. The Kreamer family donated a large collection of photographs from the late William Kreamer to the collection of the East Brunswick Museum.

I would also like to thank my parents, George and Rosemary, and my brother Todd for the behind-the-scenes help, Dawn Turner for her artistic skill, Carmella Textor, Ken Helsby, Ann Alverez, the East Brunswick Museum Board of Trustees, the Middlesex County Fair Association, and the countless number of other people who have added to my understanding of the history of East Brunswick.

Finally, I would like to thank Christine Arciszewski, who is the binding that holds this book together.

Introduction

East Brunswick Township was incorporated on February 28, 1860. Prior to this time it was part of North Brunswick and Monroe Townships. The area that makes up East Brunswick today was once home to the Lenape, New Jersey's native people, who hunted and fished in the lush fields and streams. Many local residents have found artifacts once belonging to them. Early settlers began arriving around the 1680s, settling in areas accessible to roads and rivers. They built water-powered mills along streams and began to clear trees for agricultural endeavors. Certain areas of what would become East Brunswick began to prosper during the 1700s. The Weston Mills section, located near Interchange 9 of the New Jersey Turnpike, began to grow into a small village, centered around a gristmill. Local farmers would bring grain to this area to be ground into flour. Today not much remains of the old buildings from this section.

The Old Bridge section of East Brunswick, named for an old bridge that spanned the South River, became a village of about 40 buildings by 1840. Sailing vessels would arrive at the docks to be loaded with produce and wood bound for New York City markets. Today this area has been placed on the State and National Register of Historic Places and still has many homes dating back to the 1700s. As more of the forest was cleared, it made way for additional farms, increasing the population. By 1860, the area had grown so much that the formation of a new town, named East Brunswick, was realized.

The growth of the town took place in sections. Attracted by the availability of work provided by Christopher Meyer, a German-born factory owner in Milltown, a large concentration of Germans settled in the Dutch Road section. Street names such as Hardenburg, Dutch (Deutsche), and family names like the Fishers and Hardenburgs reflect this once-ethnic community. The Dunhams Corner Road area was serviced by a school, town hall, and hollowed out tree that provided a drop off for the local mail. Halls Corner, located near Rues Lane and Cranbury Road, was named after J.C. Hall, who operated a local hotel and tavern. Herberts Corner, located near Milltown Road and Ryder Lane, was named for the Herbert family. East Brunswick also had a local horse racing track near present-day Pathmark and Race Track Road.

In 1888, Helmetta formed its own form of government and separated from East Brunswick. In the following years, South River, Spotswood, and part of Milltown also broke away and became separate towns from East Brunswick. By the 1930s, however, East Brunswick began to grow again. New houses and schools were constructed. Several housing developments and major roads were built. After World War II the housing and population booms brought large scale building and construction. The 1950s saw the construction of mass housing developments, a trend that continues to this day. East Brunswick, once a rural farm community, has grown into a large suburban community. It has a proud and fascinating history and remains a community with many ethnic and cultural backgrounds, making it a wonderful and fascinating place to live.

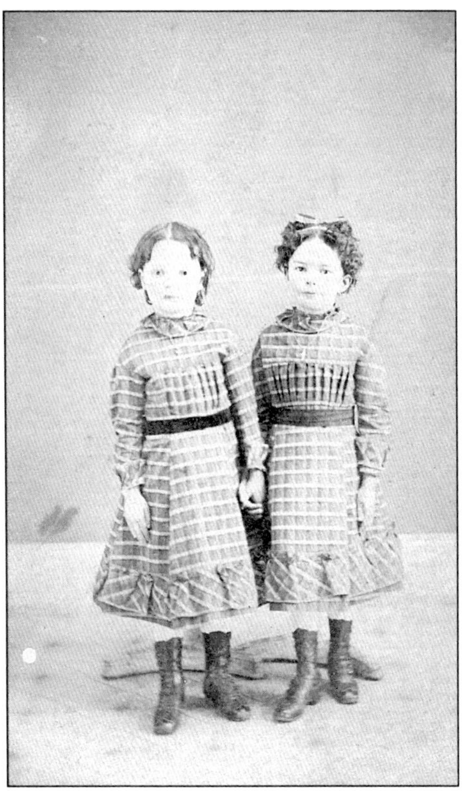

PHOTOGRAPH OF TWO YOUNG GIRLS, C. 1870. Found in the attic of an old East Brunswick house, this photograph was part of a family album. Unfortunately, like so many photographs, the two girls' identities have been lost through time. Their stern gaze is the only reminder of the life they once lived so long ago. (Collection of the East Brunswick Museum.)

One

The Early Years

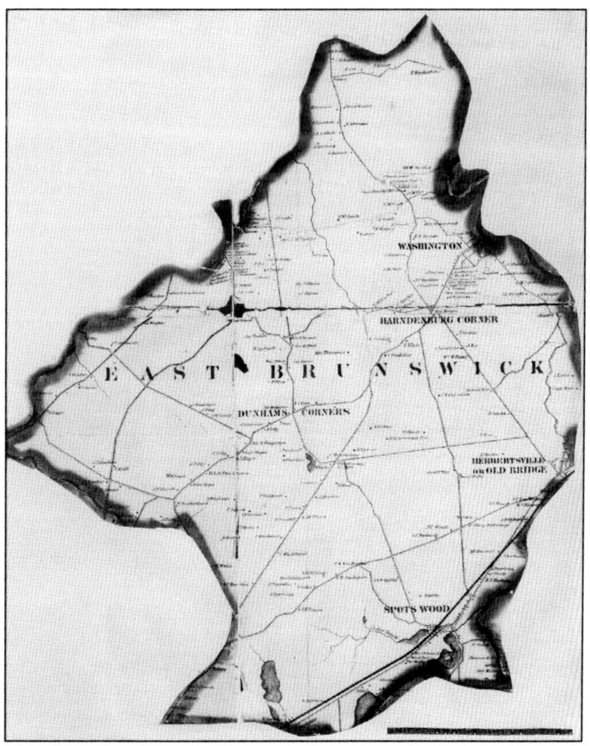

A MAP OF EAST BRUNSWICK, 1861. Created out of North Brunswick and part of Monroe, the township of East Brunswick was incorporated on February 28, 1860. The Old Bridge section near the Old Bridge Turnpike and Main Street is called Herbertsville, after General Obadiah Herbert, an important citizen. Washington, later renamed South River, would break away from East Brunswick in 1898. Helmetta Borough would break away in 1888, Spotswood in 1908, and part of Milltown in the 1890s. (Collection of East Brunswick Museum.)

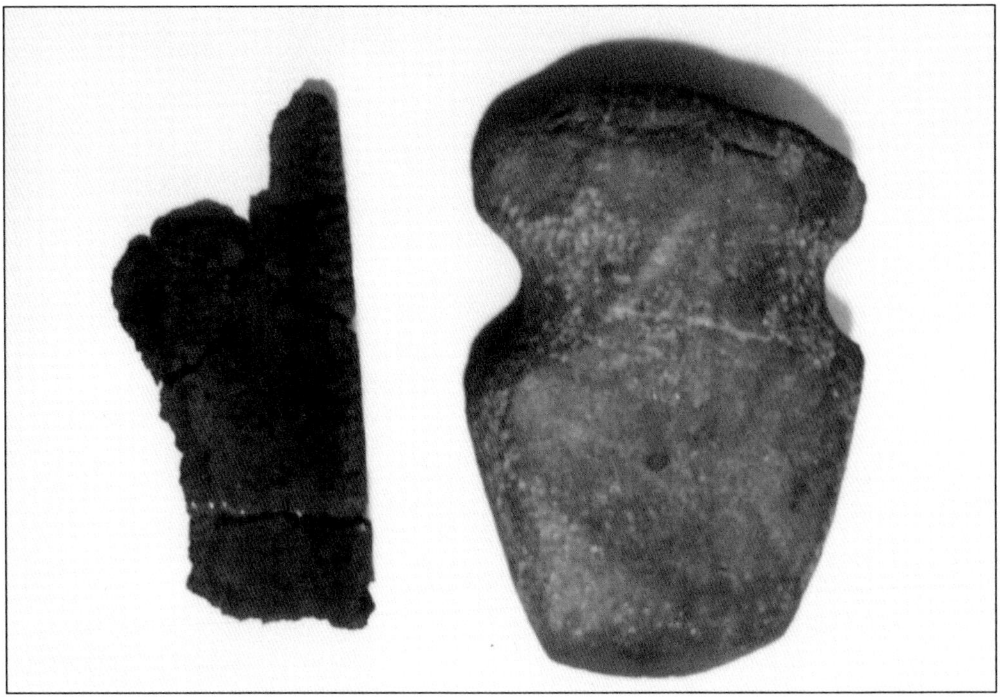

A 3,000-year-old Stone Ax and Reconstructed Pot Rim. Prior to settlement by Europeans, the Lenape, New Jersey's native people, hunted and fished in the streams and forest that make up present-day East Brunswick. (Collection of East Brunswick Museum.)

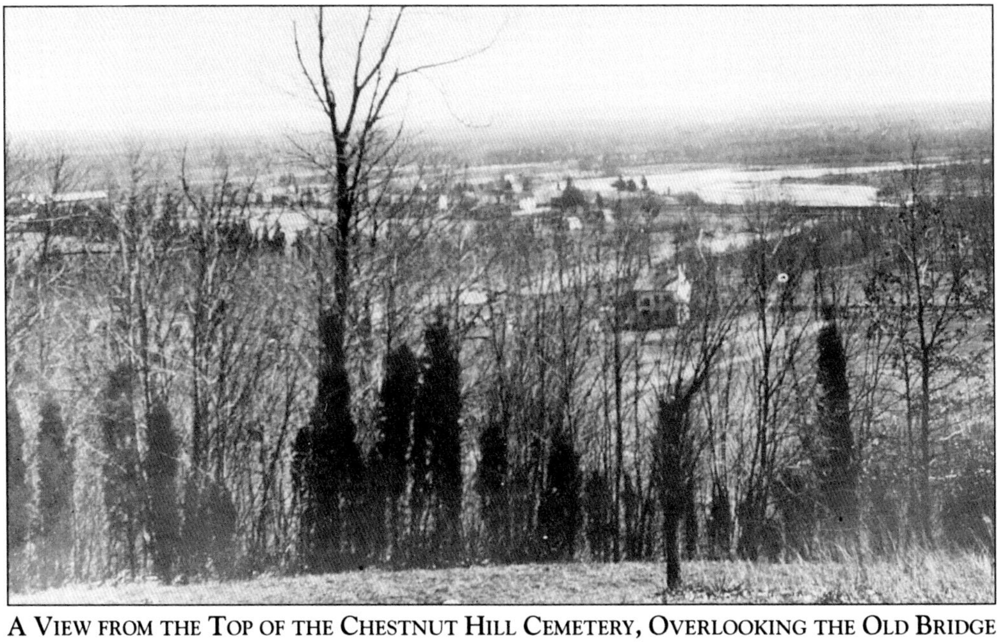

A View from the Top of the Chestnut Hill Cemetery, Overlooking the Old Bridge Section of East Brunswick. This area was ideal for early settlers because of its proximity to well-traveled routes by water and land. With the arrival of the railroad it became a conduit for goods manufactured and grown in the area to be transported to marketplaces in New York City. (Collection of East Brunswick Museum.)

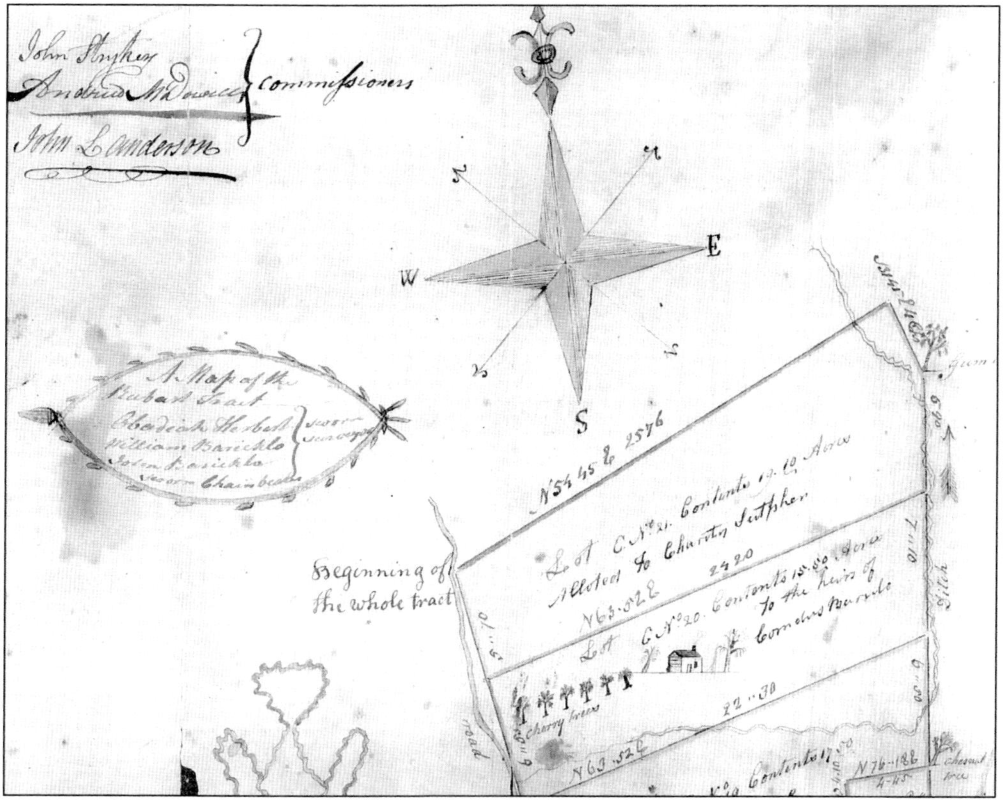

SURVEY MAP BY OBADIAH HERBERT. Mr. Herbert was a surveyor that worked in central New Jersey in the early nineteenth century. For a time, he lived in the Old Bridge section of East Brunswick. This map was drawn by him around 1820 with measurements in chains and links. (Collection of the East Brunswick Museum.)

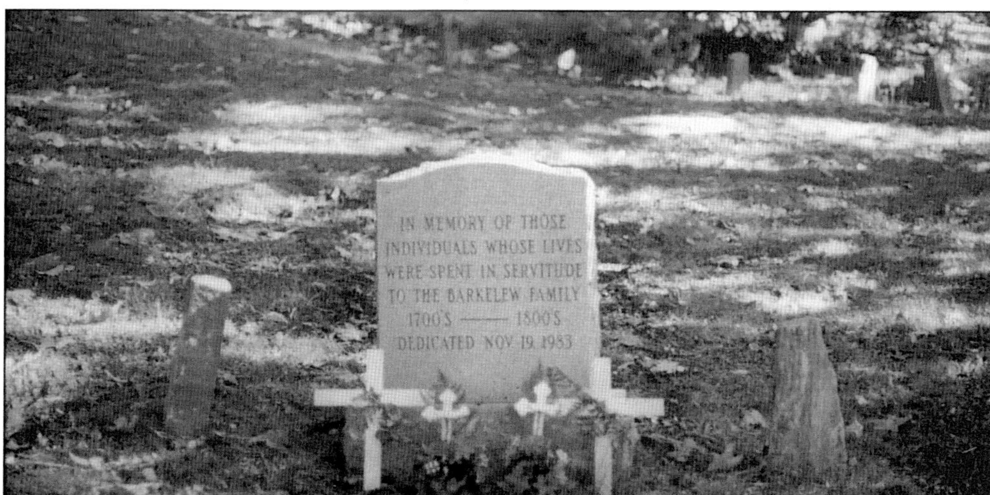

AFRICAN-AMERICAN SLAVE GRAVES. In the early 1980s, several graves were discovered along River Road in East Brunswick. The burials belonged to African-American slaves that worked for the Barkelew family in the late 1700s. The burials were disinterred and moved to Chestnut Hill Cemetery in 1983. (Photograph by Christine Arciszewski.)

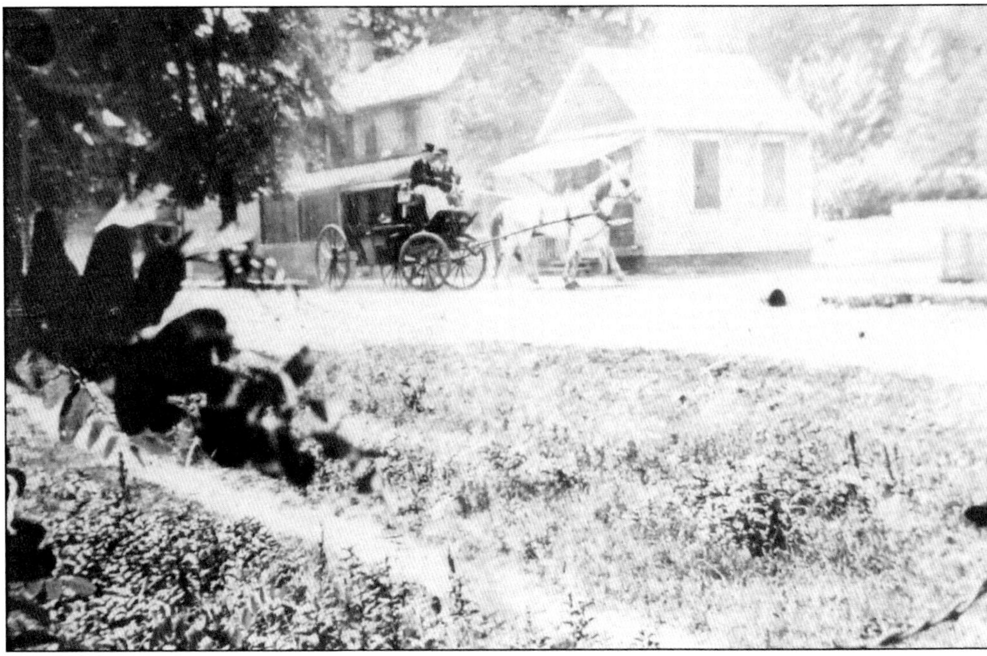

THE ALICE APPLEBY HOUSE AND A STAGE WAGON, C. 1900. Stages would travel along the Old Bridge Turnpike and the Bordentown Amboy Turnpike (Main Street). The Bordentown Amboy Turnpike was laid out between Bordentown and South Amboy, New Jersey, in 1684. Stage lines were established to run on this route by the 1740s. (Collection of East Brunswick Museum.)

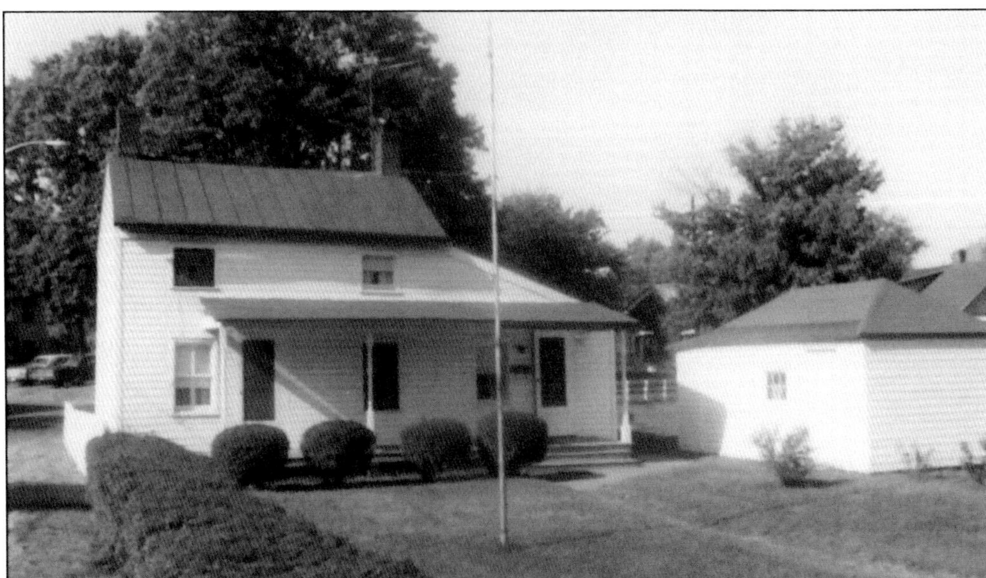

THE SCHAB HOME. This house, originally built in 1790, was owned by Mrs. Schab around the turn of the century. Recent renovations uncovered laudanum bottles in the wall. Laudanum was a painkiller used in the late 1890s that contained opium. The owner discarded the bottles by cutting a hole in the wall and dropping them in. The house still stands today near the corner of Maple Street and Rutgers Road. (Collection of Alberta Yuhas.)

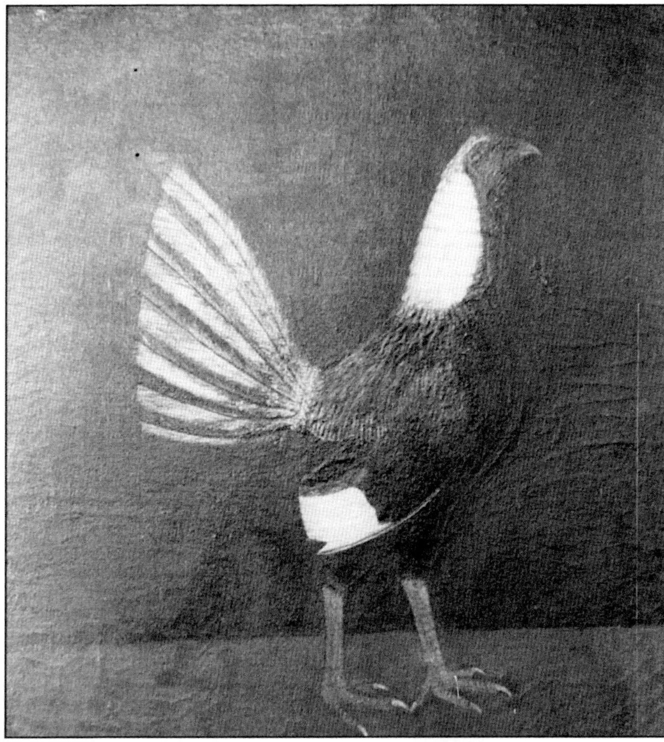

A PAINTING FROM THE 1700S. This painting was found several years ago during renovations in an 18th-century East Brunswick home. It appears to have been painted on part of a sail canvas. Sloops and other types of sailing vessels sailed up to the head of navigation on the South River. This was at the Old Bridge section of East Brunswick. (Photograph by Christine Arciszewski; collection of Barry and Jeanne Cole.)

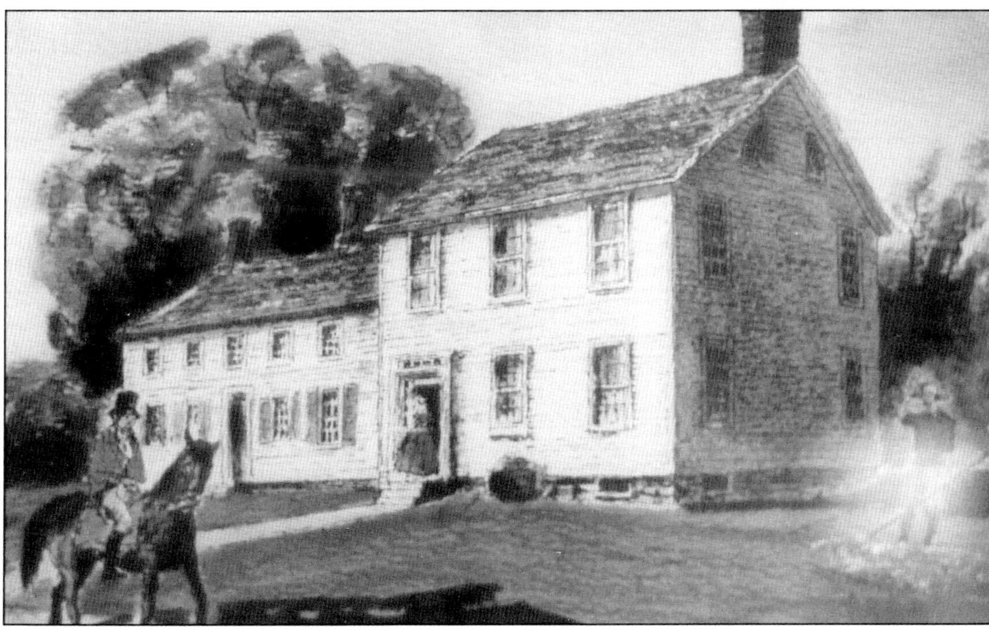

THE ONE-TIME HOME OF OBADIAH HERBERT. This home is located on the corner of the Old Bridge Turnpike and Main Street. Obadiah was an prominent individual in the Old Bridge section, as he surveyed land, owned docks, and built a shipyard along the South River. For some time, this section of town was called Herbertsville in honor of him. He added the right section of the house in 1810. The lower left section is said to have been built in 1763. (Collection of Alberta Yuhas.)

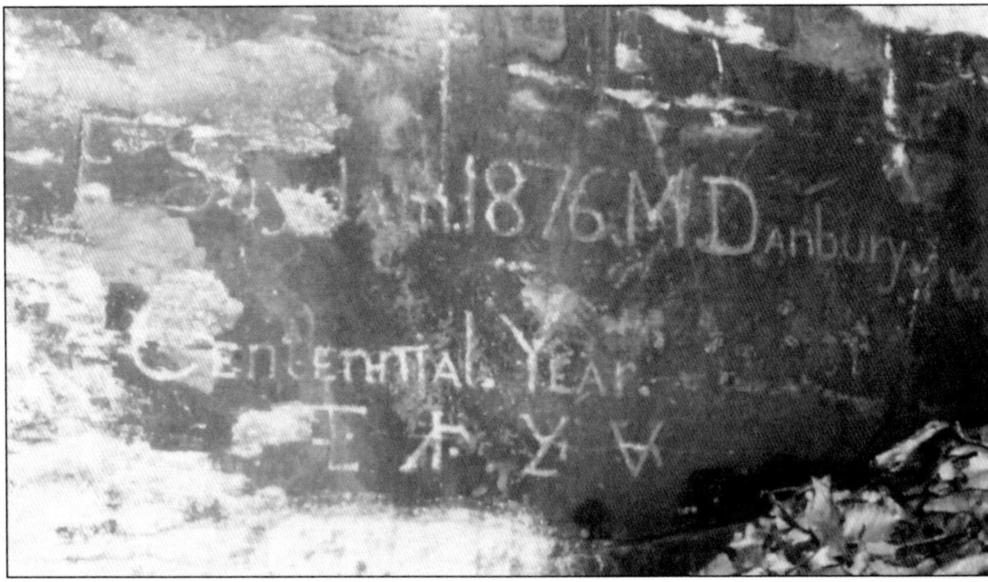

MYSTERIOUS ROCK CARVINGS. In 1876 M. Danbury and Elias Suydam carved their initials, mysterious symbols, and a skull and crossbones along the shale outcroppings on Lawrences Brook, Westons Mill Pond, and the Raritan River. Along with the symbols, the two men also carved the words "Centenial Year" and "Red Rover." *Red Rover* was a pirate novel written by James Fenimore Cooper in 1839. It is not clear why the two men did this. The one thing that can be inferred is that the men were skilled in stone carving and may have been apprentices to local stone carvers. (Photograph by Christine Arciszewski.)

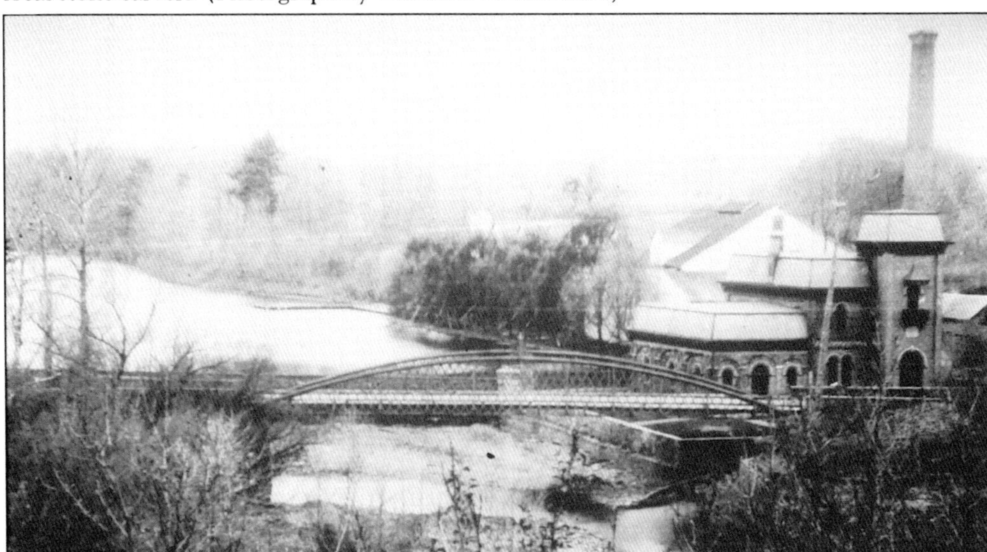

THE WESTON'S MILL SECTION OF EAST BRUNSWICK, LOCATED NEAR THE PRESENT-DAY INTERCHANGE 9 ON THE NEW JERSEY TURNPIKE. The large building to the right of the photograph was a water pumping station for New Brunswick. It was constructed in the 1870s and torn down sometime in the 1930s. The dam that created Weston's Mill pond can still be seen today. The bridge has since been replaced with a more modern bridge and is now part of Tower Center Drive. (Collection of East Brunswick Museum.)

Two

People

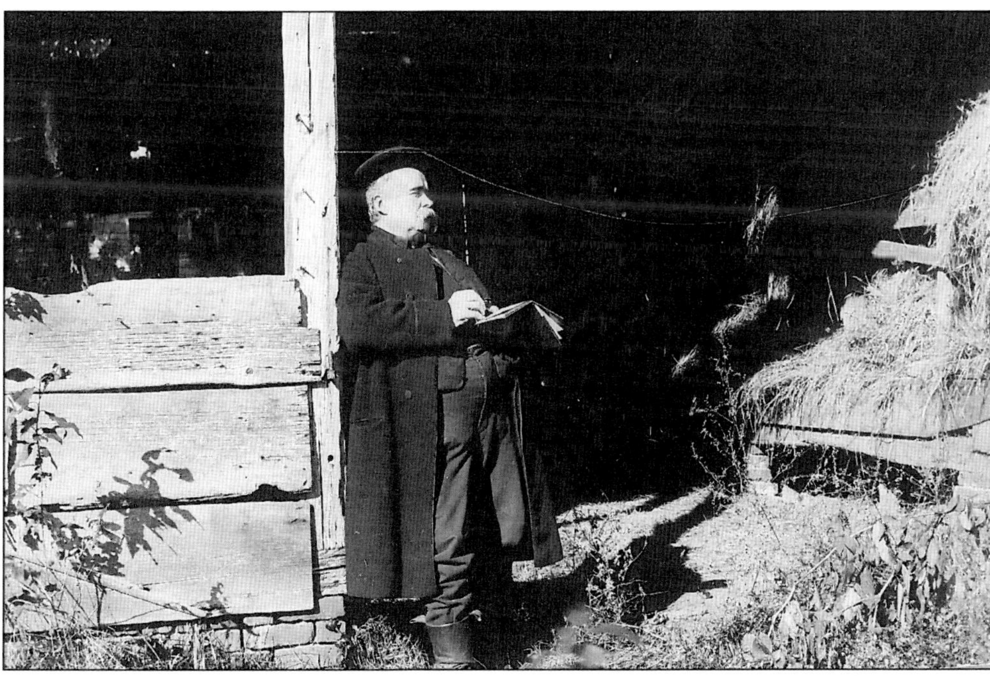

JAMES CRAWFORD THOM, C. 1880. J.C. Thom was a famous American artist who, for a time lived, on Kossman Street in a house that is still standing. He studied at an artist colony in Perth Amboy along with Louis Comfort Tiffany, of stained-glass fame. Thom died in 1898 and is buried at the Chestnut Hill Cemetery on the Old Bridge Turnpike. (Collection of East Brunswick Museum.)

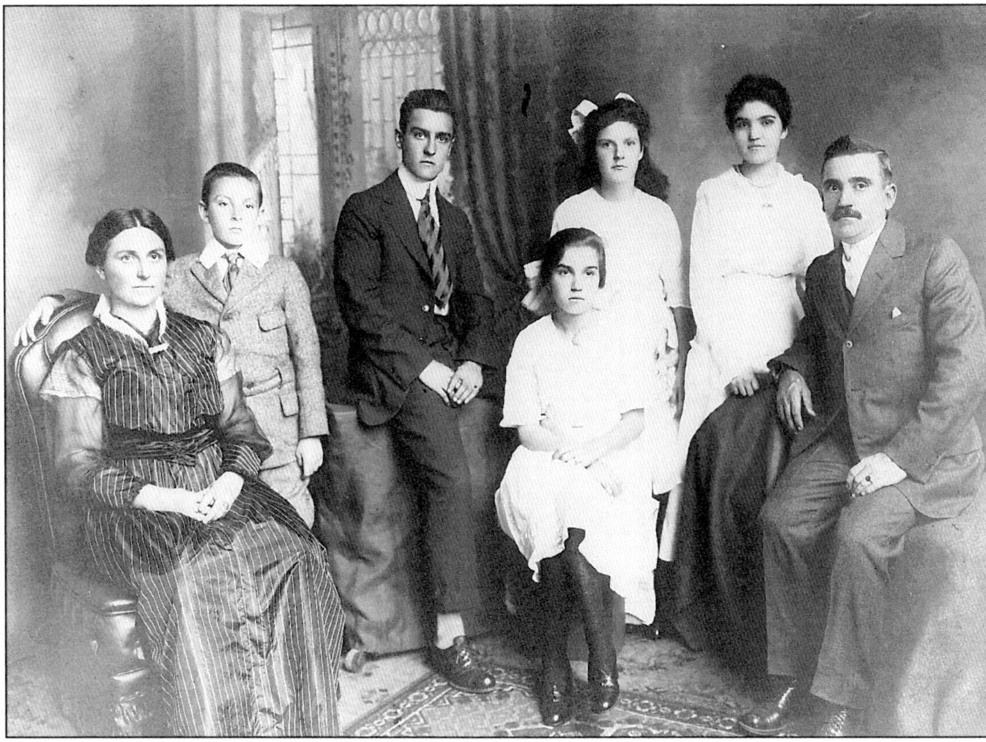

THE THOM FAMILY, SEPTEMBER 1916. The son and children of James Crawford Thom pose for a photograph. From left to right are Annie, Horace, Salvatore Jr., Ada (seated), Dorothy, Louise, and Salvatore Sr. (Collection of William Kraemer.)

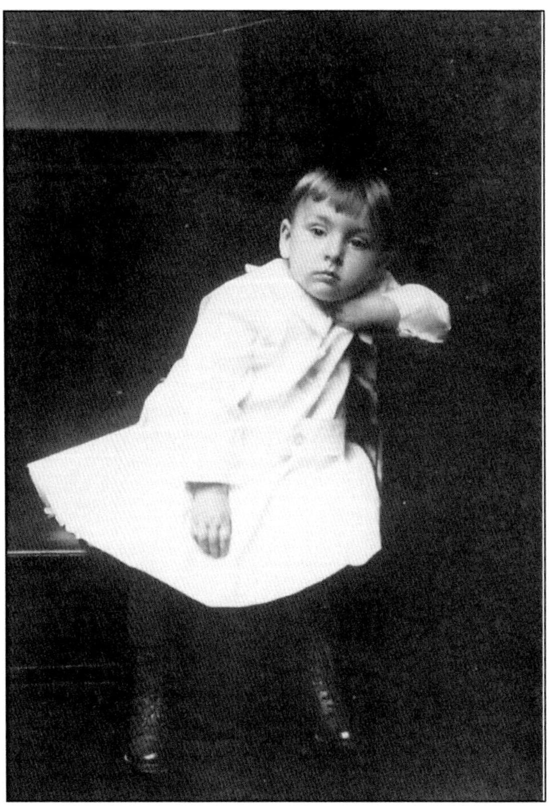

HORACE THOM. Mr. Thom was the grandson of famous East Brunswick artist James Crawford Thom. He was delivered by Doctor Ira Crandall in 1907 at a cost of $12.50. (Collection of East Brunswick Museum.)

LOUISE GILES THOM. Mrs. Thom was the first wife of James Crawford Thom. She died in 1881. (Collection of East Brunswick Museum.)

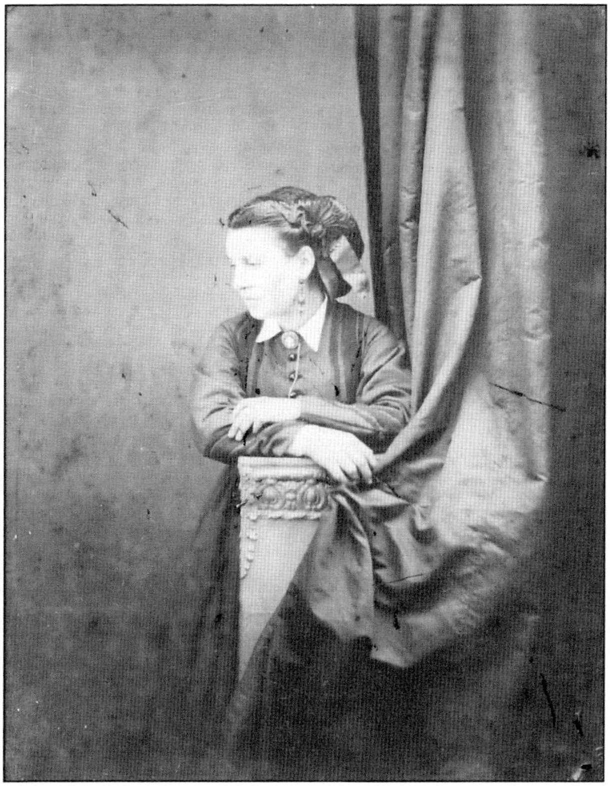

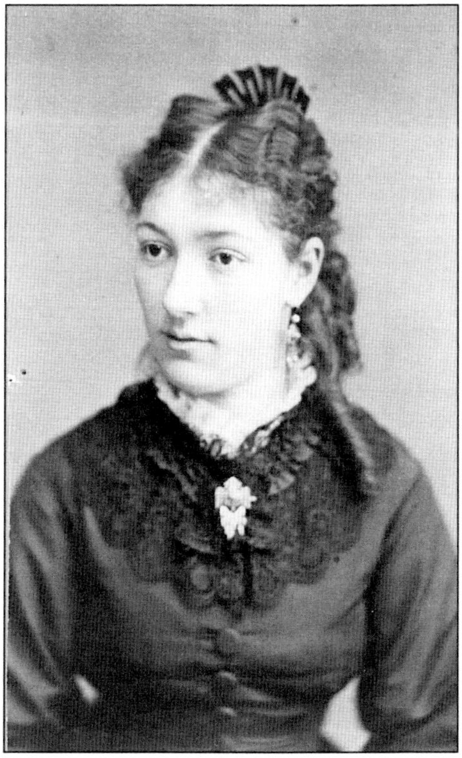

STELLA DISBROW, C. 1880. Mrs. Disbrow was the wife of Doctor Stephen J. Disbrow. The family lived on Main Street in the Old Bridge section of East Brunswick. (Collection of Mark Nonestied.)

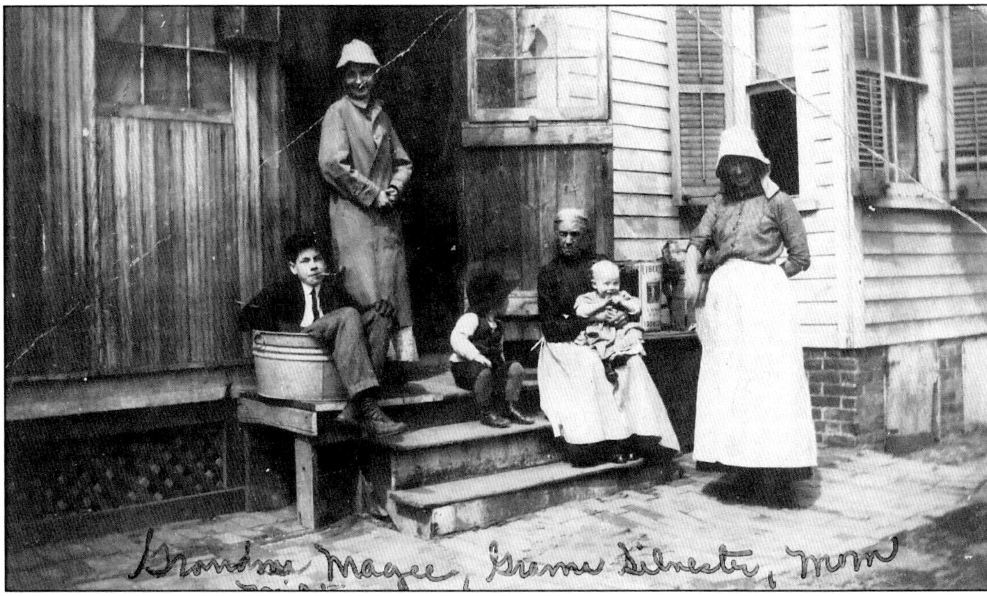

THE MAGEE AND SILVESTER FAMILY. The family posed for a picture on the side stoop, *c.* 1920. (Collection of Florence Mount.)

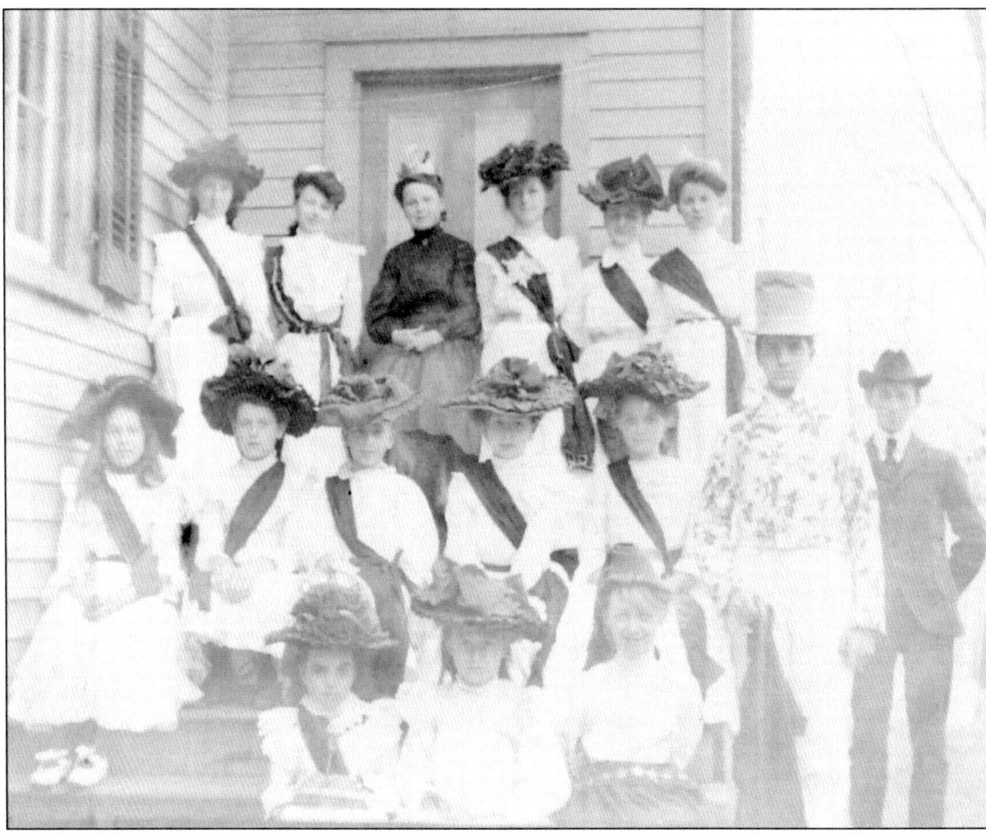

A GROUP GATHERING AT TOWN HALL, C. 1915. (Collection of East Brunswick Museum.)

MURRAY CHITTICK. Mr. Chittick posed in his World War I uniform. His childhood home still stands in the township's historic district. (Collection of Alberta Yuhas.)

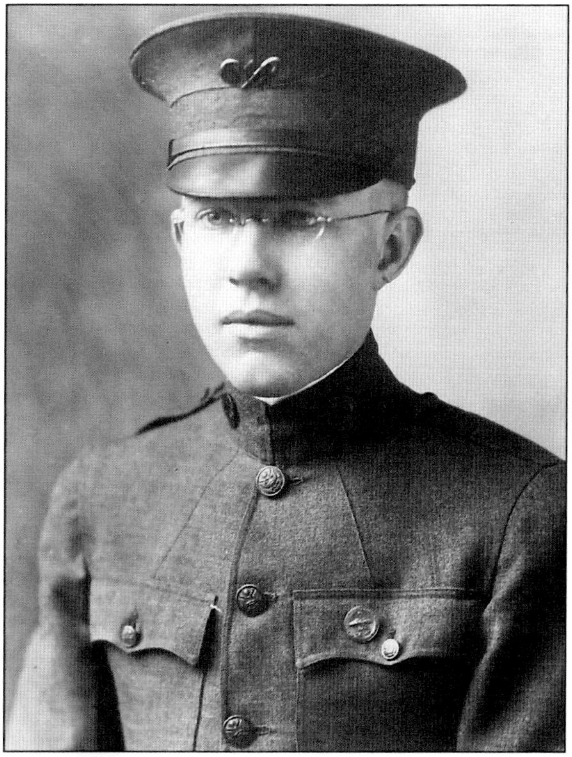

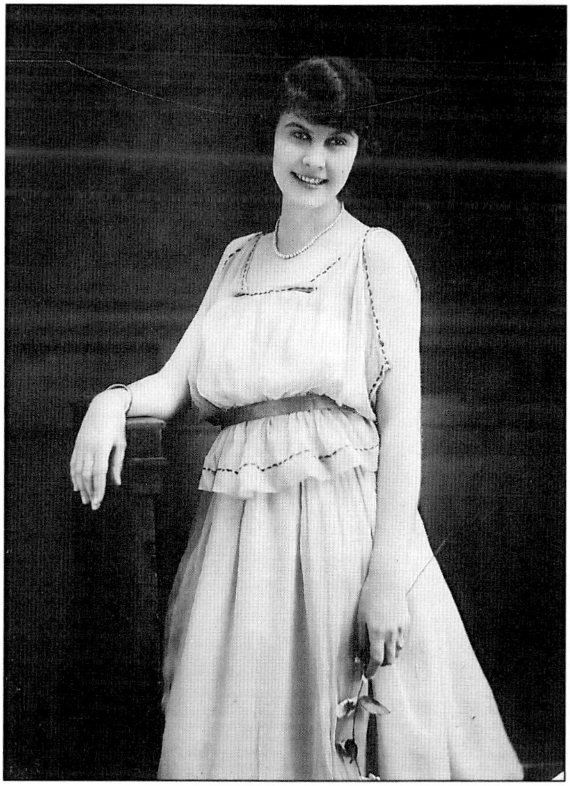

HENRIETTA DEIKER CHITTICK. Mrs. Chittick was the wife of Murray Chittick. She was a schoolteacher for 40 years. (Collection of Alberta Yuhas.)

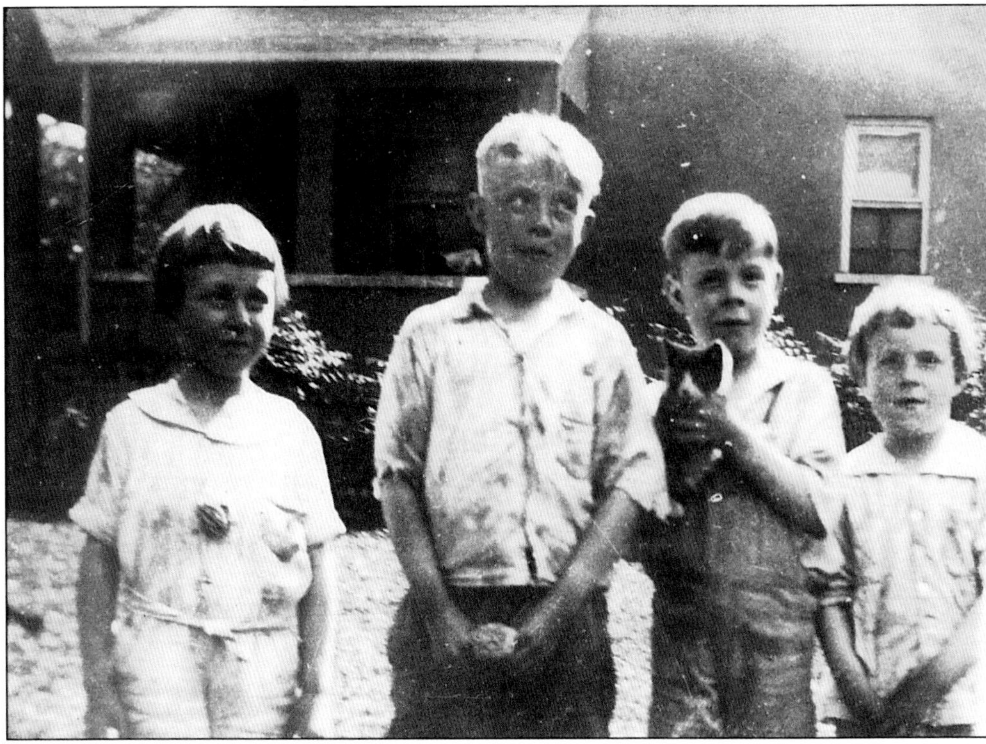

Local Rascals. These four boys look like they got caught with their hand in the cookie jar when this photograph was taken in 1940. (Collection of Florence Mount.)

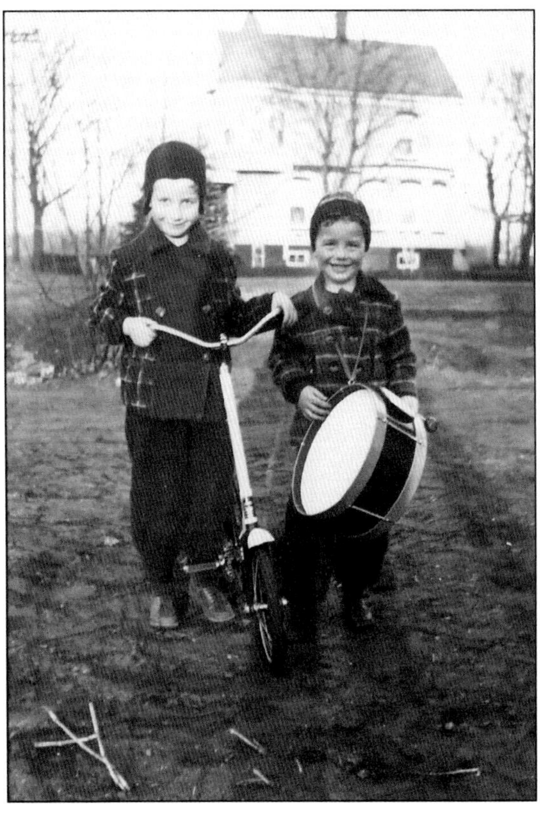

Two Young Boys with Their Latest Toys, c. 1938. The house in the background still stands on the corner of Kossman Street and River Road. (Collection of Florence Mount.)

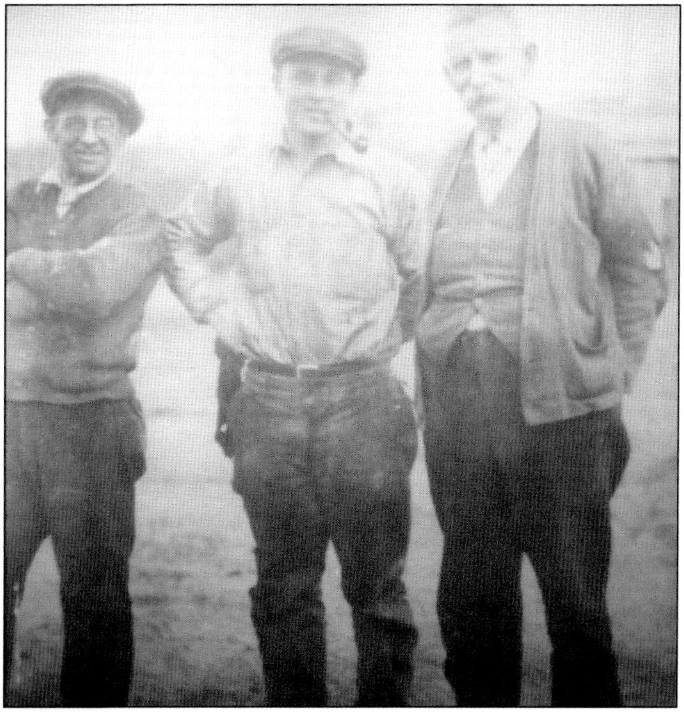

Charles Reid (right) with other Co-workers from the Old Bridge Enamel Brick and Tile Company. Mr. Reid was said to have had a breakfast consisting of, among other things, six eggs and six pancakes. (Collection of Alberta Yuhas.)

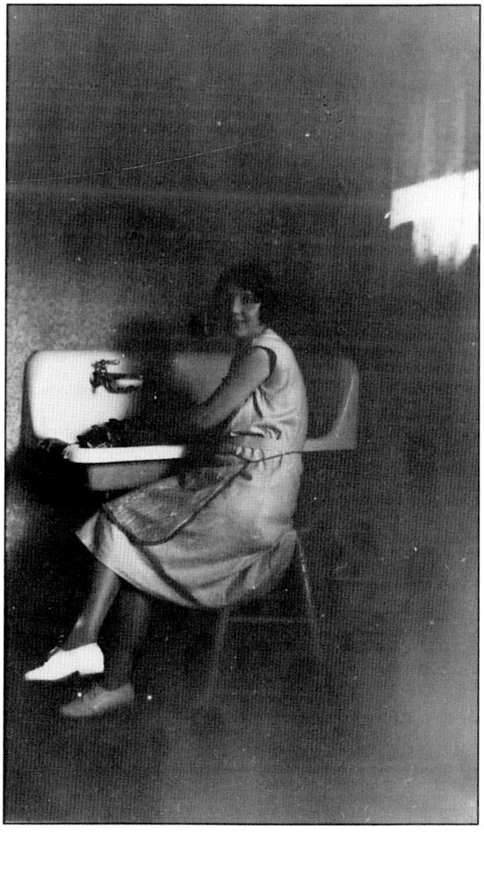

Mrs. Reid of Kossman Street. She was photographed cleaning garden vegetables in her modern kitchen in 1931. (Collection of Florence Mount.)

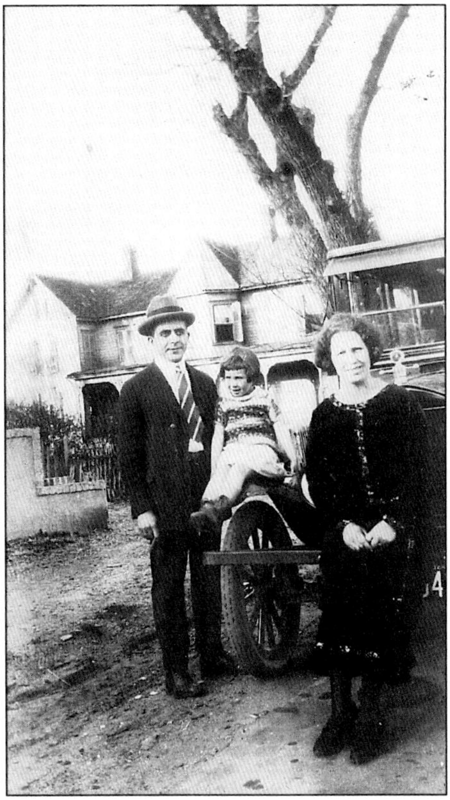

NICK RAIMONDI AND FAMILY, 1924. Nick Raimondi, his wife, and their child are seen posing in front of their automobile on Main Street. (Collection of East Brunswick Museum.)

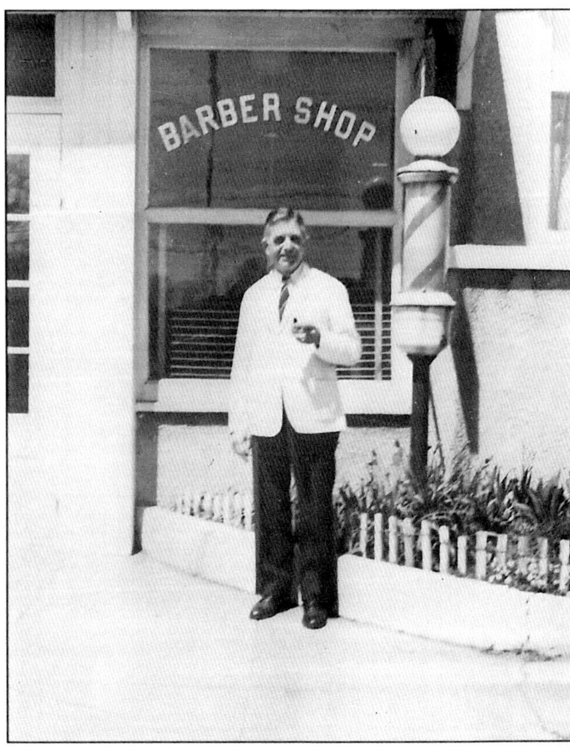

A BARBER SHOP, C. 1930. Nick Raimondi was a local barber in the Old Bridge section of East Brunswick for 45 years. (Collection of East Brunswick Museum.)

GRANDMA SQUIRE, C. 1870. The Squires family lived in the Old Bridge section near Squires Street. (Collection of East Brunswick Museum.)

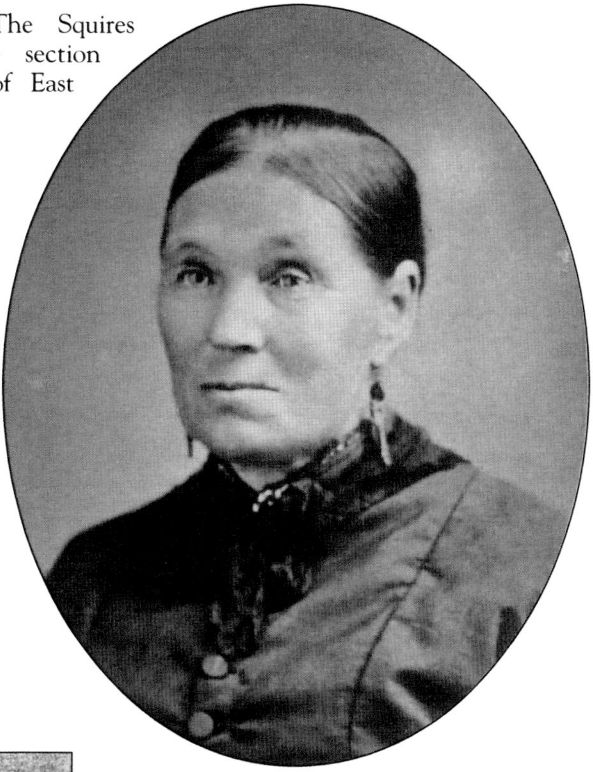

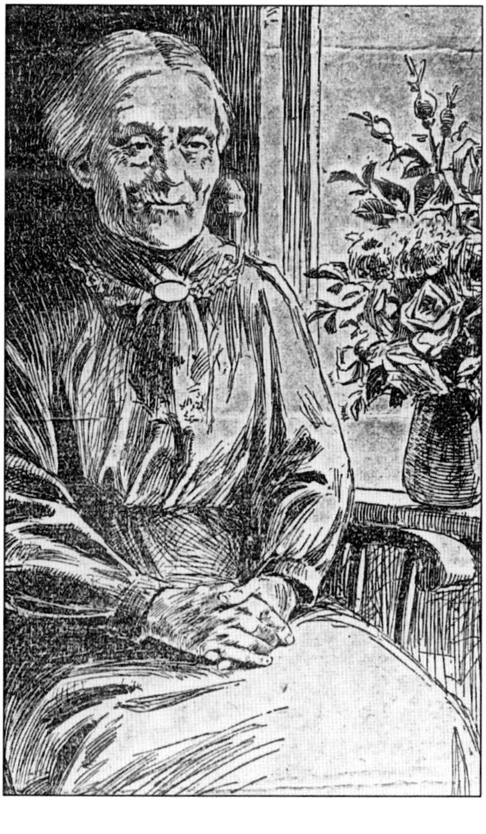

MRS. CATHERINE HERBERT, THE WIFE OF GENERAL OBADIAH HERBERT. Catherine was born in 1799 and died in 1899, after almost living to see three centuries. Her husband was a surveyor and shipbuilder, and also owned considerable property in the Old Bridge section. For some time, this part of town was referred to as Herbertsville. (Collection of East Brunswick Museum.)

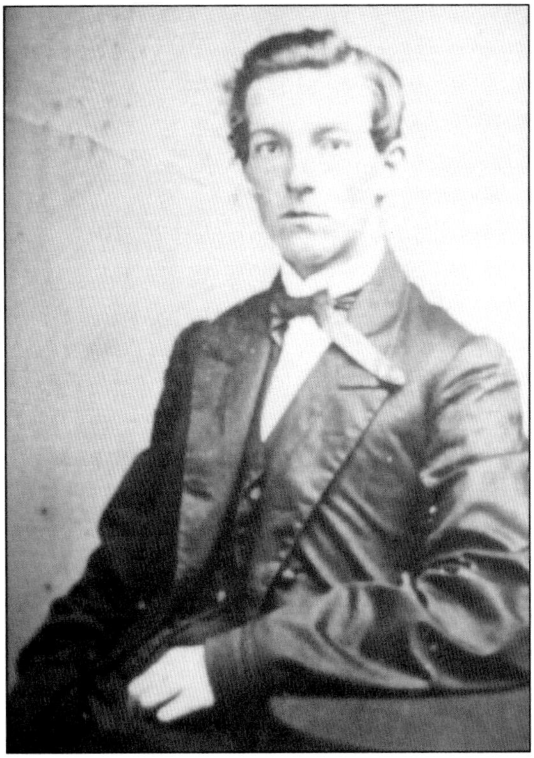

William Augusts Rogers, 1860. William H. Rogers had ten children, one of whom was William A. Rogers, who was born in 1843. When the Civil War broke out in 1861, he went off to fight and was killed at the Battle of Chancellorsville in 1863. His body was never recovered. A marble obelisk on the top of Chestnut Hill Cemetery was placed there by his family as a fitting memorial to their fallen son. (Collection of Katheryn Rogers.)

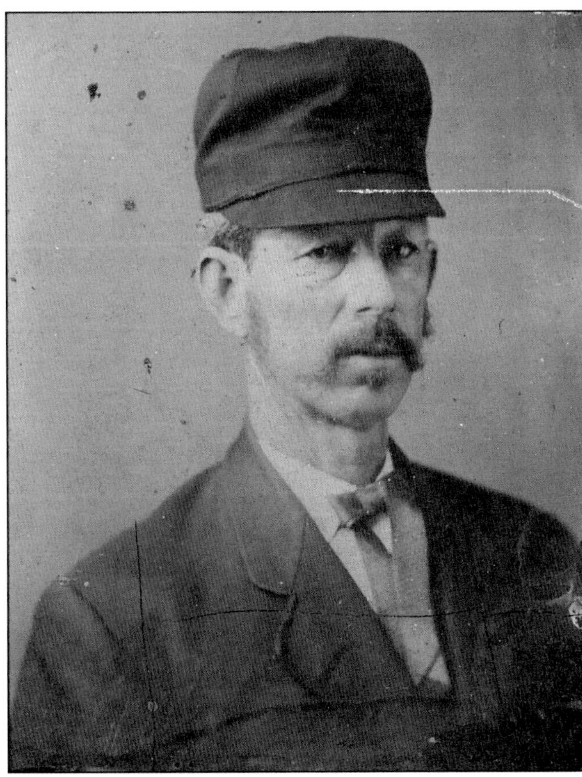

John Magee, c. 1865. Members of the Magee family were early settlers in this area. John Magee fought in the Civil War. (Collection of Alberta Yuhas.)

AN 1863 TINTYPE PHOTOGRAPH. This young man, one of John Magee's brothers, also served in the Civil War. (Collection of East Brunswick Museum.)

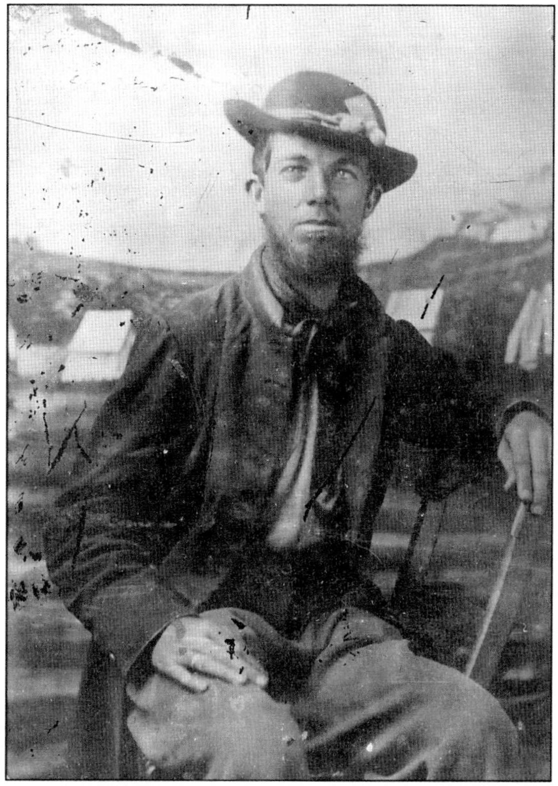

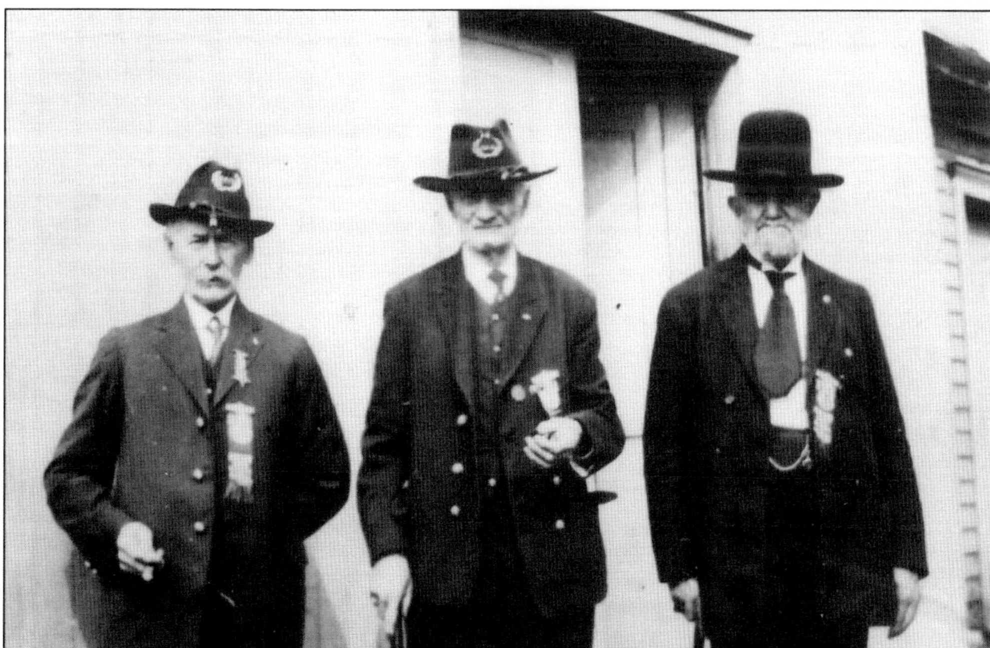

THE LAST THREE CIVIL WAR VETERANS FROM THE OLD BRIDGE SECTION, C. 1915. From left to right are Henry Beebe, Mr Van Hise, and Herb Appleby. (Collection of East Brunswick Museum.)

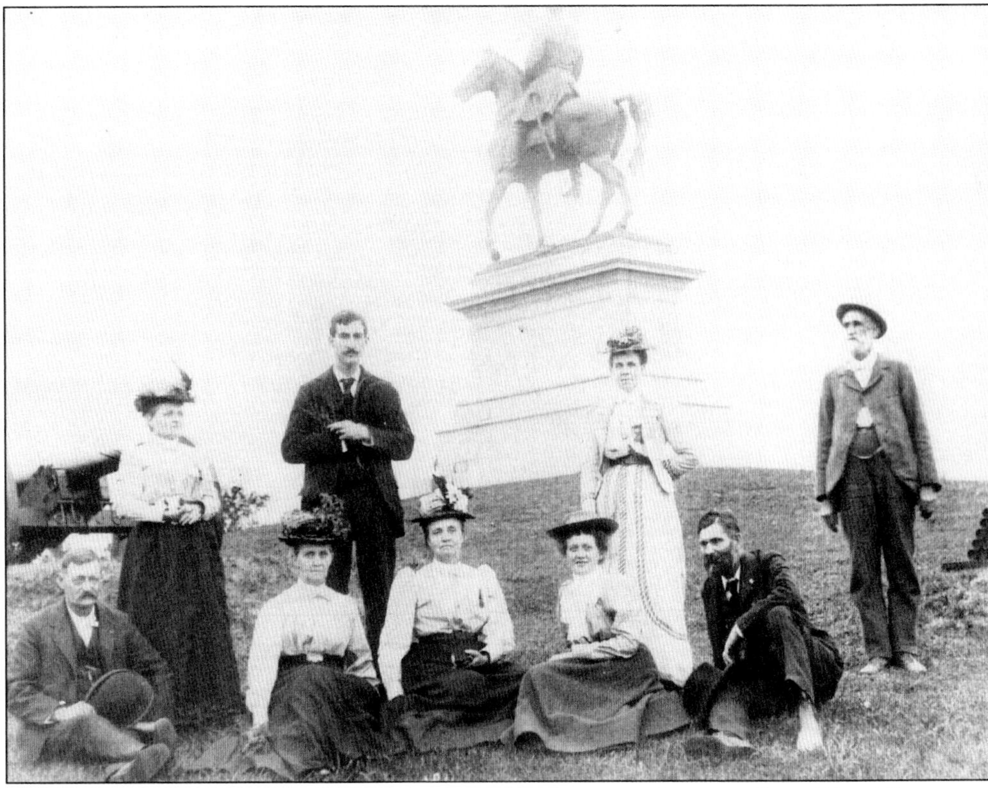

SEVERAL CIVIL WAR VETERANS FROM THE OLD BRIDGE SECTION AND THEIR FAMILIES. These men took their families on a tour of Gettysburg, Pennsylvania, in the 1890s. (Collection of Helen Appleby Silvester.)

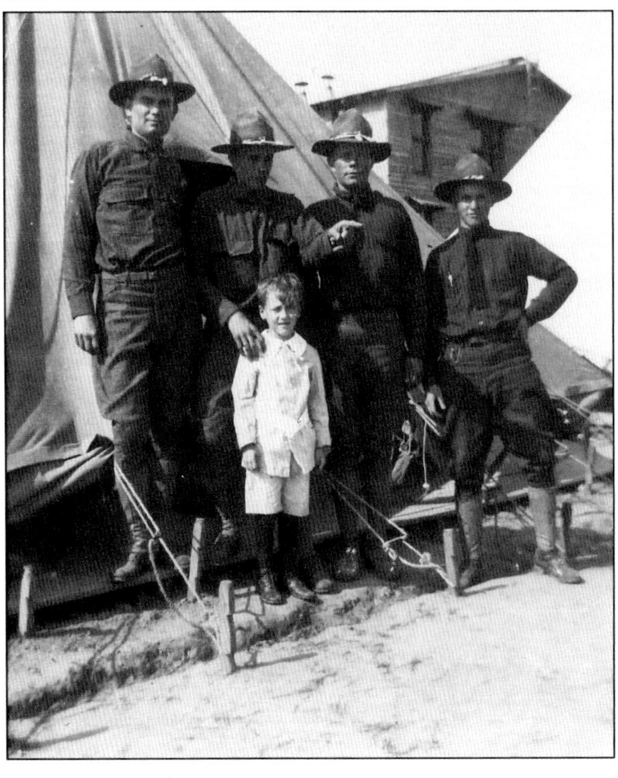

LOCAL RESIDENTS AT CAMP DIX DURING WORLD WAR I. (Collection of East Brunswick Museum.)

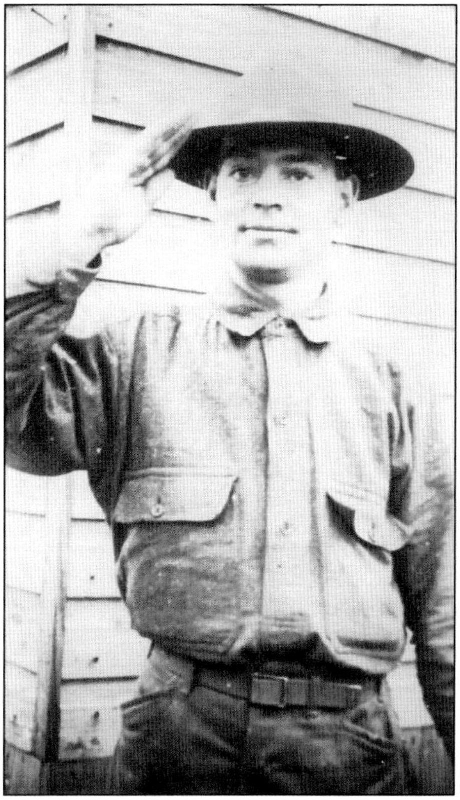

AUGUSTUS HILLYER. Mr. Hillyer lived in the Old Bridge section of East Brunswick and enlisted during the First World War. He died in 1918 from the flu epidemic, and is buried at the Chestnut Hill Cemetery. (Collection of William Kraemer.)

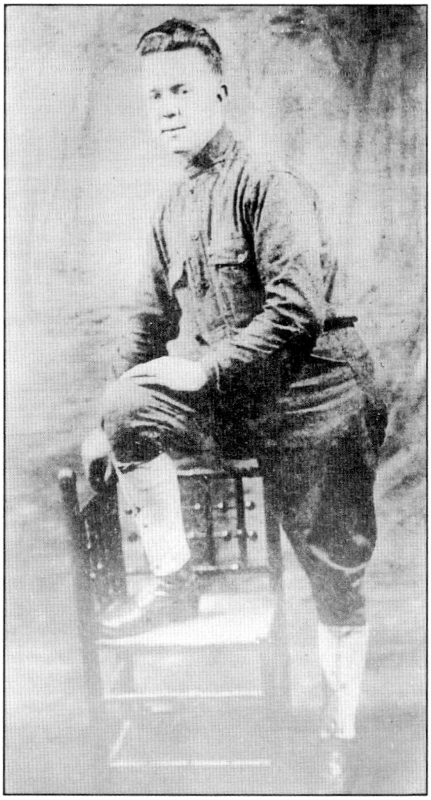

HAROLD RUSHER. Mr. Rusher enlisted for World War I but never got to fight, as he died in 1918 from the flu epidemic. He was buried at Chestnut Hill Cemetery in a coffin with a glass viewing lid. About 50 years later, his body was moved from Chestnut Hill Cemetery to a family plot at Tennent Church Cemetery in Manalapan. (Collection of William Kraemer.)

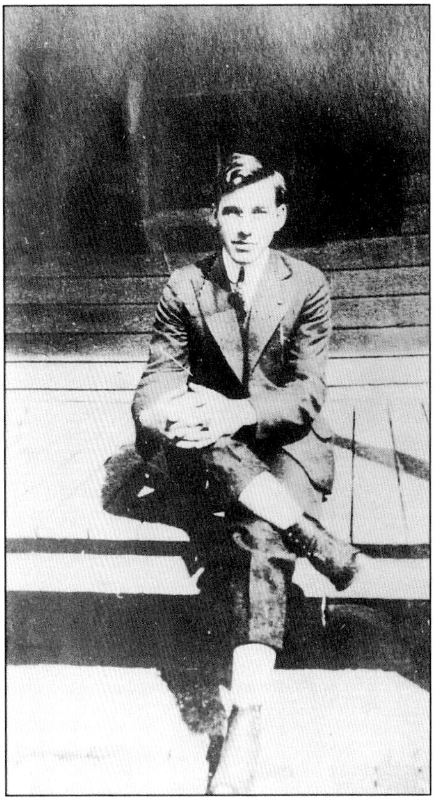

ELLSWORTH SILVESTER. Mr. Silvester enlisted in the army to fight in World War I. He died at Camp Dix from the flu epidemic in 1918 and is buried at the Chestnut Hill Cemetery. The flu epidemic of 1918 was the worst epidemic of the 20th century. Over 20 million people died worldwide. It effected many people living in East Brunswick and the surrounding communities. Several cemeteries have mass graves containing victims of the epidemic. (Collection of Silvester Family.)

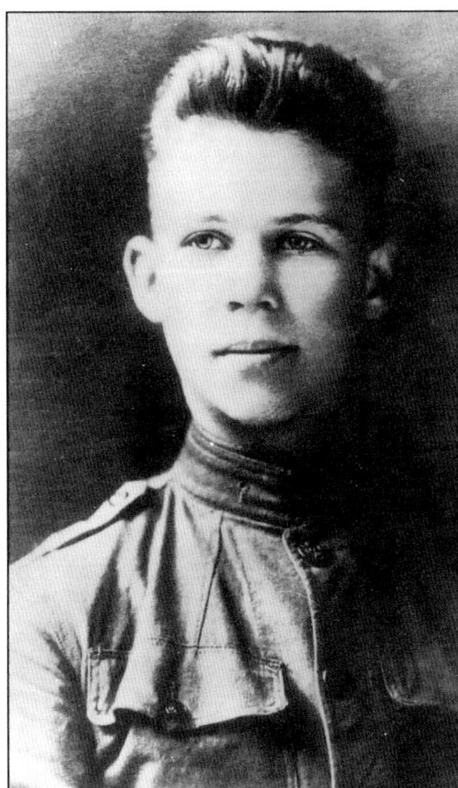

JOSEPH CRANDALL. The Crandall family lived in the Old Bridge section of East Brunswick. Joseph was killed at the Battle of Chateau Theirry in 1918. A fellow soldier wrote the following in a letter to the Crandall family: ". . . Sgt. Crandall being deserted by guides held his section by the road side. He was hit in the leg by a shell fragment early in the action, but remained with his section in spite of physical pain. Some two hours later a second fragment tore through his shoulder blade . . . and caused instantaneous death." He was awarded the Distinguish Service Cross posthumously. (Collection of the East Brunswick Museum.)

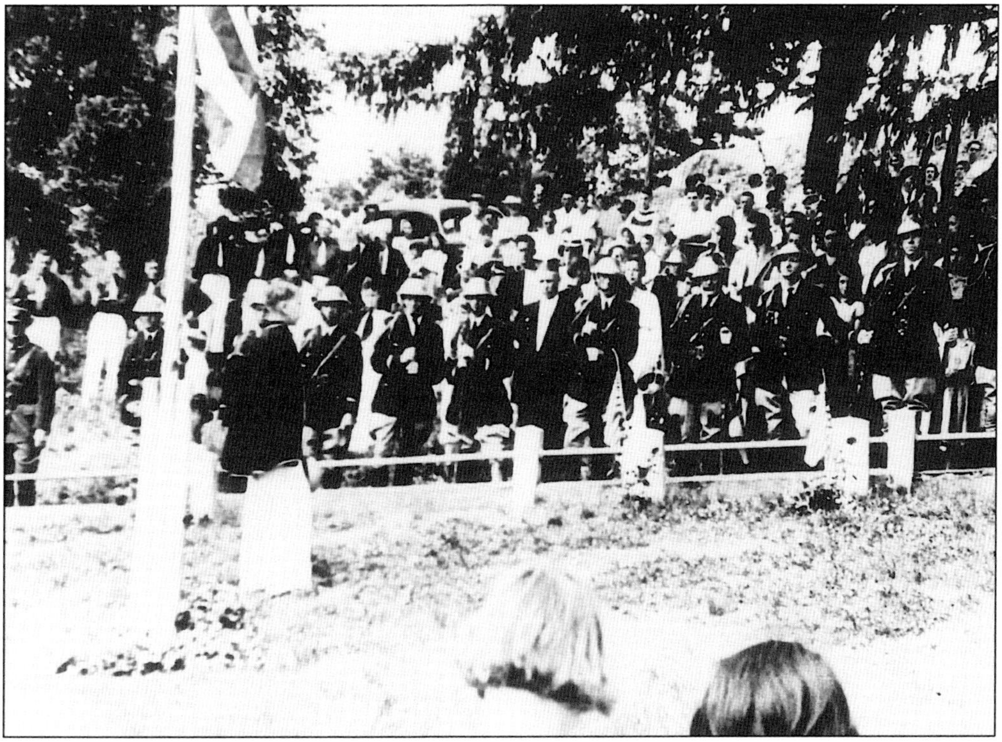

MEMORIAL DAY SERVICES AT CHESTNUT HILL CEMETERY, C. 1930. The young boy in the center is reciting the Gettysburg Address. The memorial service took place in the cemetery's Civil War veteran plot. (Collection of East Brunswick Museum.)

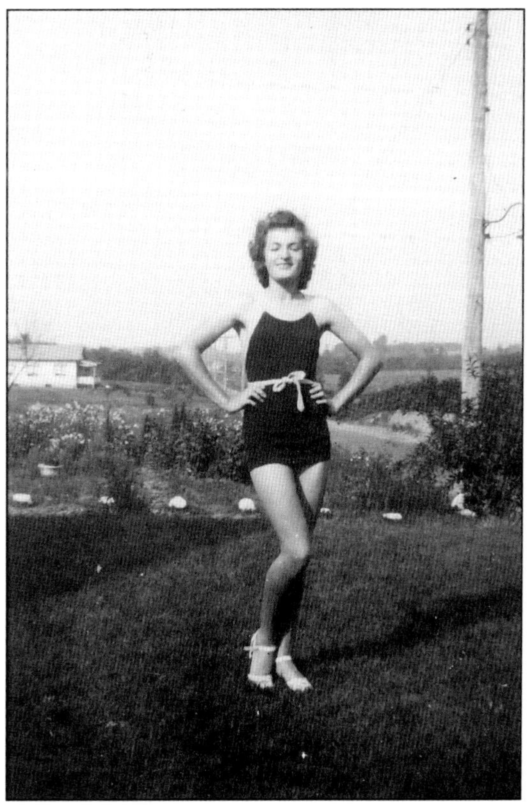

HELEN ZDANOWICH, C. 1940. The house in the background in still standing on Rue's Lane, near East Waverley Drive. (Collection of Arciszewski Family.)

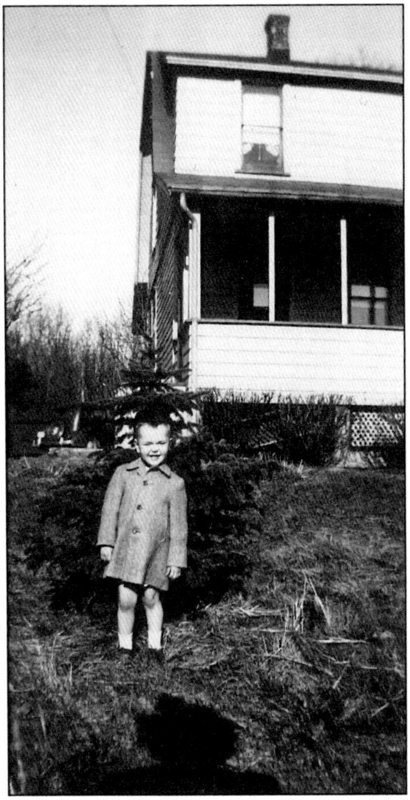

A Member of the Gatarz Family in front of the Homestead on Ryders Lane. This home was demolished in 1965 to allow the construction of the Aldersgate Methodist Church. (Collection of Aldersgate Methodist Church.)

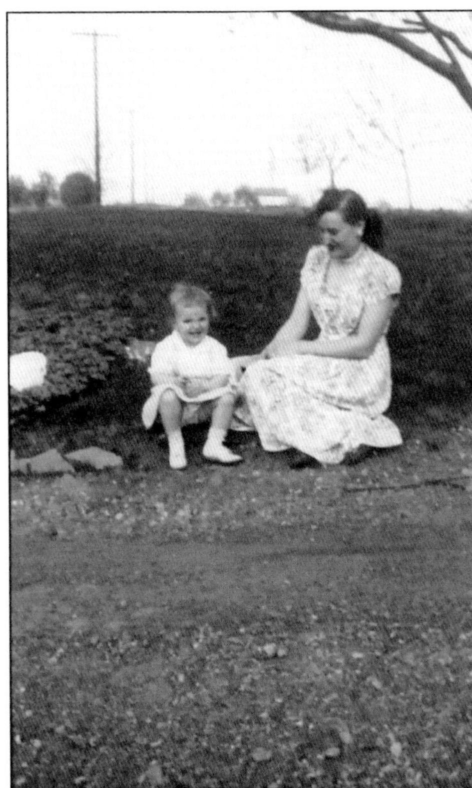

Helen Arciszewski and Baby Elizabeth, 1951. The two were visiting the old farmstead where Helen lived as a child. Rue's Lane, looking north to Winton Road, is in the background. (Collection of Arciszewski Family.)

JULIA C. YATES, C. 1900. Julia was a prominent resident of the Old Bridge section, where she worked as a music teacher and local artist. (Collection of East Brunswick Museum.)

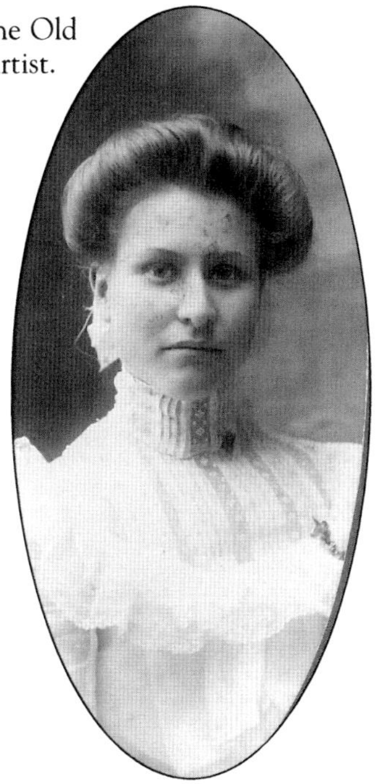

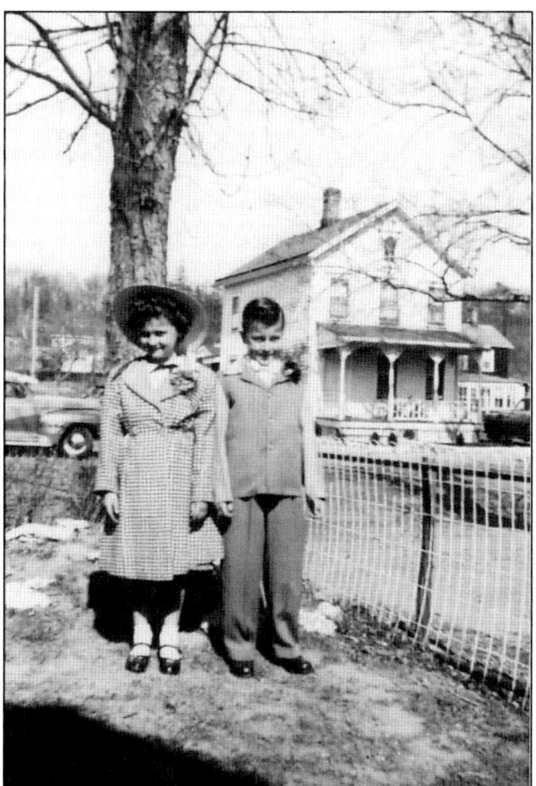

THE YATES FAMILY HOME, C. 1948. The home in the background was built in 1874 for Captain Yates, who operated a boat on the South River carrying produce and goods to New York City. It still stands today on Kossman Street and is owned by Frank and Betty Galganski. A young Betty Galganski is shown here standing to the left. Recent renovations uncovered the old Yates' family Bible and Captain Yates' spy glass. (Collection of Alberta Yuhas.)

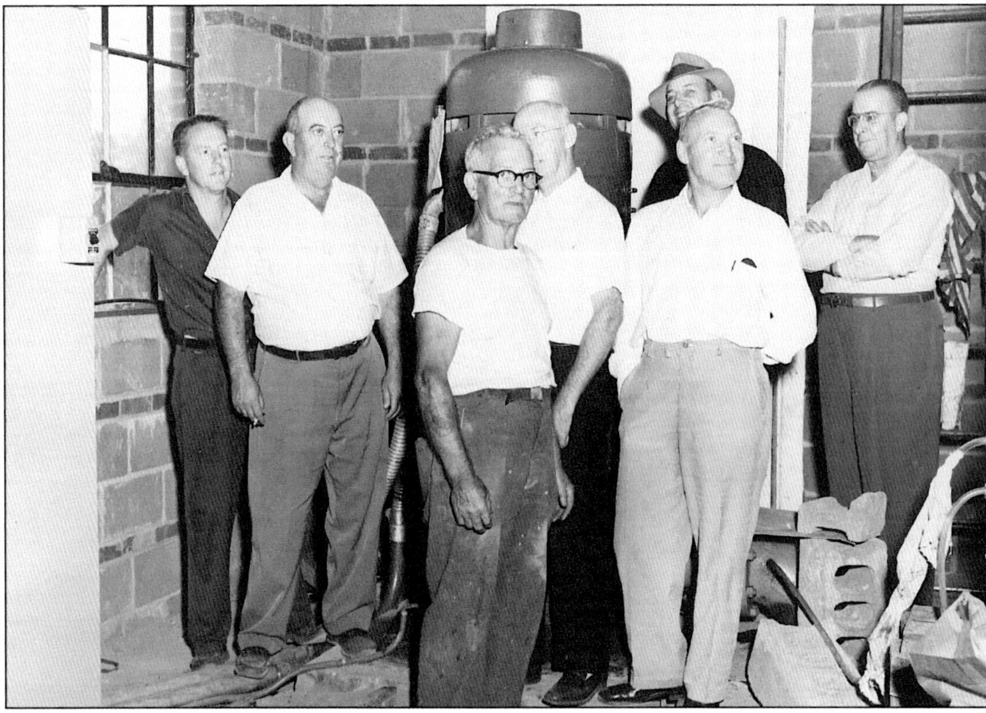

Township Employees in Front of the New Wellhouse, Pump, and Filter, c. 1950s. Charles Sullivan, a longtime East Brunswick resident, stands to the right rear of the machine. Vernon L. Appleby is to his right. (Collection of East Brunswick Museum.)

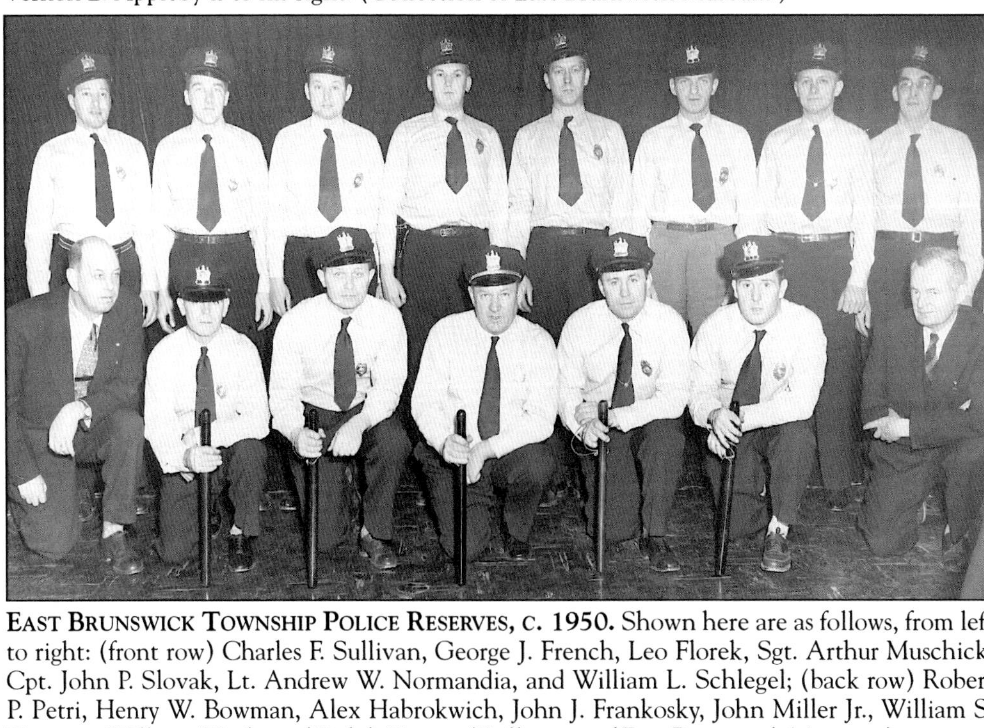

East Brunswick Township Police Reserves, c. 1950. Shown here are as follows, from left to right: (front row) Charles F. Sullivan, George J. French, Leo Florek, Sgt. Arthur Muschick, Cpt. John P. Slovak, Lt. Andrew W. Normandia, and William L. Schlegel; (back row) Robert P. Petri, Henry W. Bowman, Alex Habrokwich, John J. Frankosky, John Miller Jr., William S. Tennant, William Wirth, and Ralph Young. (Collection of East Brunswick Museum.)

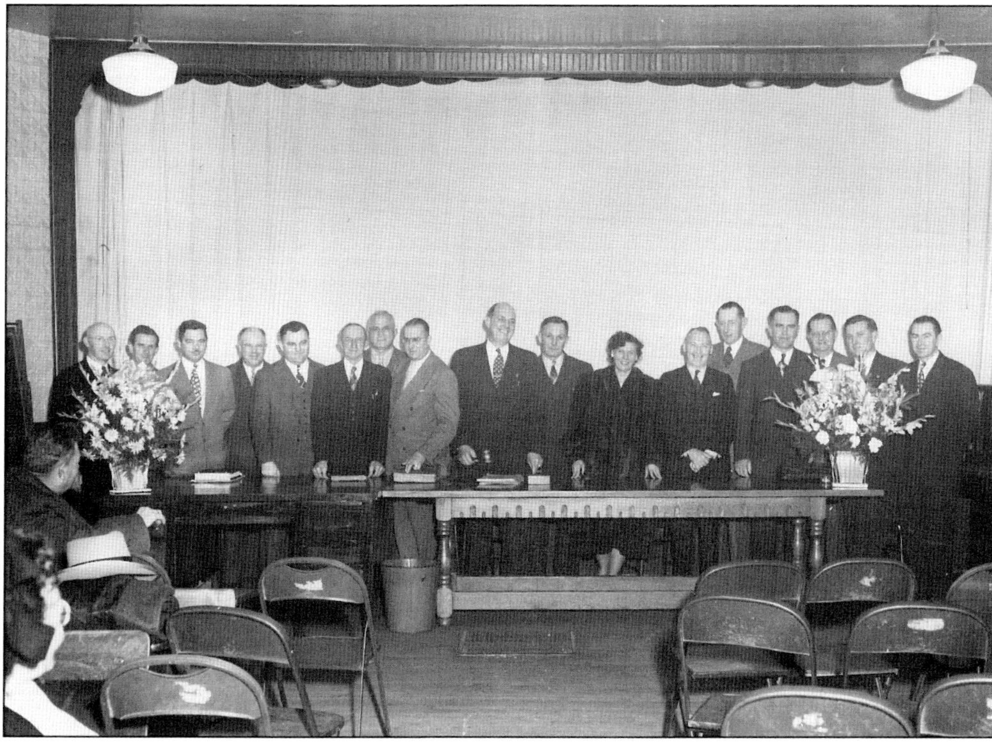

PEOPLE IN THE OLD TOWN HALL ON KOSSMAN STREET, C. 1948. (Collection of East Brunswick Museum.)

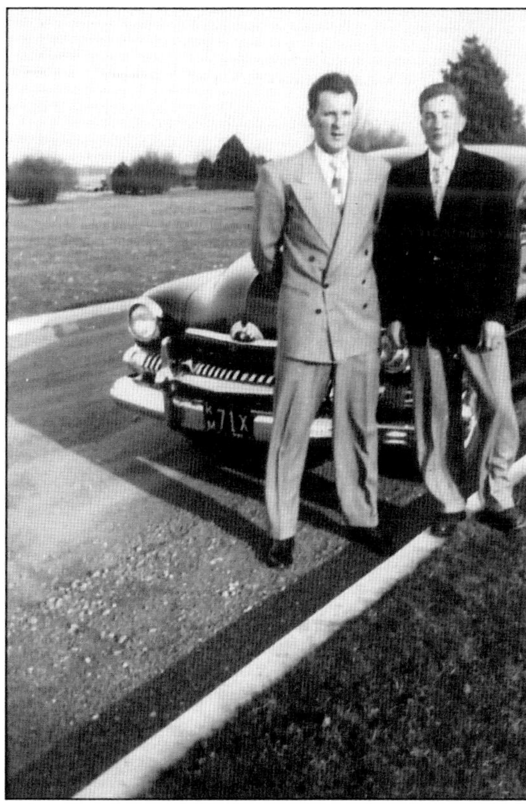

JOSEPH ARCISZEWSKI. Mr. Arciszewski (left) shows off his new 1951 Mercury to Alex Zdanowich (right) along Rue's Lane. (Collection of Arciszewski Family.)

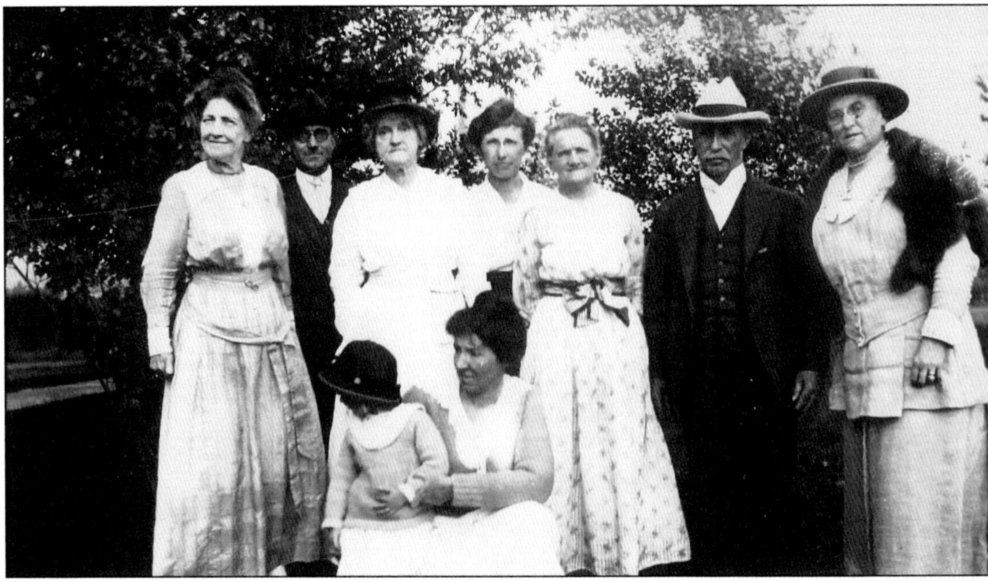

MEMBERS OF THE ROGERS FAMILY AROUND 1920. The Rogers family moved to the Old Bridge section of East Brunswick, now the Historic District, around 1820. The family owned considerable property and a sailing vessel that transported wood to New York City. The Rogers house still stands today at 26 Maple Street. (Collection of East Brunswick Museum.)

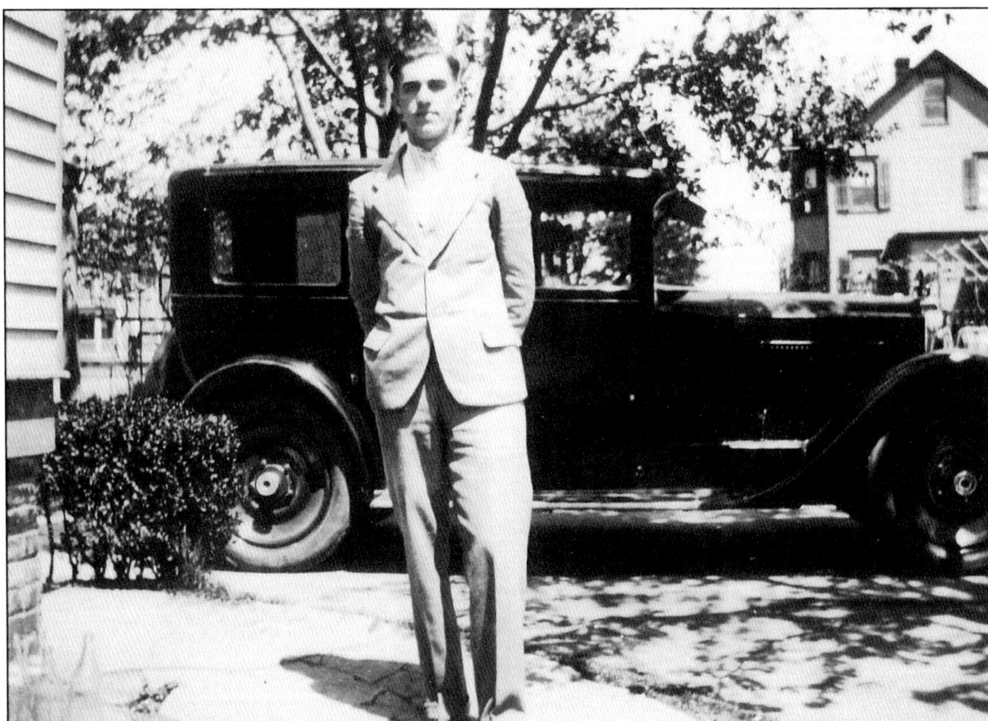

CHARLES AUER. Mr. Auer would later marry Grace Smith. He became a prominent individual in East Brunswick, and was involved in civic and government endeavors. (Collection of East Brunswick Museum.)

JOHN JOSEPH SMITH. Mr. Smith was the father of longtime East Brunswick resident Grace Auer. (Collection of East Brunswick Museum.)

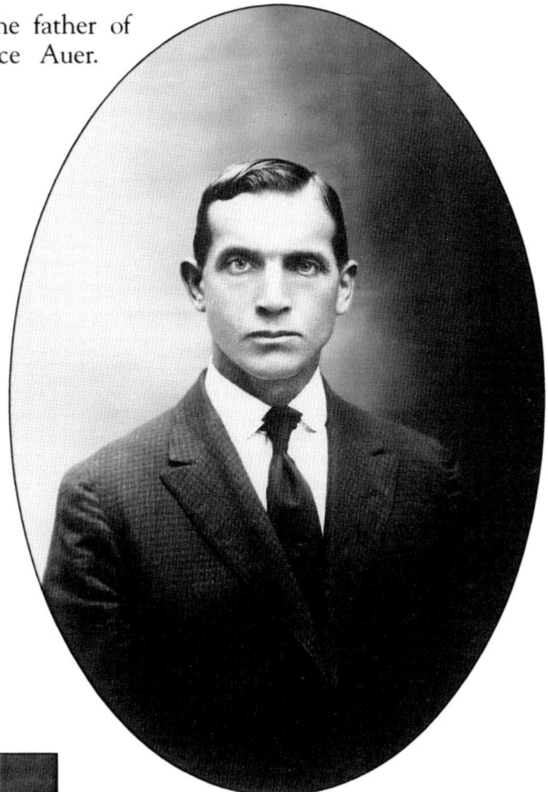

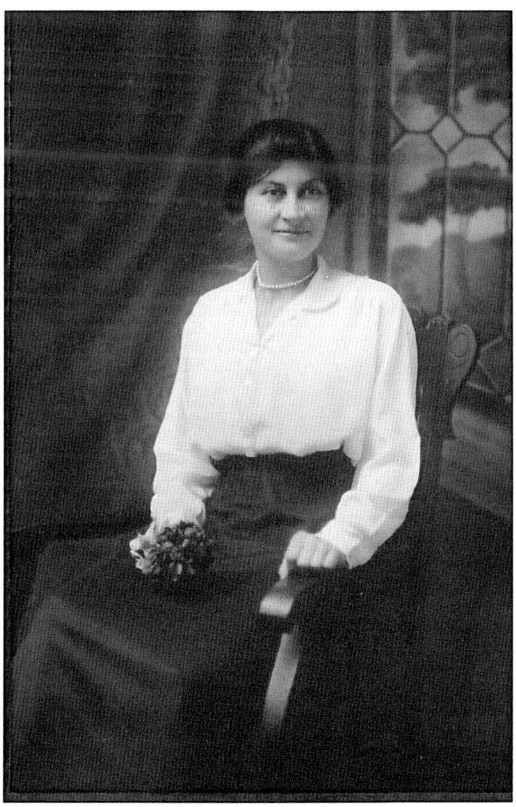

ELLA HART, C. 1920. Ella Hart lived on a farm near Harts Lane. (Collection of East Brunswick Museum.)

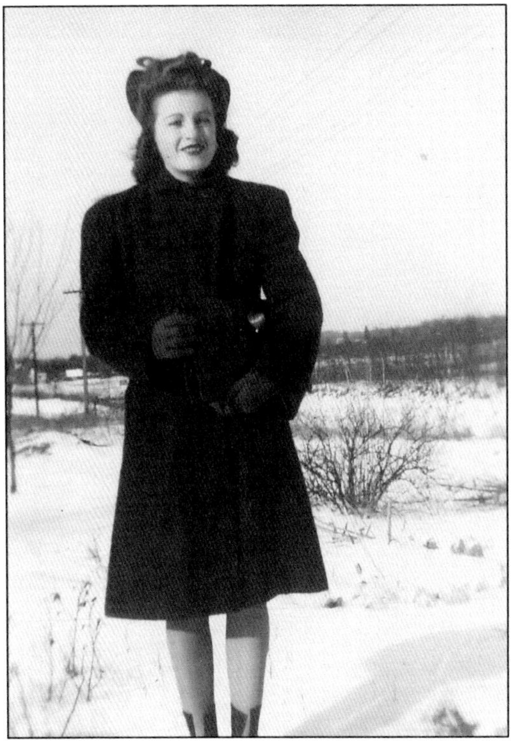

OLGA ZDANOWICH, C. 1944. The fields to the right of the photograph are on Rue's Lane across from Waverley Drive, where Catholic Charities is today. (Collection of Arciszewski Family.)

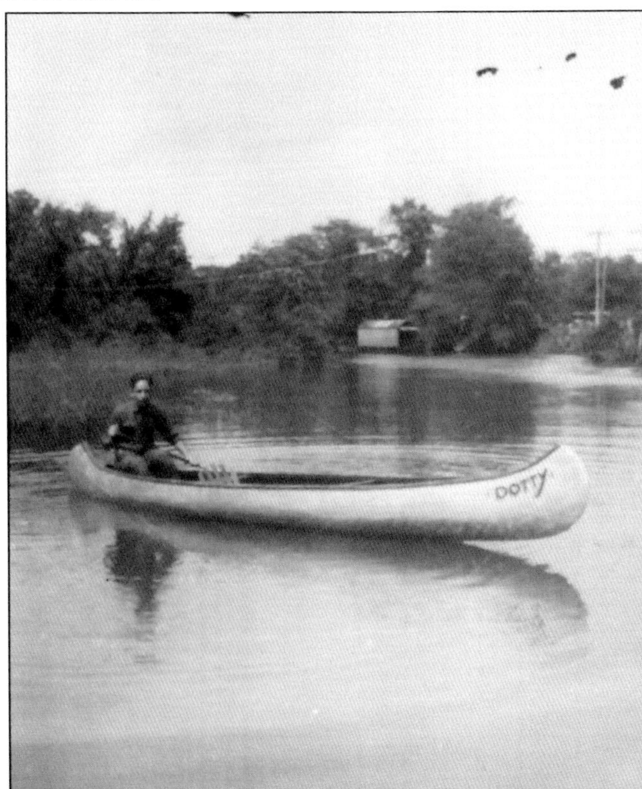

WILLIAM KRAEMER, C. 1927. Bill Kraemer moved to East Brunswick from Brooklyn in 1910. He fell in love with his future wife, Martha, who lived in Sayreville on the South River. He would row his canoe to her house to court her. (Collection of William Kraemer.)

William and Martha Kraemer on Their Wedding Day, 1929. The couple lived in what used to be a one-room schoolhouse. Martha and Bill both passed away in 1996, after being married for over 65 years. (Collection of Kraemer Family.)

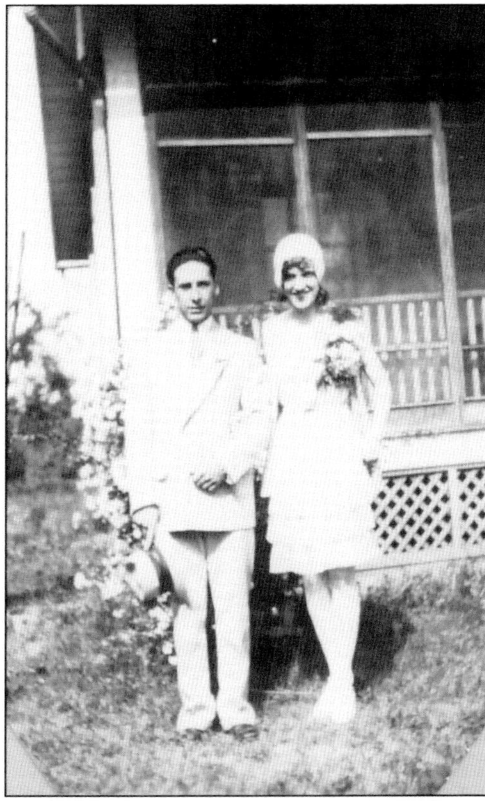

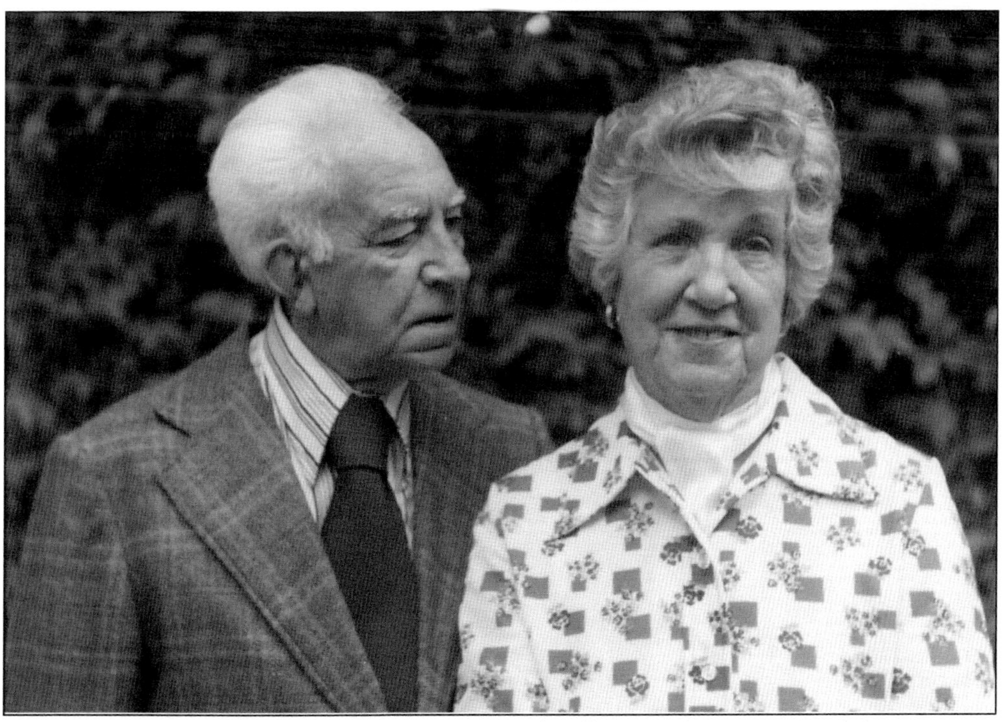

Bill and Martha Kraemer in Recent Years. (Collection of Kraemer Family.)

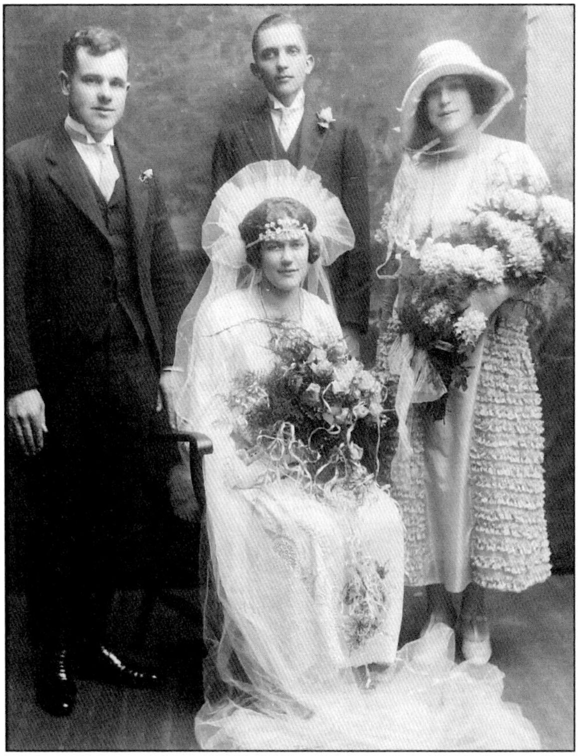

THE WEDDING OF LAURENCE SMITH (LEFT) AND ANN OTTERBEIN (SEATED), 1923. Laurence Smith lived on Milltown Road, where his apple orchard is still maintained by Smiths Farm. Also pictured are George Smith and Veronica Otterbein. (Collection of East Brunswick Museum.)

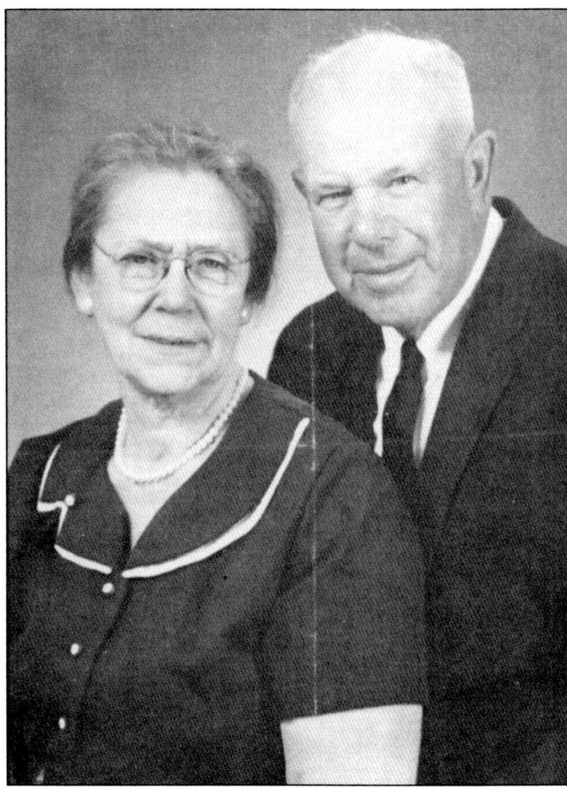

MR. AND MRS. LAWRENCE SMITH IN 1968. (Collection of East Brunswick Museum.)

Three

Recreation

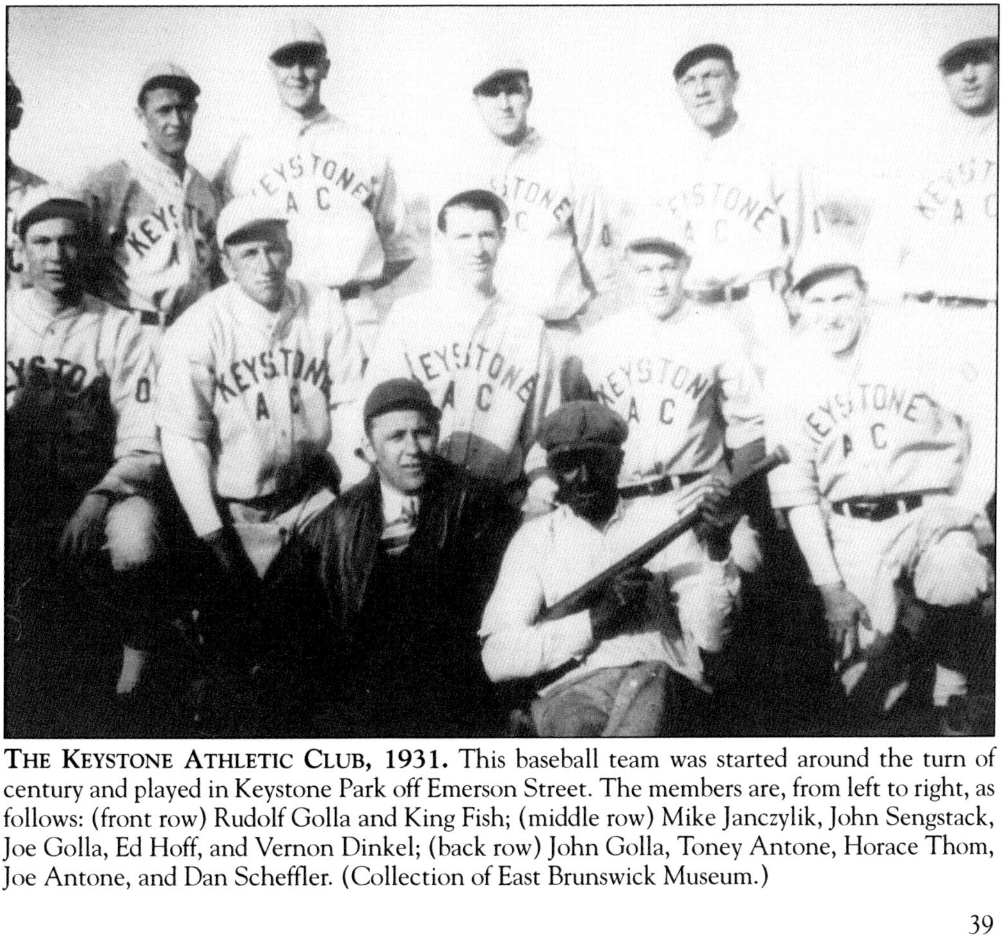

The Keystone Athletic Club, 1931. This baseball team was started around the turn of century and played in Keystone Park off Emerson Street. The members are, from left to right, as follows: (front row) Rudolf Golla and King Fish; (middle row) Mike Janczylik, John Sengstack, Joe Golla, Ed Hoff, and Vernon Dinkel; (back row) John Golla, Toney Antone, Horace Thom, Joe Antone, and Dan Scheffler. (Collection of East Brunswick Museum.)

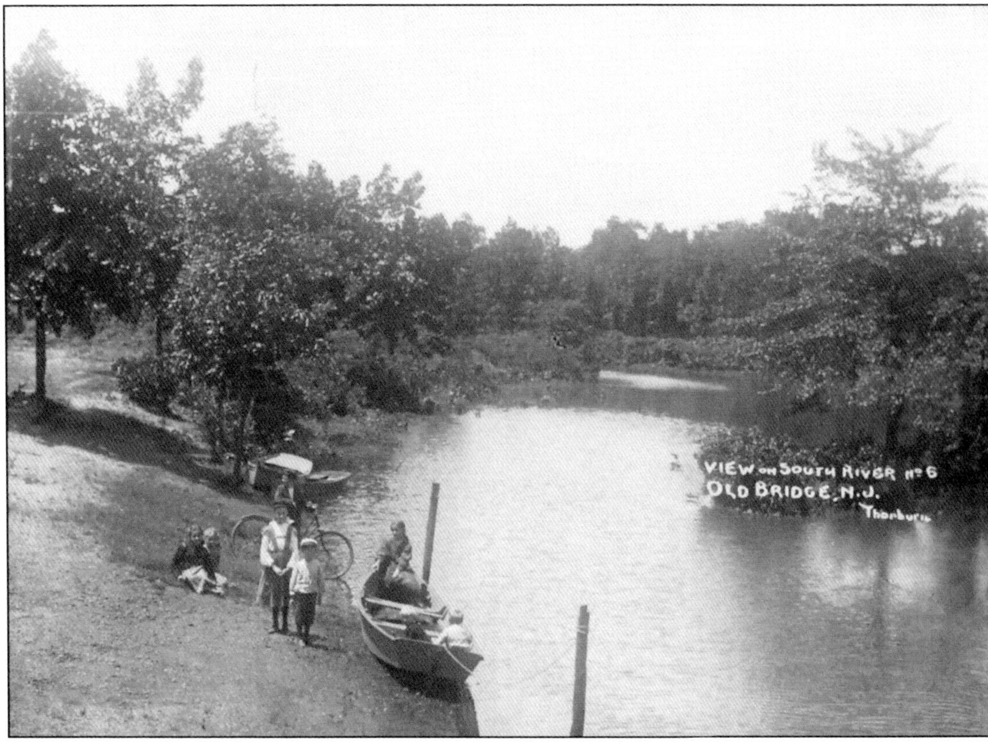

A View of the South River. The South River was used by local residents, who greatly enjoyed the recreation and beauty of it. (Collection of William Kraemer.)

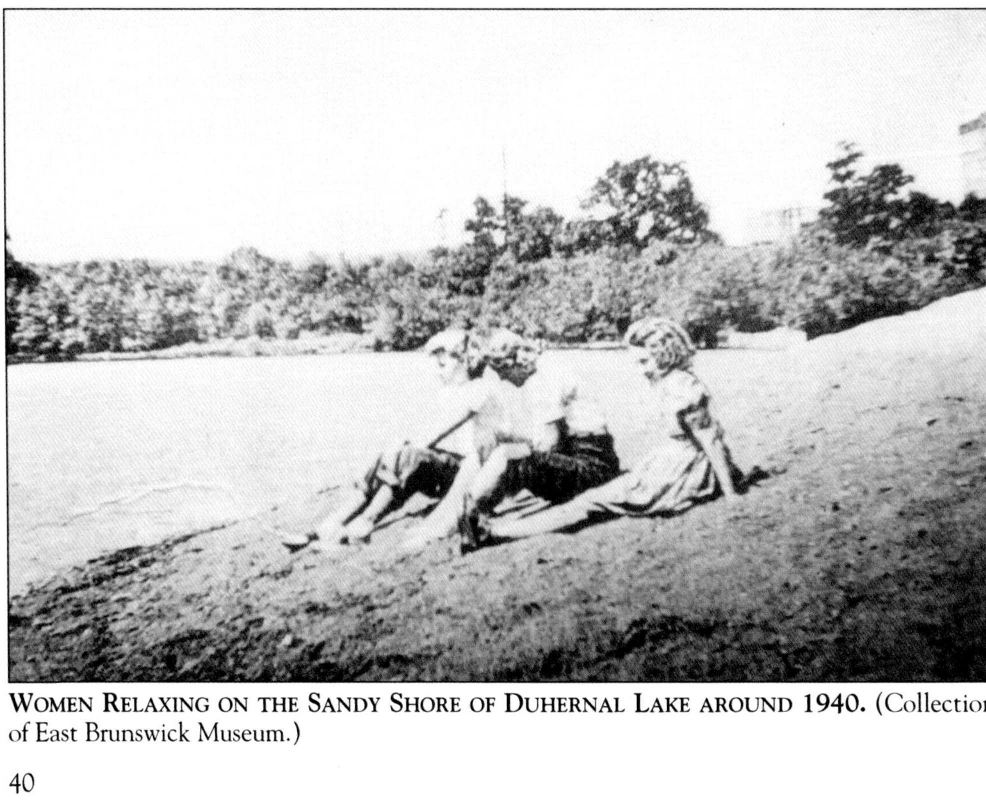

Women Relaxing on the Sandy Shore of Duhernal Lake around 1940. (Collection of East Brunswick Museum.)

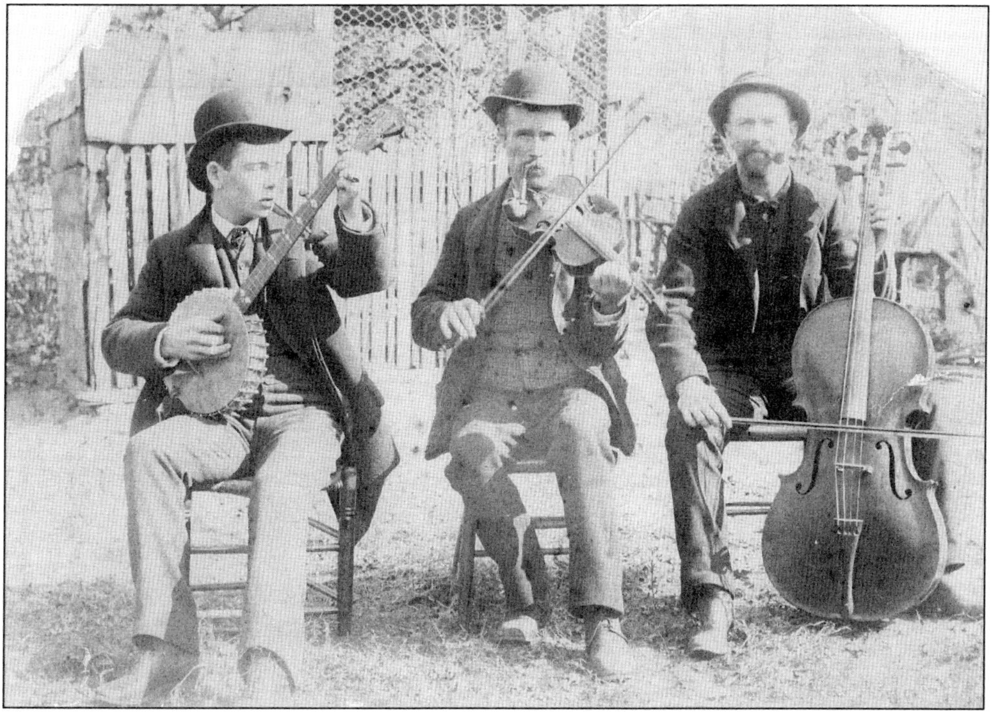

A THREE-PERSON STRING BAND, C. 1890. These men lived in the Old Bridge section. (Collection of Mark Nonestied.)

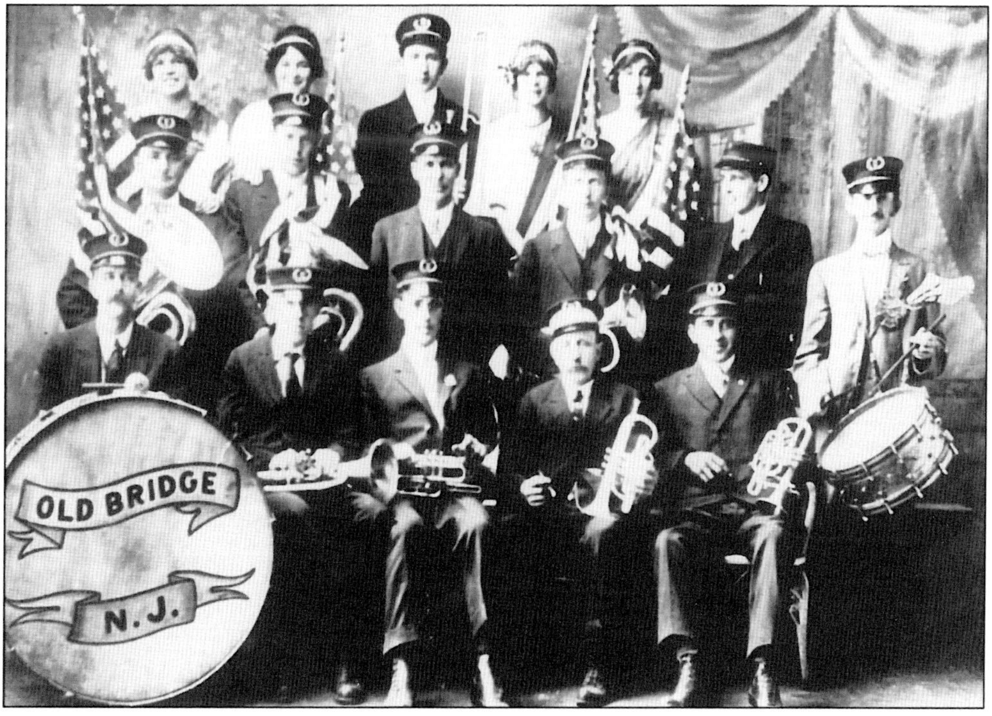

A LOCAL BAND FROM THE OLD BRIDGE SECTION, C. 1890. (Collection of East Brunswick Museum.)

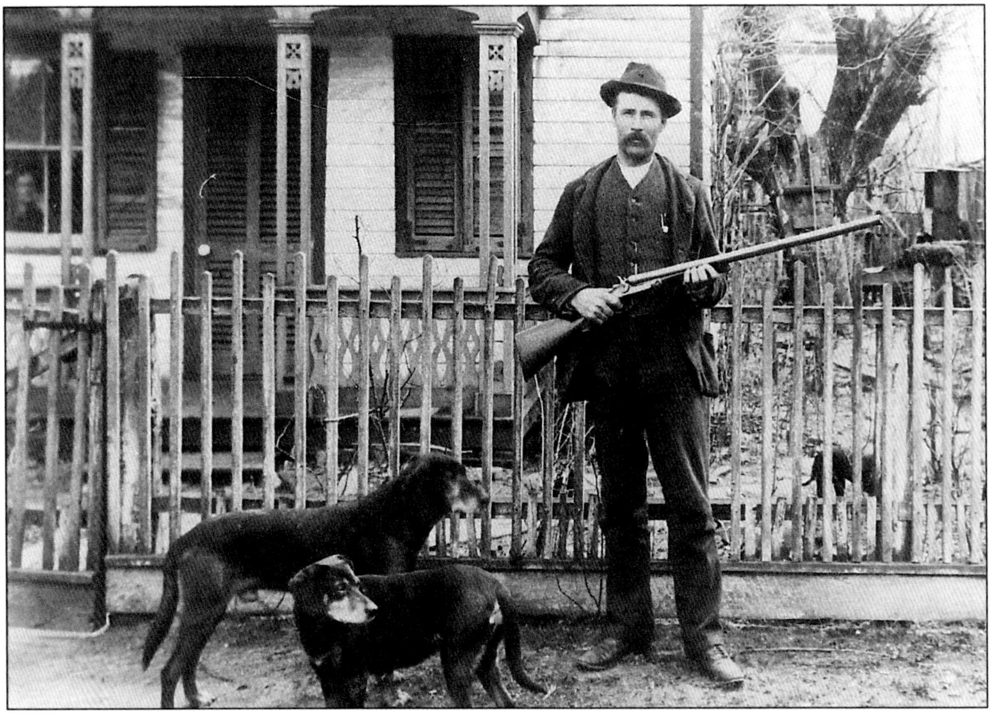

James K. Silvester, c. 1890. Mr. Silvester is shown standing with his hunting shotgun. The house in the background is still standing on Kossman Street. (Collection of Florence Mount.)

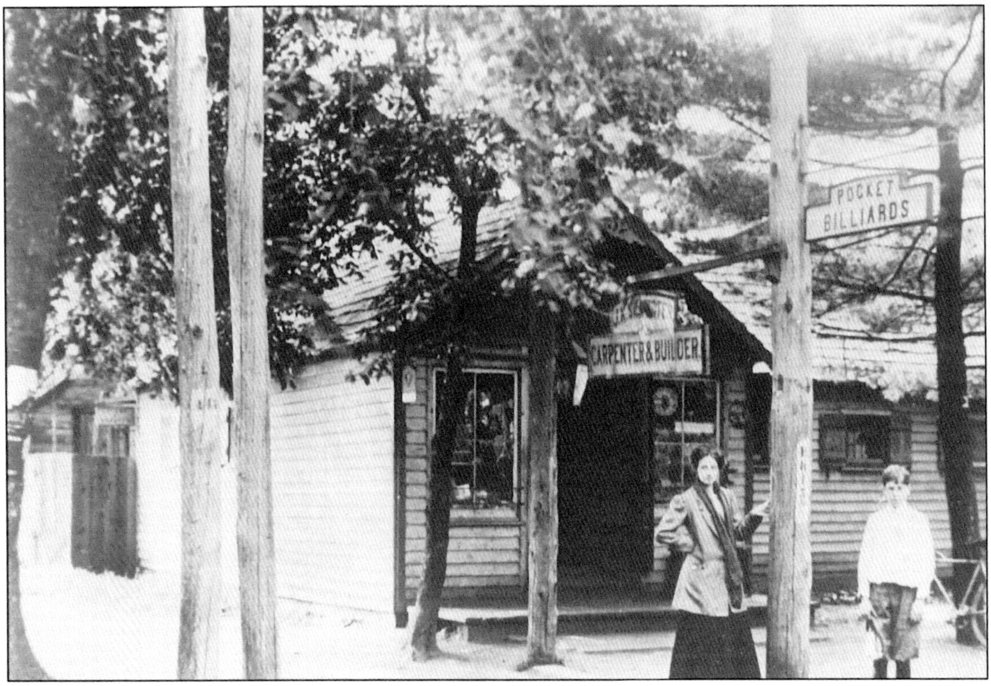

Silvester's Billiard Hall, c. 1912. James K. Silvester owned a billiard hall where the present-day Village Depot is, on Main Street in the Old Bridge section. (Collection of East Brunswick Museum.)

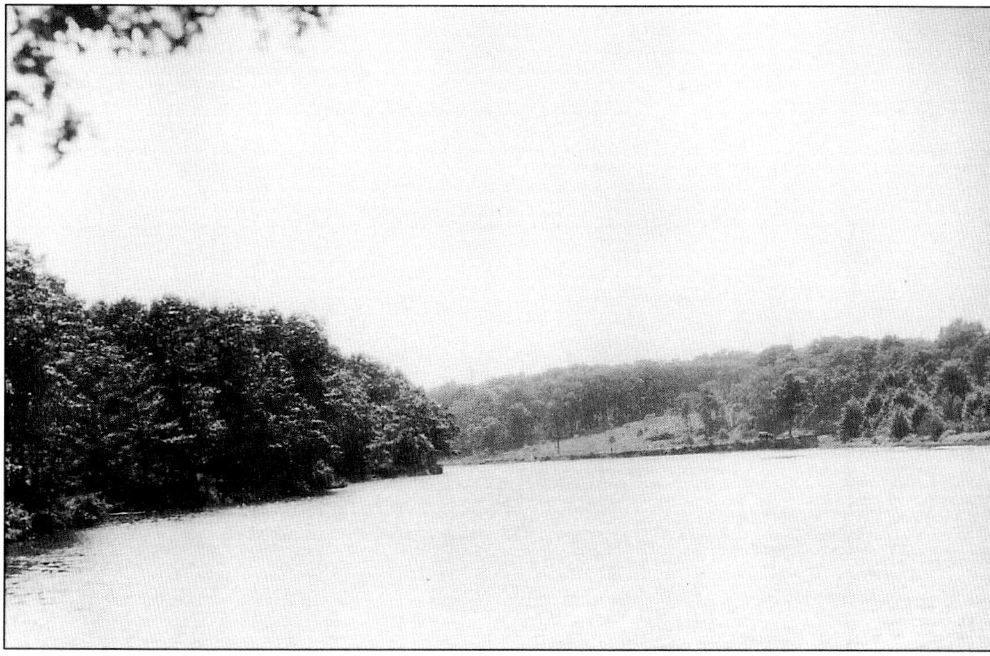

FARRINGTON LAKE AS SEEN FROM THE LAWRENCE BROOK COUNTY CLUB, C. 1938. Farrington Lake was named for Mayor Farrington of New Brunswick. It is to this day a popular recreation facility for boating and fishing. (From *Middlesex County Pictorial 1938*; collection of East Brunswick Museum.)

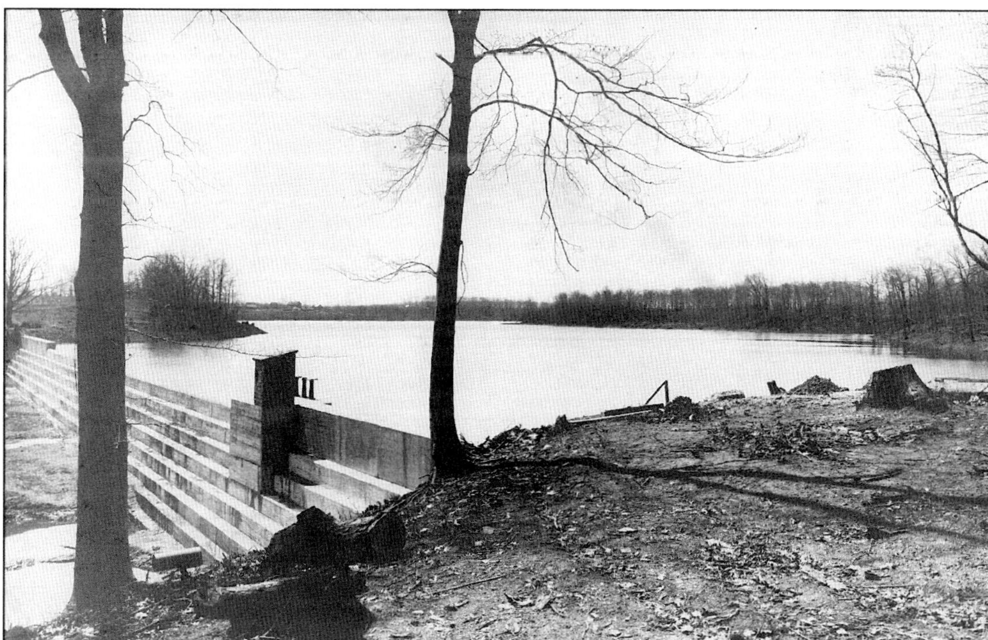

THE CONSTRUCTION OF THE FARRINGTON LAKE DAM, 1927. Farrington Lake, named for Edward Farrington of New Brunswick, was created in the 1920s by the Farrington Lake Dam. To this day it remains a popular spot for fishing and boating. Bicentennial Park would be located near the center left rear of the photograph. (Collection of East Brunswick Museum.)

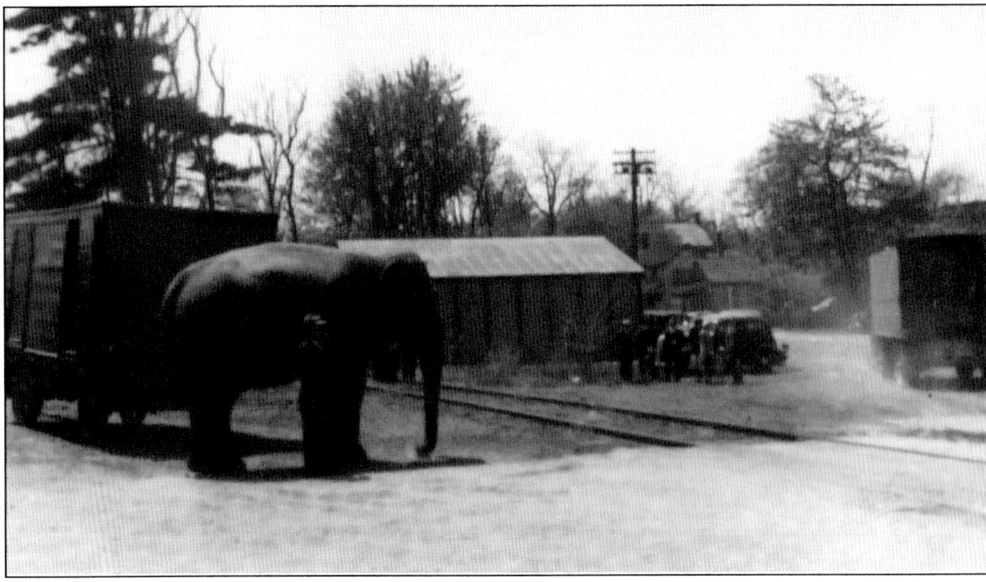

THE CIRCUS IS COMING, C. 1930. The circus arrived by train at the Old Bridge Station. Elephants pulled the circus cars up to South River. At the end of the day, the elephants cooled themselves off in the South River. (Collection of William Kraemer.)

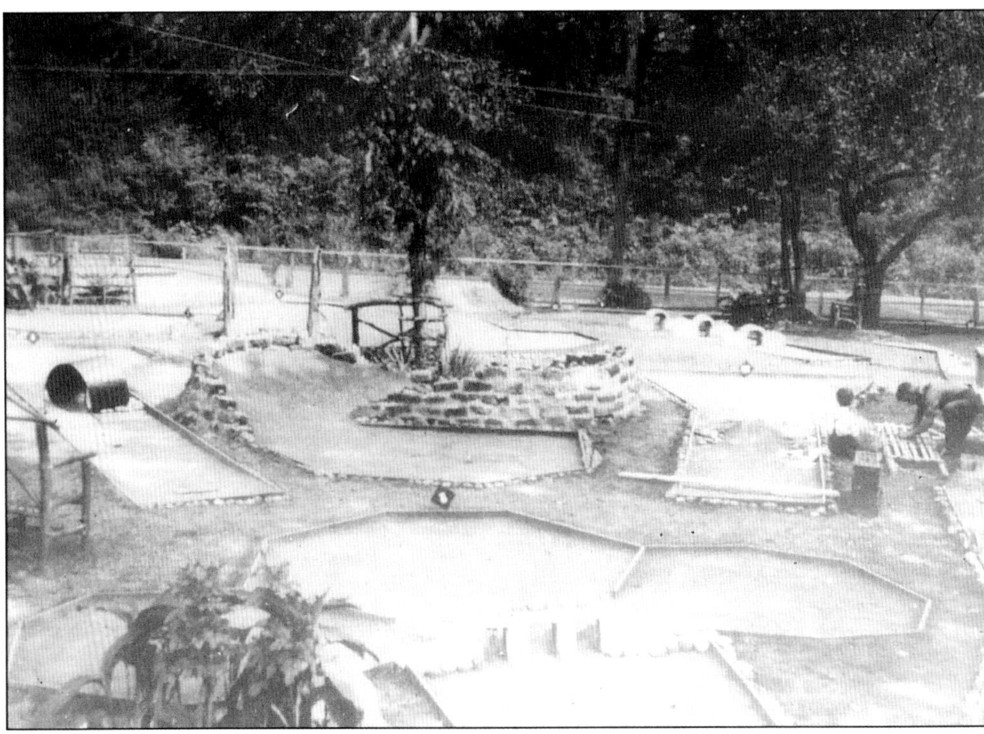

A MINIATURE GOLF COURSE, C. 1935. This golf course would eventually disappear, making way for a Route 18 northbound exit ramp onto the Old Bridge Turnpike, across from Pine Street. (Collection of the Silvester Family.)

GRACE AUER PLAYING TENNIS, C. 1930. Her husband, Charles, was on the other side of the net. (Collection of East Brunswick Museum.)

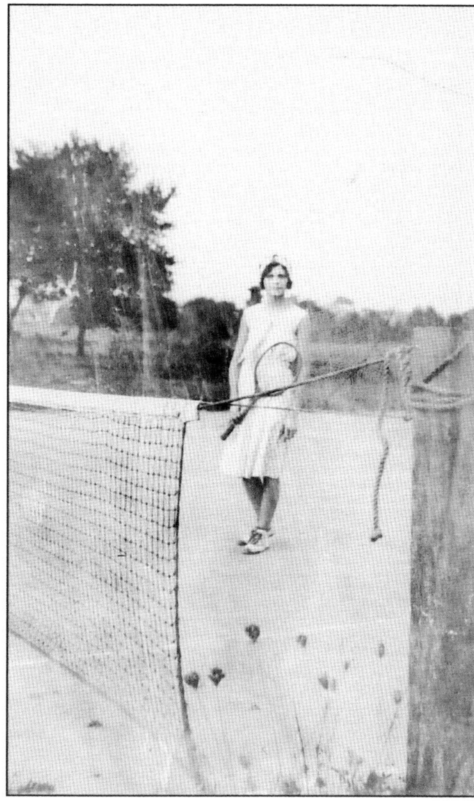

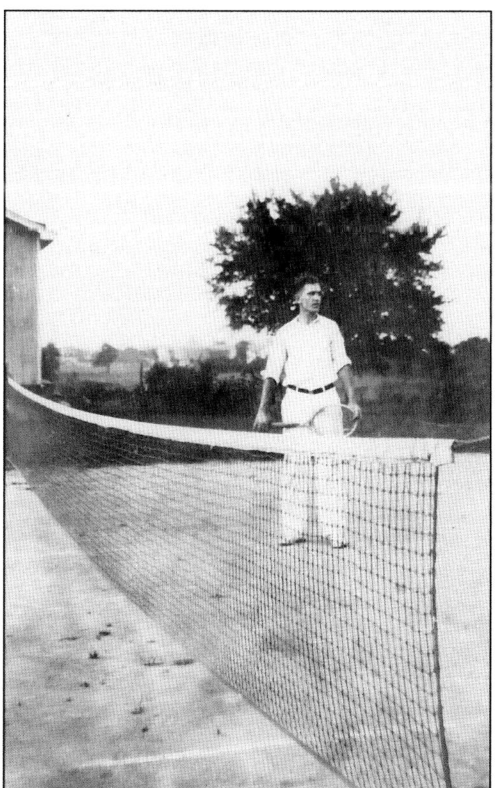

CHARLES AUER PLAYING TENNIS, C. 1930. (Collection of East Brunswick Museum.)

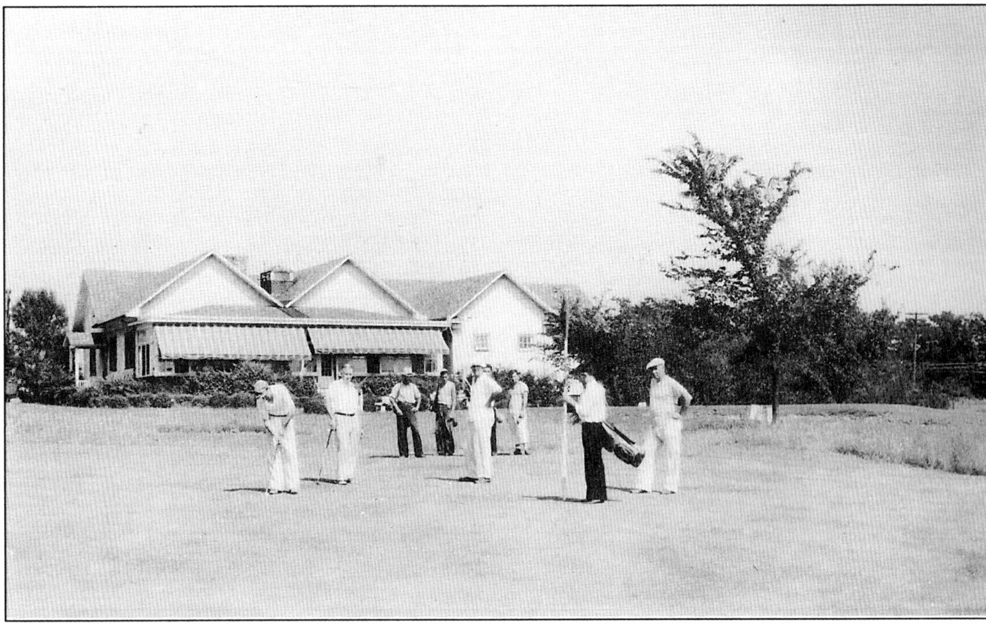

THE LAWRENCE BROOK GOLF CLUB, 1938. The club was a popular spot for golfers. (From *Middlesex County Pictorial 1938*; collection of East Brunswick Museum.)

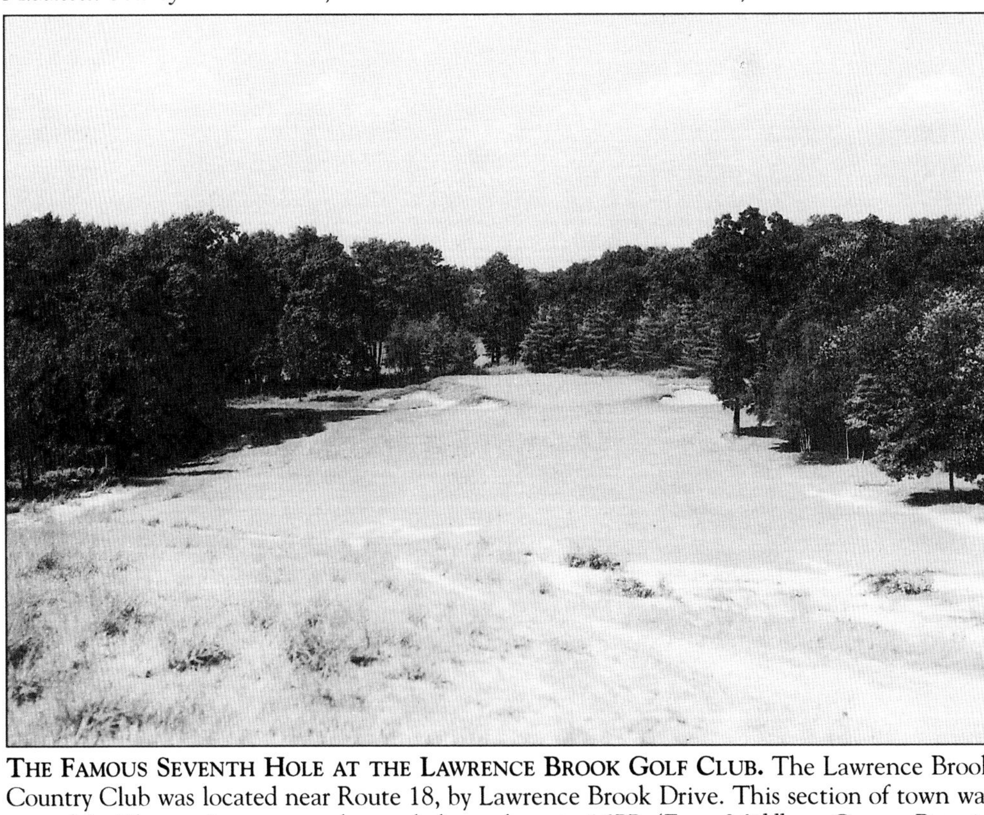

THE FAMOUS SEVENTH HOLE AT THE LAWRENCE BROOK GOLF CLUB. The Lawrence Brook Country Club was located near Route 18, by Lawrence Brook Drive. This section of town was named for Thomas Lawrence, who settled near here in 1677. (From *Middlesex County Pictorial 1938*; collection of East Brunswick Museum.)

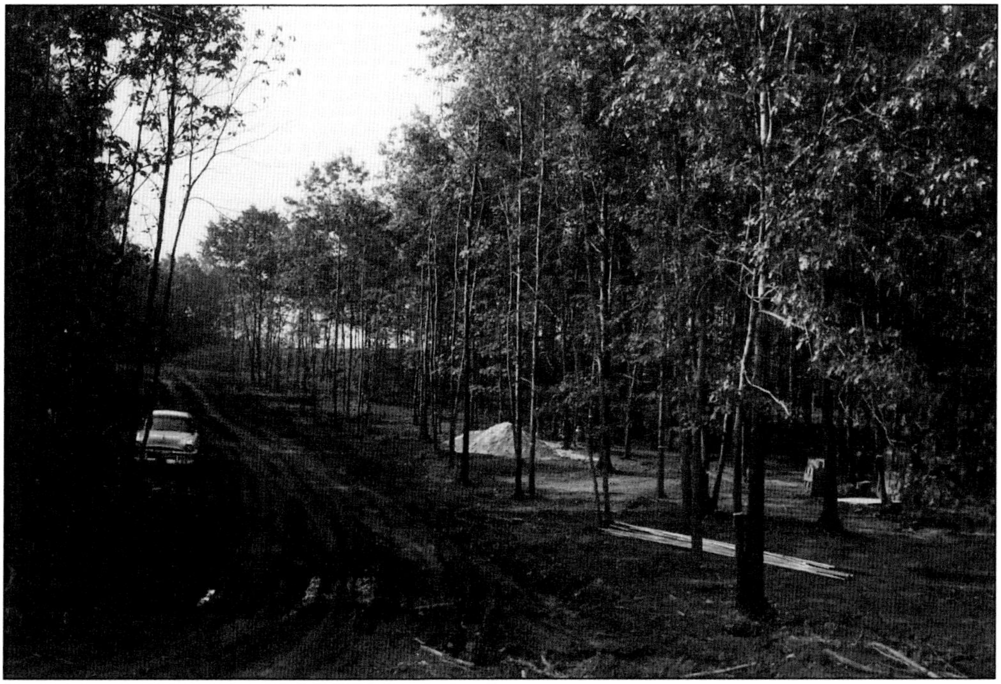

Welsh Park under Construction, c. 1955. Welsh Park was one of East Brunswick's first parks. It was originally called Birch Hill Park, but was later renamed after Frank Welsh. (Collection of East Brunswick Museum.)

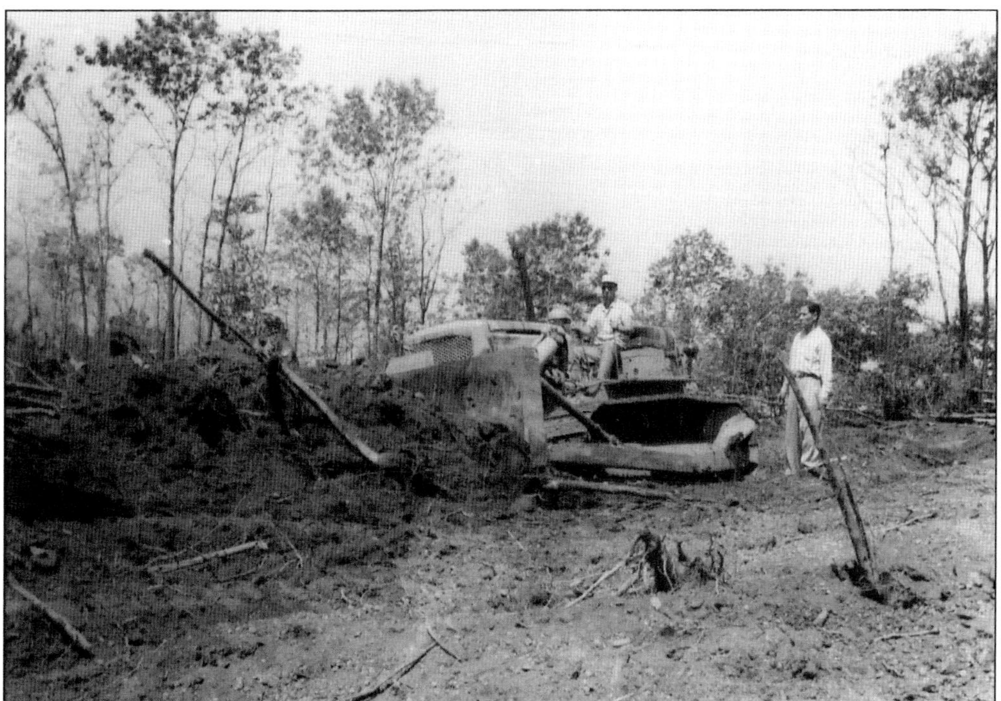

A Bulldozer Clearing Land that would later become Welsh Park, c. 1955. (Collection of East Brunswick Museum.)

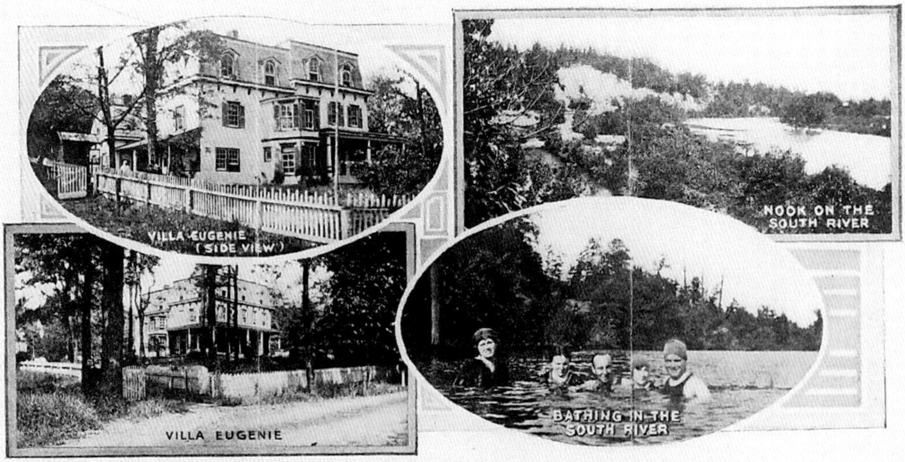

Villa Eugenie - - - Old Bridge - - - New Jersey

VILLA EUGENIE, an all-year-round establishment, in which all the allurements of a home-like atmosphere are linked with the conveniences of a select resort, is situated on the South River Shore Road in one of the most picturesque spots overlooking the river.

THE HOUSE is thoroughly modern in every detail.

THE SLEEPING ROOMS are spacious, well furnished and equipped with every provision for comfort.

THE TABLE is supplied from the Villa's own gardens, dairy and poultry flocks.

THE CLIMATE is ideal, similar to that of Lakewood.

THE CUISINE is under the personal supervision of Monsieur Jean Bickel, ex-chef of leading metropolitan hotels.

THE AMUSEMENTS include boating, bathing, fishing, tennis, croquet, dancing and hunting in season.

RATES, according to location of rooms, quoted on application. Special concessions to permanent guests.

ACCESSIBILITY: Old Bridge is in Middlesex County, N. J., seven miles from New Brunswick, the county seat, and is reached from New York in about one hour and a half via the Pennsylvania Railroad or by auto through Staten Island via Perth Amboy Ferry.

WEEK-END parties catered to.

Address: Jean Bickel, Proprietor, Villa Eugenie, Old Bridge, N. J. Telephone South River: 40 F-2

Following the years this building housed Conover's Boarding School, it was a popular resort hotel with much clientele from New York.

The Old Bridge Section of Town. This section became a popular resort area at the turn of century. The old Home Boarding School was turned into a resort hotel by Jean Bickle. An advertisement to attract people to the area displays such fun activities as bathing in the South River. (Collection of East Brunswick Museum.)

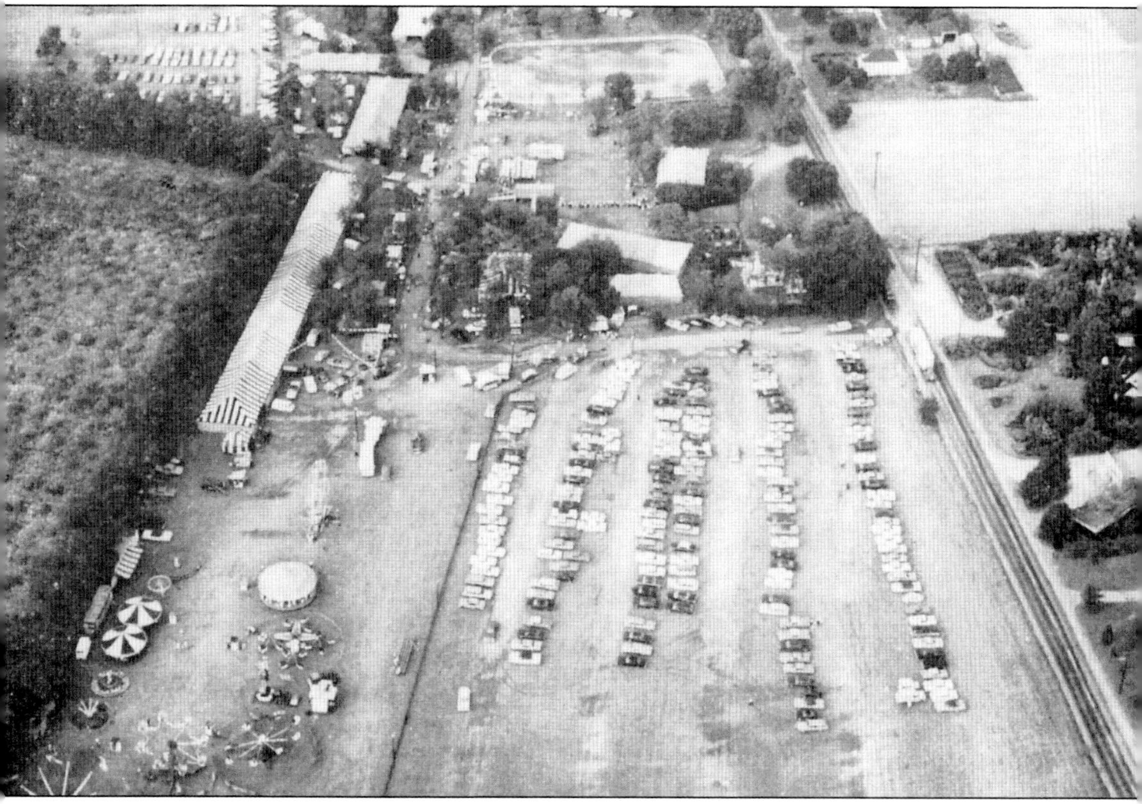

AN AERIAL VIEW OF THE MIDDLESEX COUNTY FAIR, 1970. The Middlesex County Fair originally started as a vegetable and flower show in 1938. At that time it was located in the old Grange Hall on Dunhams Corner Road. The Grange Hall is still standing today, and is used as a local recreational facility. The fair was canceled during World War II, as it was thought that the public would waste gas needed for the war effort to get there.

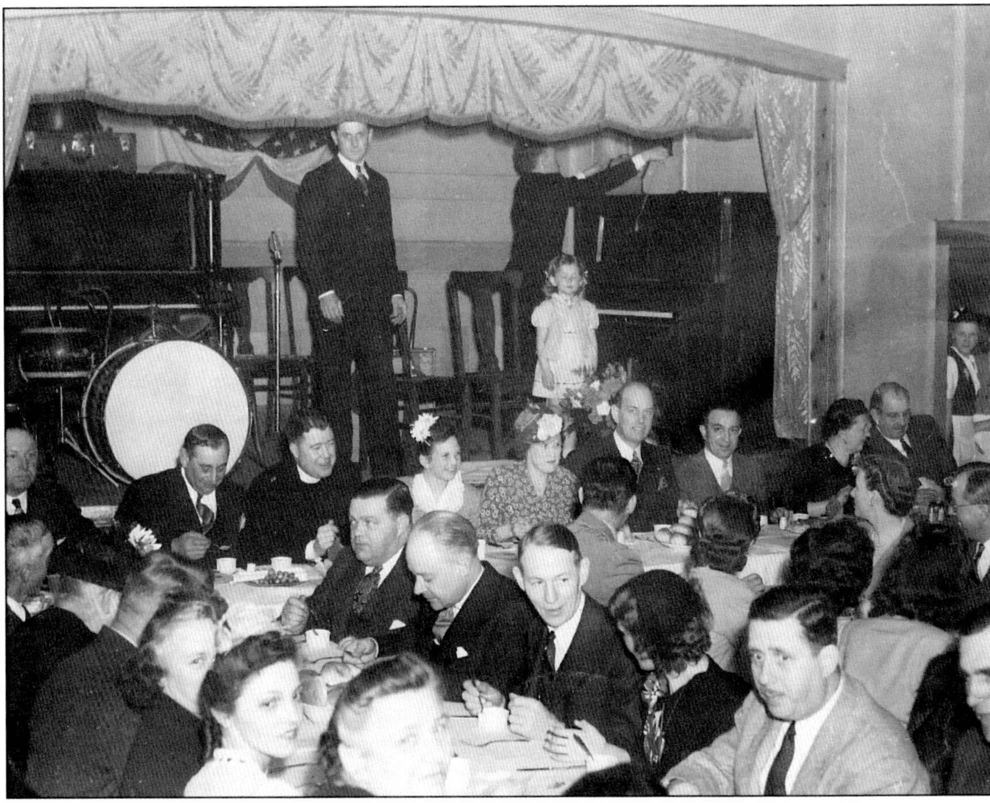

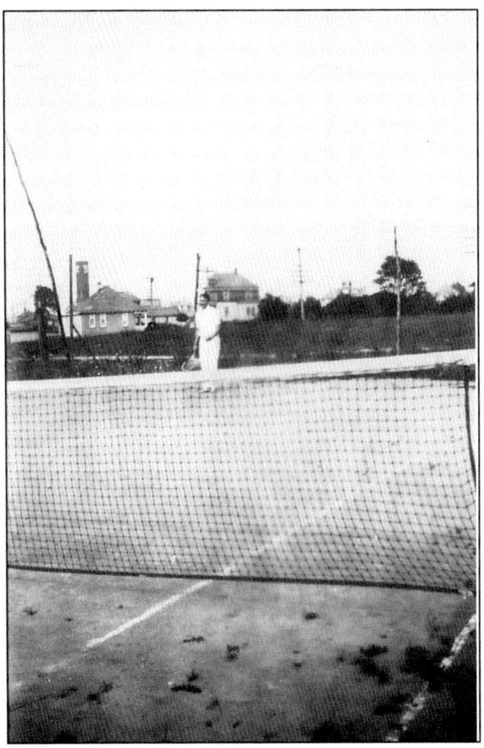

AN EAST BRUNSWICK SOCIAL EVENT, LATE 1940S. (Collection of East Brunswick Museum.)

THE AUER TENNIS COURT, C. 1930. Grace and Charles Auer had this tennis court built on their Cranbury Road farm, near the present-day East Brunswick High School. (Collection of East Brunswick Museum.)

Four

Houses and Buildings

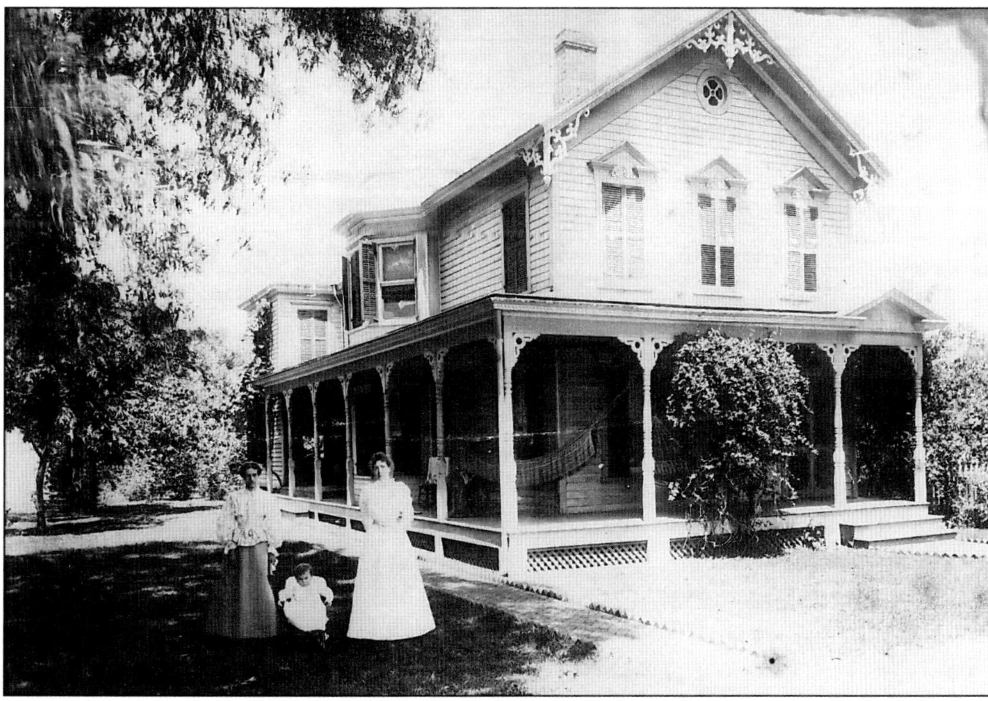

THE HOME OF STEPHEN DISBROW, C. 1890. Stephen Disbrow, a local doctor in the Old Bridge section, lived in this ornate house around the turn of the century. Although remodeled, the building still stands today at 180 Main Street, and is now a veterinarian's office. (Collection of East Brunswick Museum.)

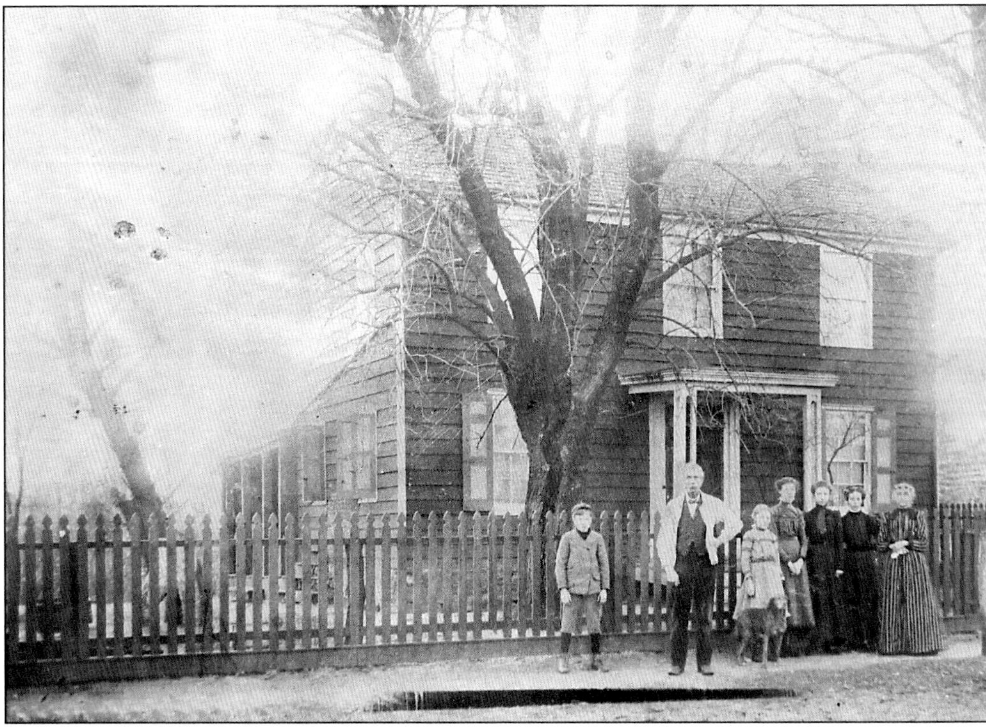

A Quaint Local Home. This house still stands at 6 Kossman Street, in the Historic District. Around the turn of the century, it was moved to its present location.

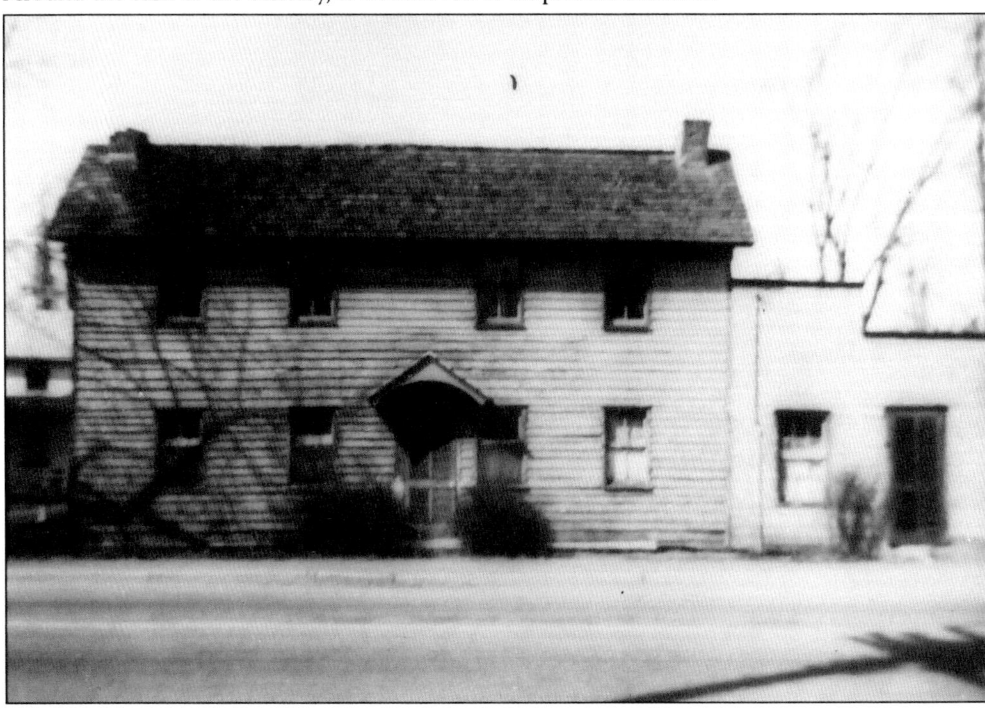

The Home of Andrew Jackson Disbrow, c. 1890. This home, once located on Main Street, is no longer standing. (Collection of East Brunswick Museum.)

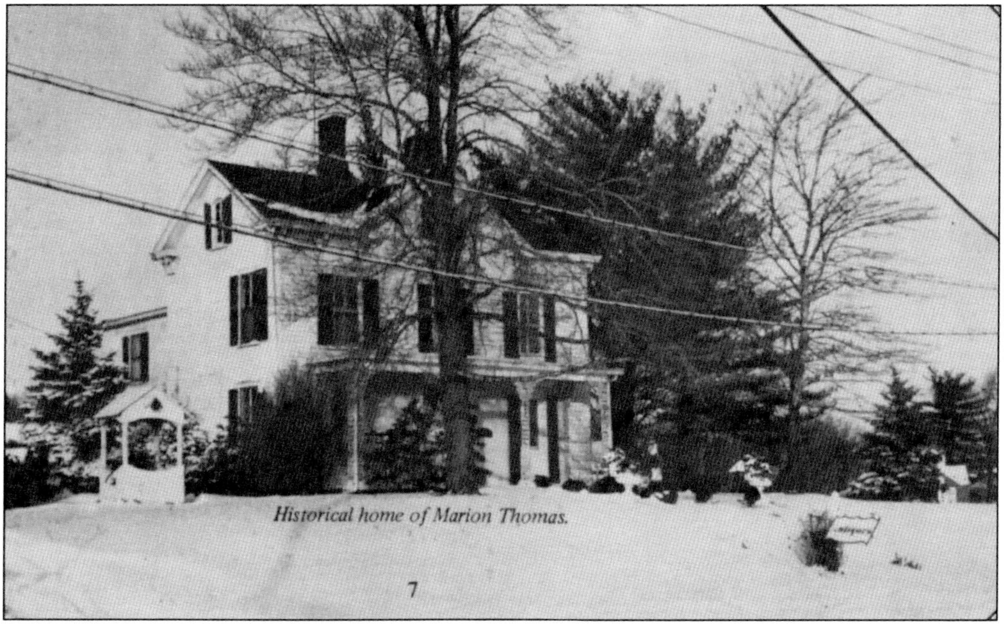

THE MARION THOMAS HOUSE, ROUTE 18. Originally built as a private residence in the early 1800s, this building was added onto and turned into the Cosmopolitan Hotel by the 1880s. In more recent times, it has been the home and antique shop of Marion Thomas. It still stands today, behind a clear sound barrier on Route 18. (Collection of East Brunswick Museum.)

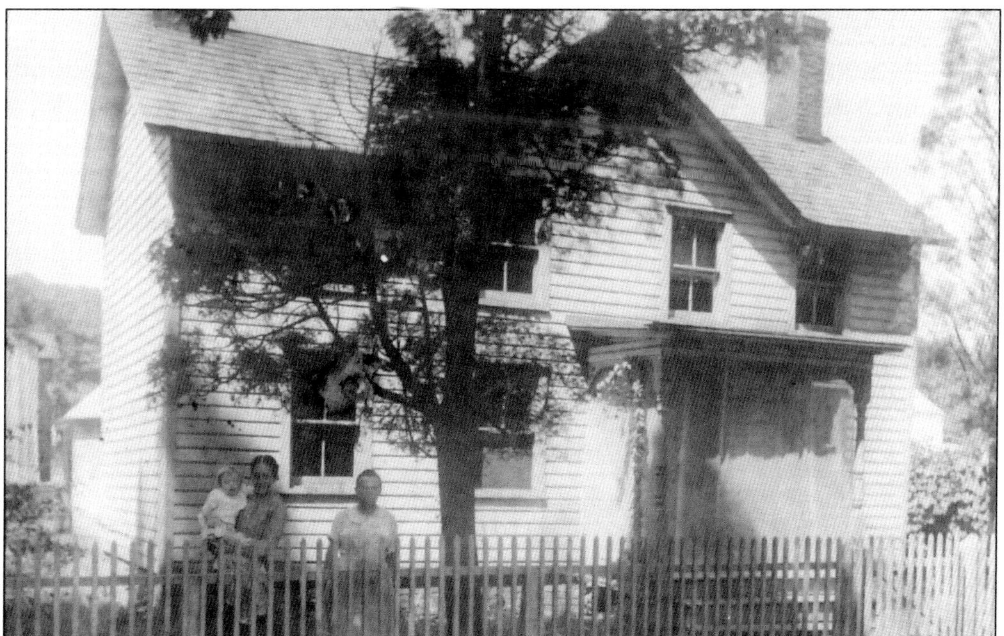

NO. 12 KOSSMAN STREET, C. 1890. This house was used as a restaurant as early as 1867. It is owned by the Cosgrove family, and looks much the same today as it does here. (Collection of Alberta Yuhas.)

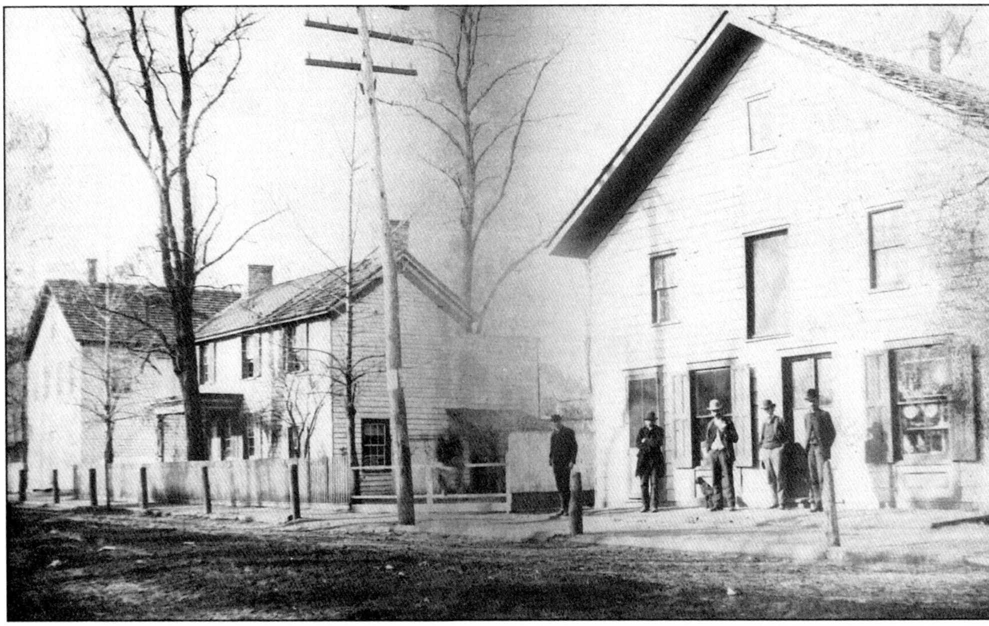

MAIN STREET, C. 1870. This view shows the home of Alice Appleby. The two general stores on either side of the house burned down at the turn of century. (Collection of East Brunswick Museum.)

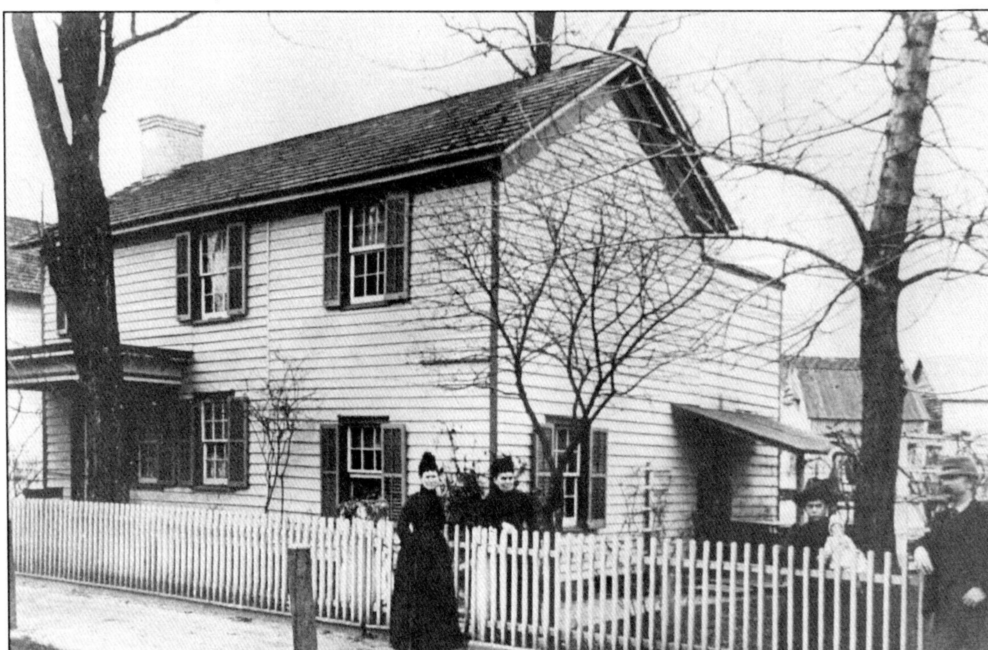

ALICE MURRAY APPLEBY DEVOE (ON THE SIDEWALK), C. 1890. Standing outside the fence is Alice Murray Appleby, who was born in the home in 1868. She later moved to Spotswood and died there in 1913. Her son, Fred Devoe, donated this house to East Brunswick Township in 1944 to be used as a library and civic center. The building still stands today at 166 Main Street. (Collection of East Brunswick Museum.)

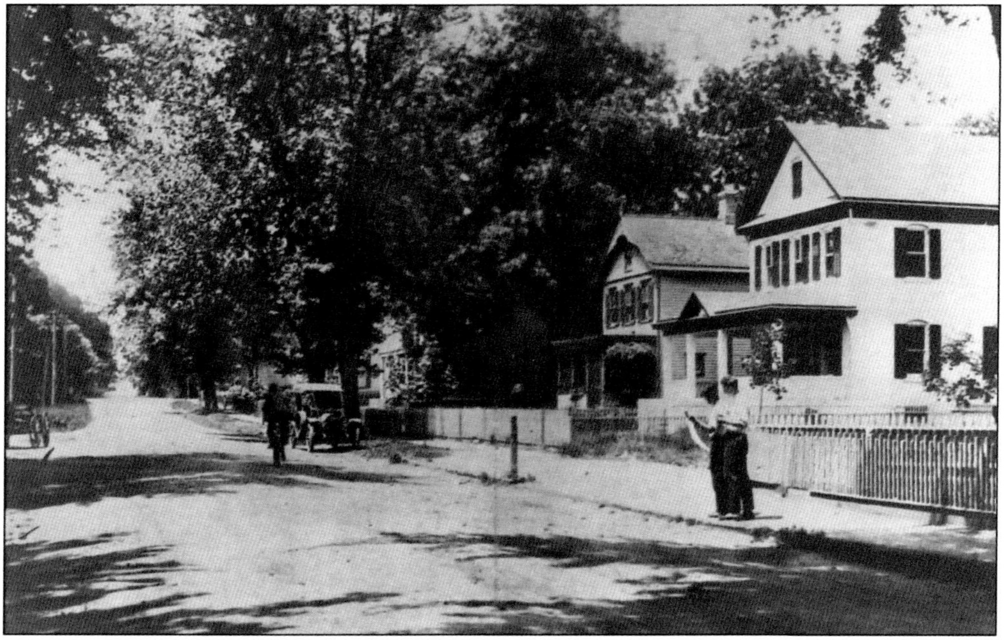

Main Street, Looking toward the Corner of the Old Bridge Turnpike, c. 1910. The building to the immediate right was the home of Murray Chittick. Murray's father, George, built the home around the turn of the century after the old house burned down. This home still stands today on Main Street and is constructed out of hollow tile, making it fireproof. (Collection of East Brunswick Museum.)

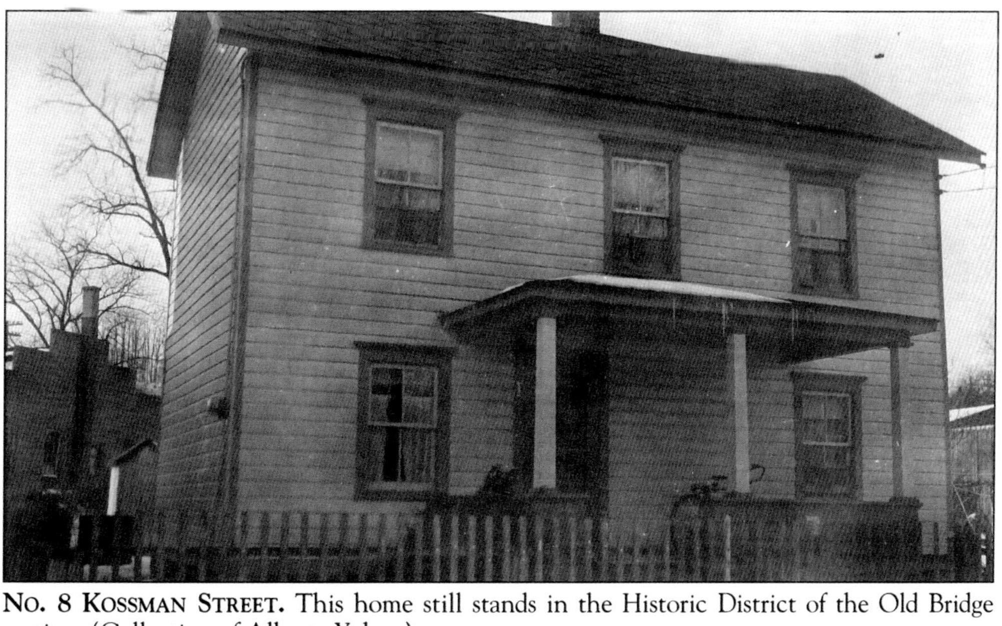

No. 8 Kossman Street. This home still stands in the Historic District of the Old Bridge section. (Collection of Alberta Yuhas.)

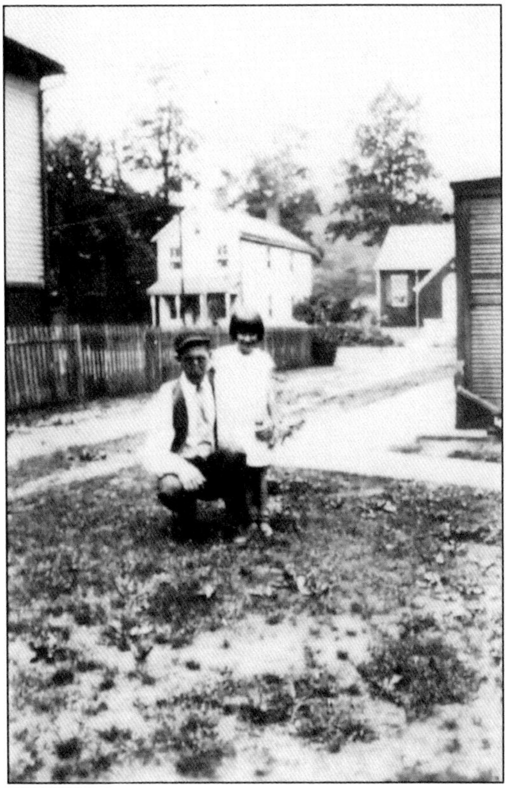

JOHN ALBECKER, 1930. The home in the background belonged to Rachel Slover Wright, who was murdered in the house in 1906. The murderer was never caught, but a local newspaper vowed that, if found, the newly purchased electric chair at the state prison would be put to use. (Collection of Alberta Yuhas.)

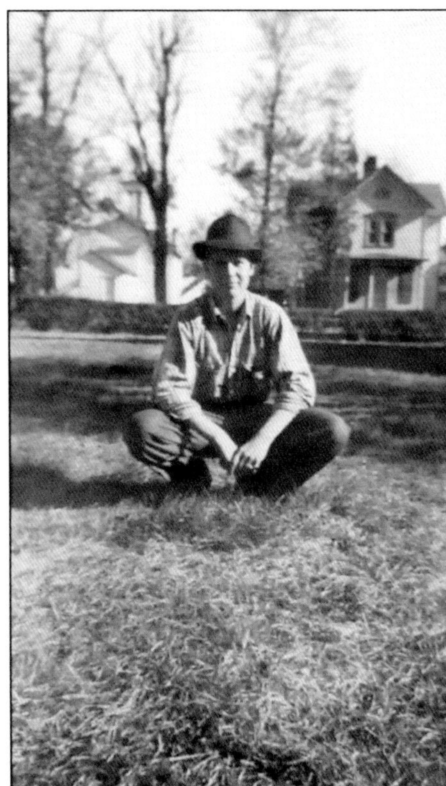

THE HOME OF HANNAH DISBROW, 1871. The house in the background to the right belonged to Hannah Disbrow, who lived there with her six children. Her husband was killed in the Civil War. Hannah was a skilled dressmaker and used these skills to help support her family. The structure is still standing today at 27 Kossman Street and is the home of John and Alberta Yuhas. (Collection of John and Alberta Yuhas.)

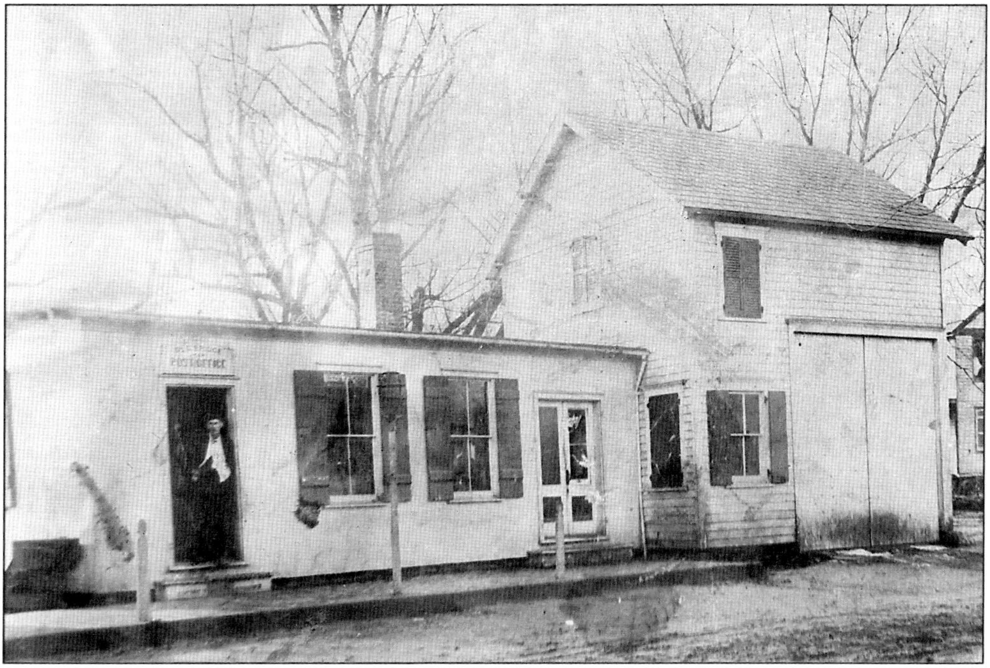

THE POST OFFICE, C. 1880. At one time the old post office was located behind the weigh station at the corner of the Old Bridge Turnpike and Main Street. The mail would arrive by train and then be sorted in this building. (Collection of East Brunswick Museum.)

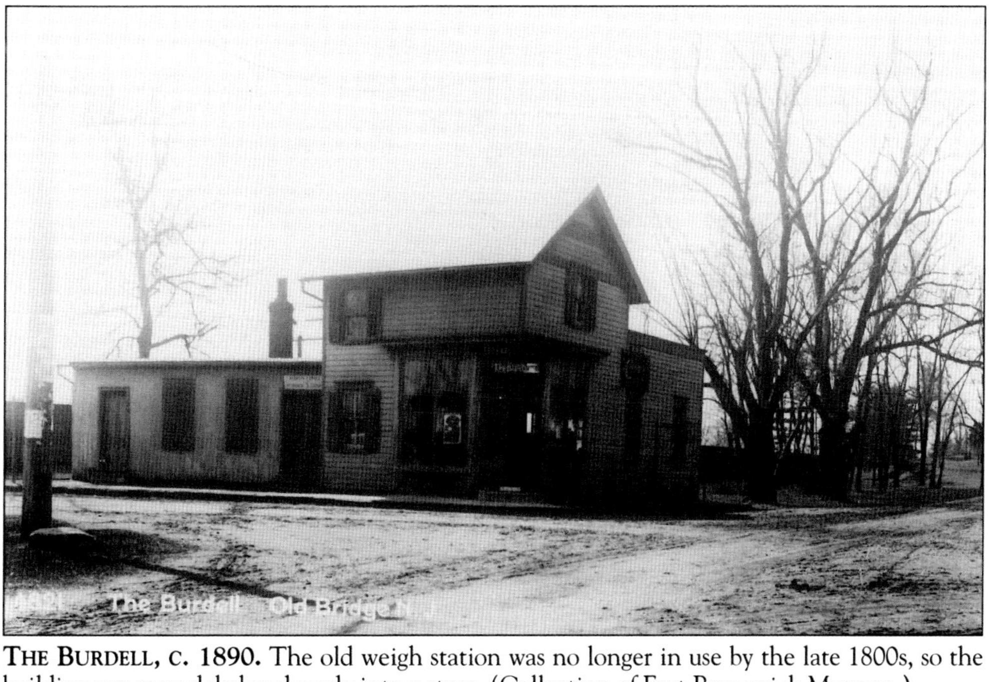

THE BURDELL, C. 1890. The old weigh station was no longer in use by the late 1800s, so the building was remodeled and made into a store. (Collection of East Brunswick Museum.)

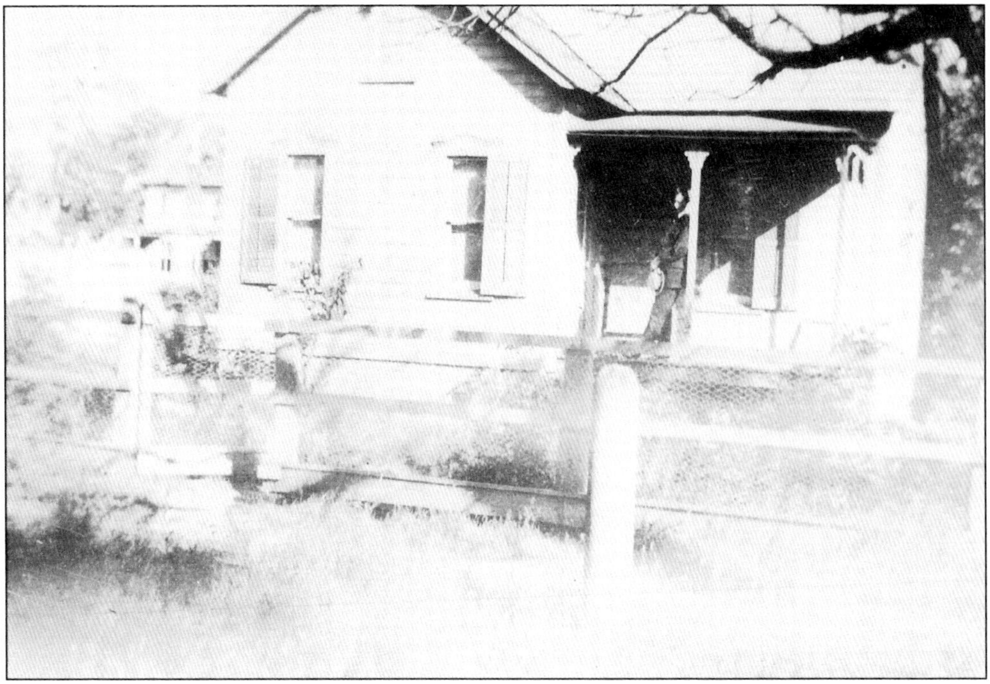

THE HOME OF MILTON B. CARPENTER, 9 OAK STREET, THE OLD BRIDGE SECTION, C. 1923. (Collection of Florence Mount.)

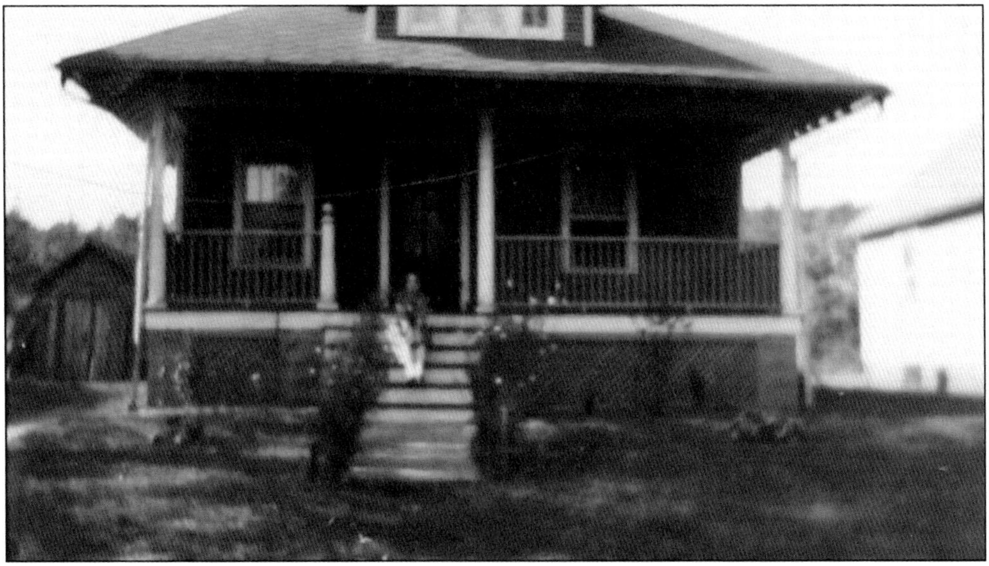

THE REID FAMILY HOME. This house, located at 46 Kossman Street in the township's Historic District, was purchased as a kit home from a Sears and Roebuck Catalog in 1926 at a cost of about $1,500. Its current owners, Carl and Penny Barry, have restored the home. (Collection of Florence Mount.)

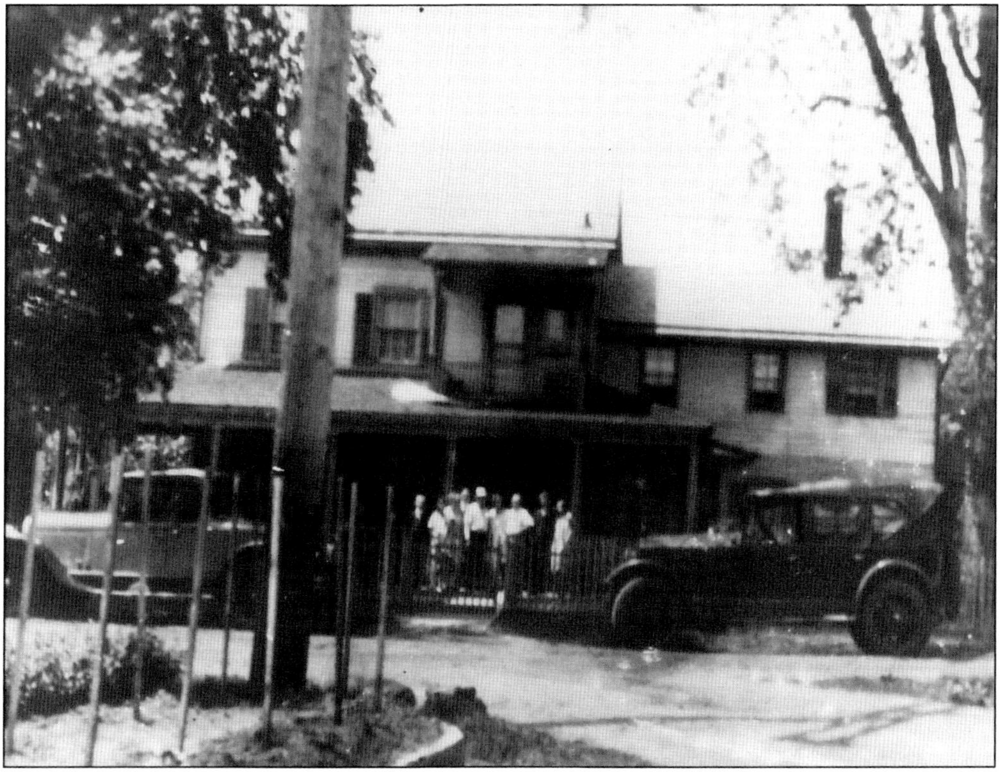

THE FORMER ST. THOMAS CHURCH RECTORY, C. 1931. Originally built as a home in the 1700s, this structure later served as a rectory for St. Thomas Church. It is still standing on the corner of River Road and Kossman Street in the Old Bridge section. (Collection of East Brunswick Museum.)

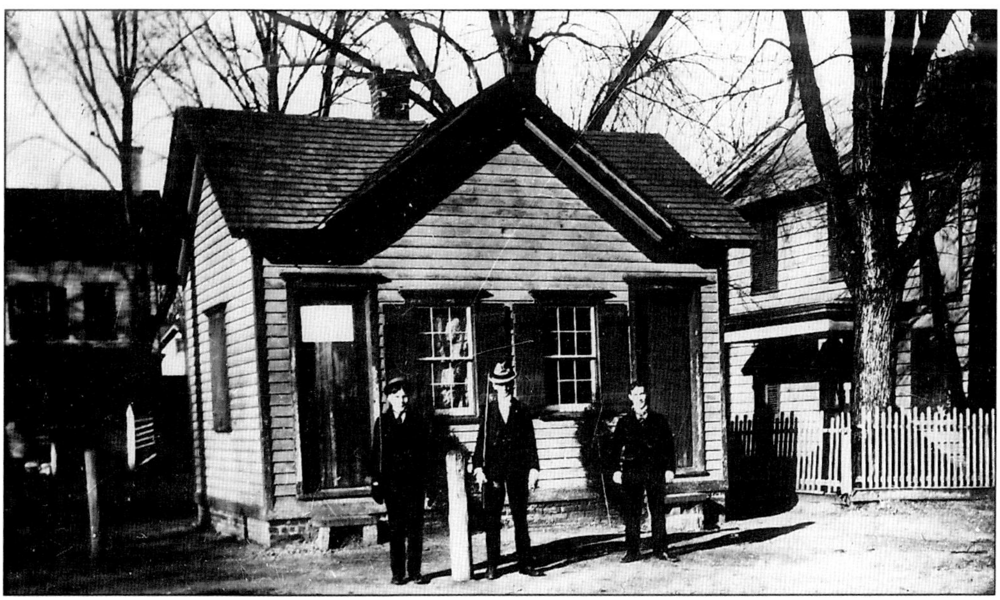

A BARBERSHOP, C. 1900. Mr. Latscher operated a barbershop in the Old Bridge section of East Brunswick. (Collection of East Brunswick Museum.)

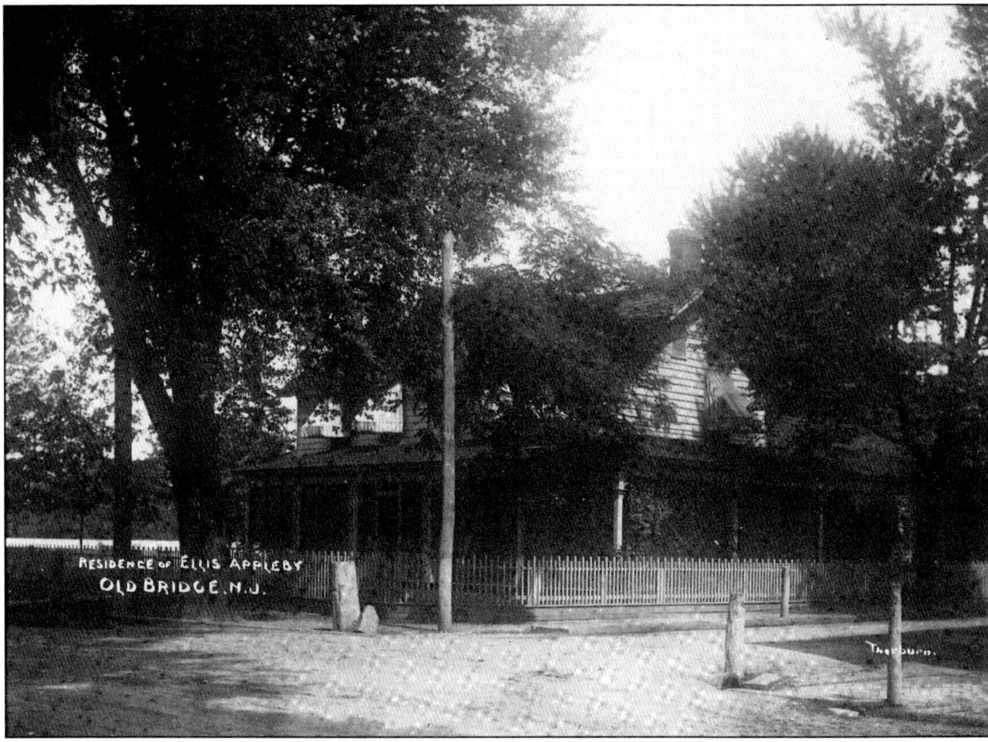

THE APPLEBY HOME, BUILT IN THE EARLY 1800S. This was an early home of the Appleby family, who lived on Main Street in what is now the Historic District of the Old Bridge section. James Appleby, along with his brother Leonard, operated a general store. The home still stands on the corner of Main Street and Emerson Road. (Collection of East Brunswick Museum.)

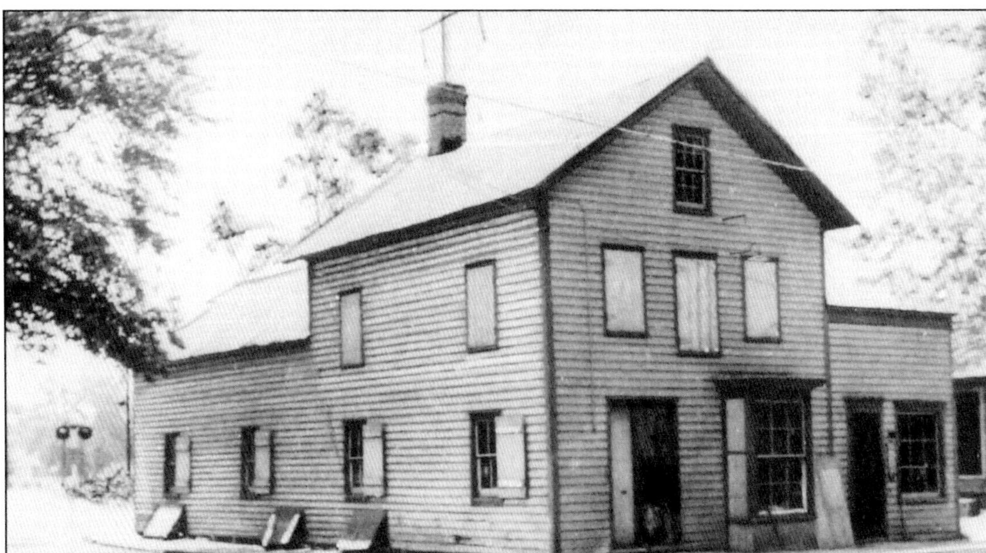

APPLEBY'S GENERAL STORE, C. 1900. It was said that if they didn't have what you wanted, they could get it for you. The general store first opened up in 1826, and would serve the public for over 140 years before finally closing in 1962. The building still stands on the corner of Emerson Street and Main Street. (Collection of East Brunswick Museum.)

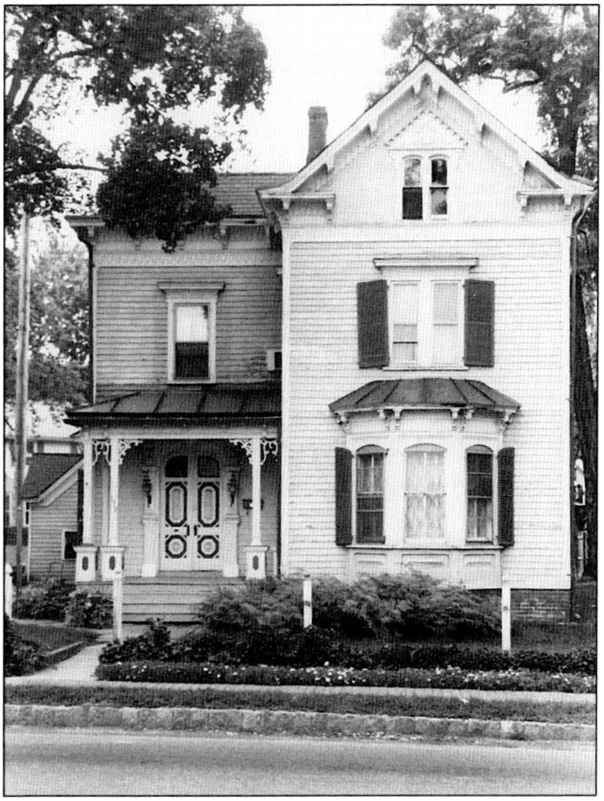

THE HOME OF DOCTOR IRA CRANDALL. This Italianate house was built in the late 1860s. Doctor Crandall made house calls in a horse-drawn carriage until he was able to purchase an automobile. The house still stands near the intersection of Main Street and the Old Bridge Turnpike. (Collection of Arciszewski Family.)

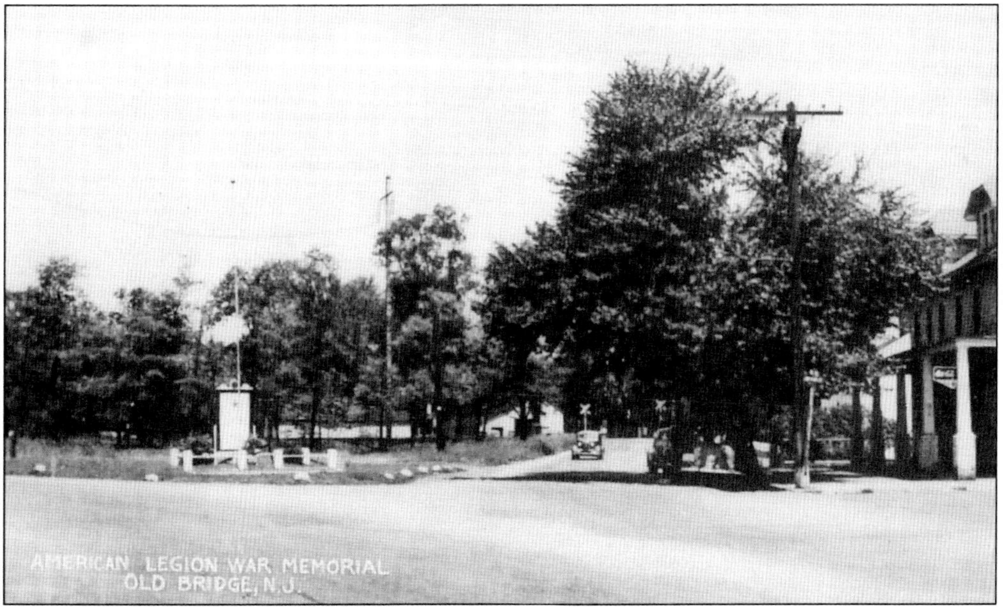

THE AMERICAN LEGION WAR MEMORIAL, C. 1945. This memorial was located on a triangular piece of property on Emerson Road (right) and Matawan Road (left). A newer memorial and the American Legion Hall occupy the site today. (Collection of East Brunswick Museum.)

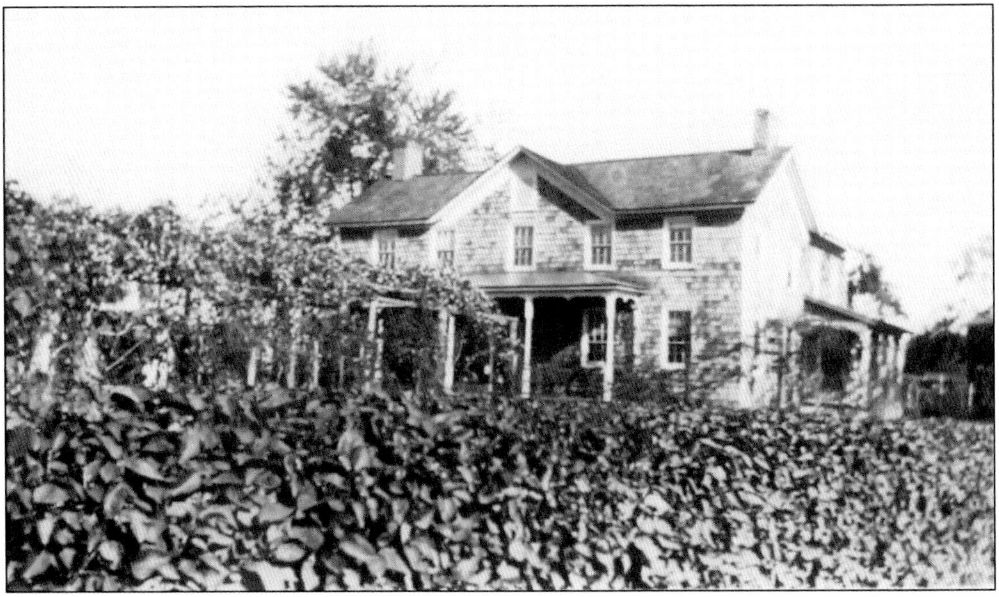

The Rogers House, c. 1920. This home was originally built prior to 1780. In the 1800s, it was owned by Captain William Rogers, who operated a sloop on the South River between Old Bridge and markets in New York City. A grape arbor connected his house to his daughter's house just next door. (Collection of William Kraemer.)

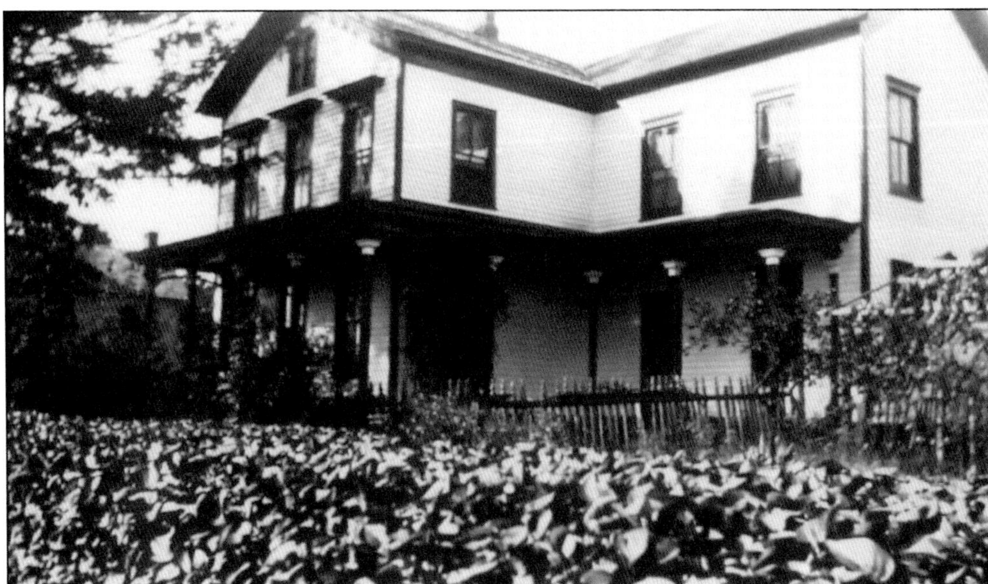

The Rogers-Brown Home, c. 1920. William Rogers' daughter and her husband lived in this house, which was built prior to 1868. It still stands at 22 Maple Street; however, a fire in recent years destroyed the wing to the right of the photograph. (Collection of William Kraemer.)

Five

Schools

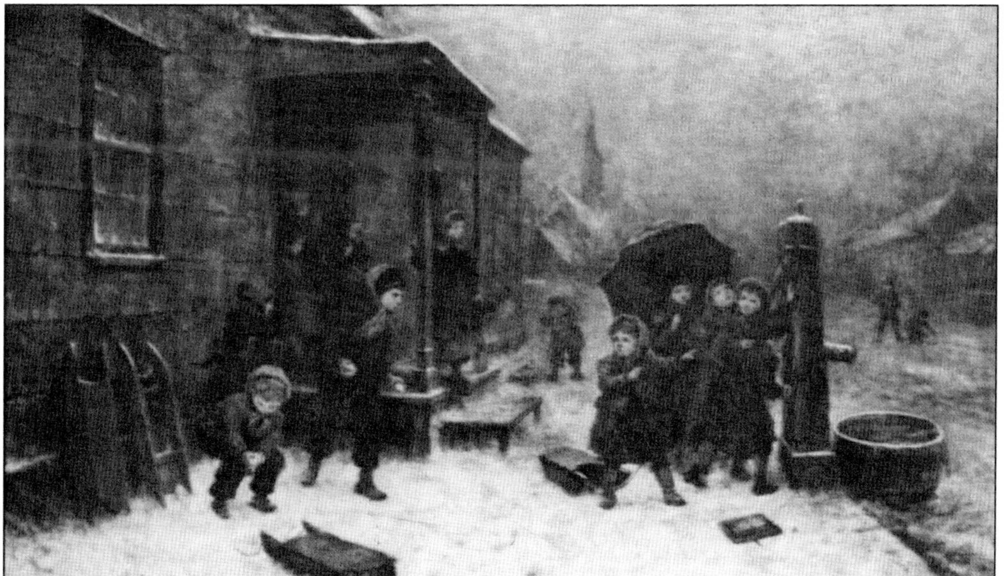

A C. 1880 PAINTING BY LOCAL ARTIST JAMES CRAWFORD THOM. The subject of this painting, titled *Winter in Old Bridge*, is the local one-room schoolhouse on Kossman Street in the Old Bridge section of East Brunswick, now the township's Historic District. Several of the students shown here are preparing for a snowball fight. The school building was later moved a block from its original site to 32 Kossman Street, where it still stands as a local residence. It is the oldest schoolhouse in East Brunswick, having been built prior to 1850. (Collection of East Brunswick Museum.)

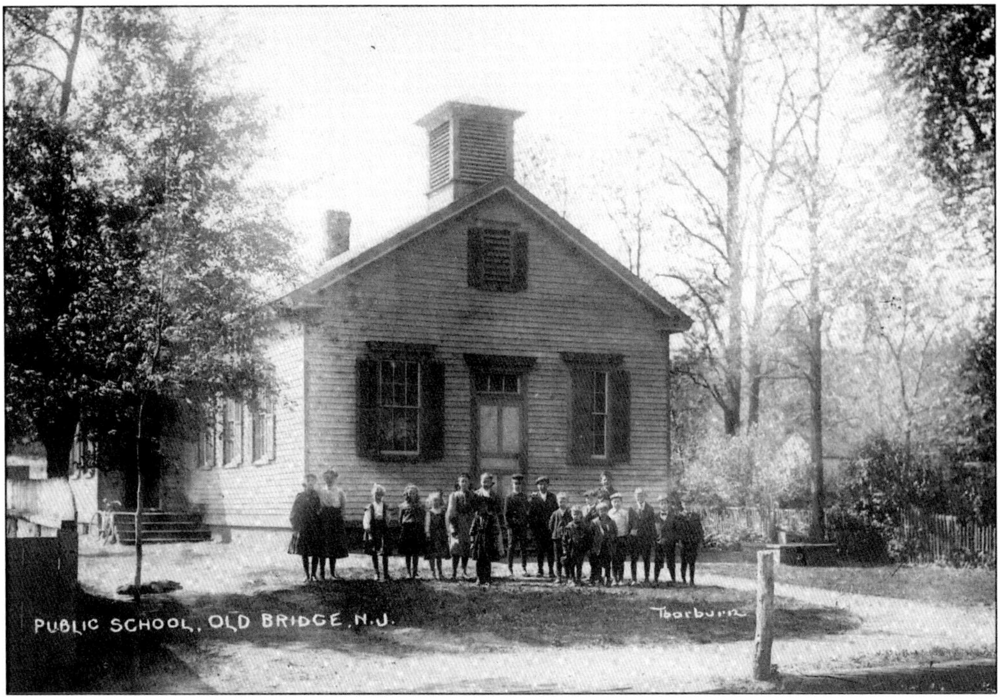

PUBLIC SCHOOL #2, C. 1890. After the one-room schoolhouse became overcrowded, a new larger building was constructed. (Collection of East Brunswick Museum.)

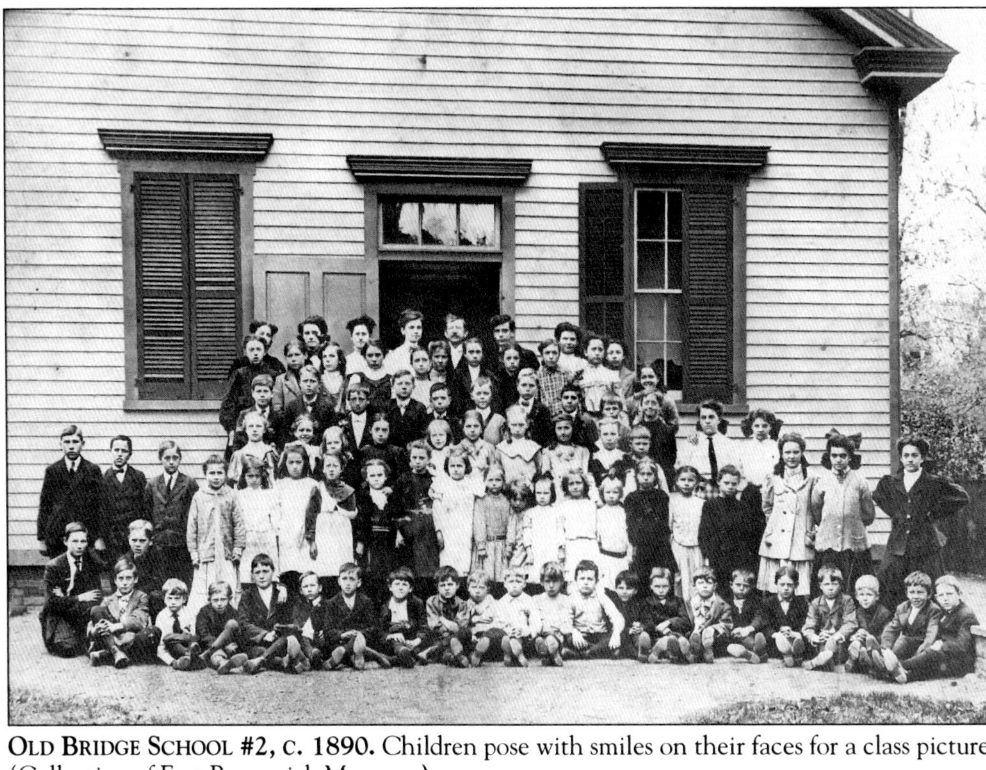

OLD BRIDGE SCHOOL #2, C. 1890. Children pose with smiles on their faces for a class picture. (Collection of East Brunswick Museum.)

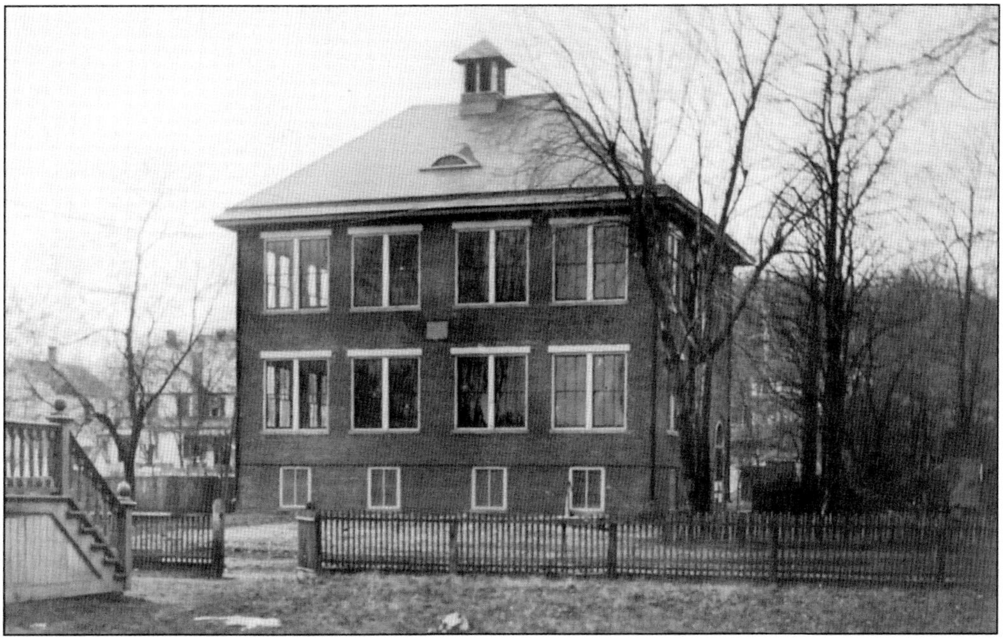

CRANDALL SCHOOL, C. 1910. Originally called Old Bridge School #3, this building would later be renamed Crandall School in honor of Joseph Crandall, a local boy killed in World War I. This building had separate entrances for boys and girls. A bell on the top of the building signalled the start of classes. (Collection of Alberta Yuhas.)

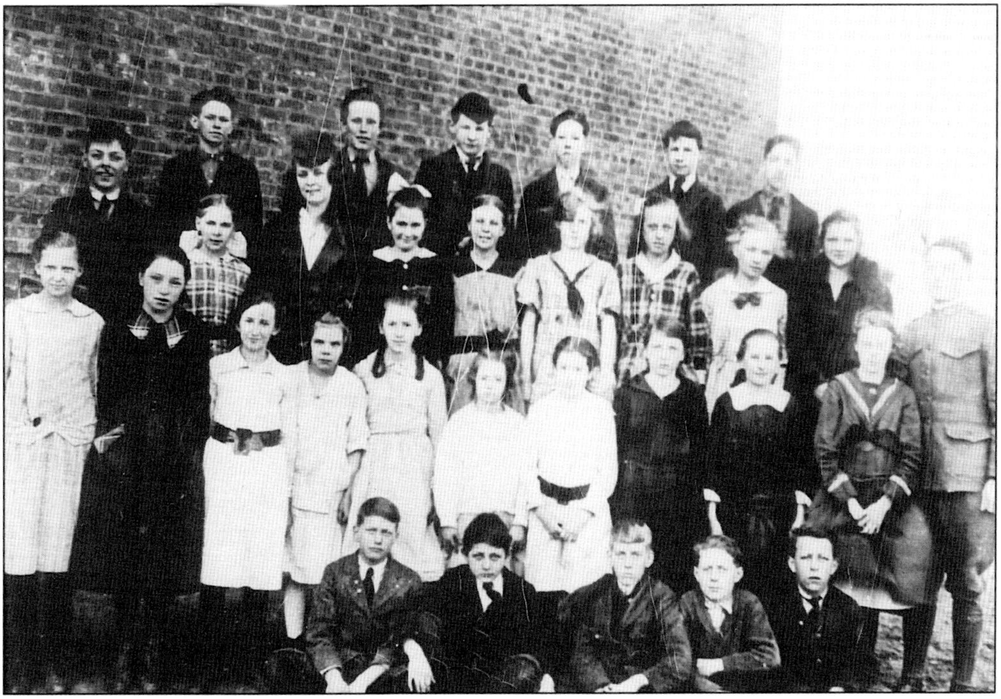

A 1920 CLASS PHOTOGRAPH. The teacher, a World War I veteran, wears his uniform with pride as his class stands for their picture. (Collection of East Brunswick Museum.)

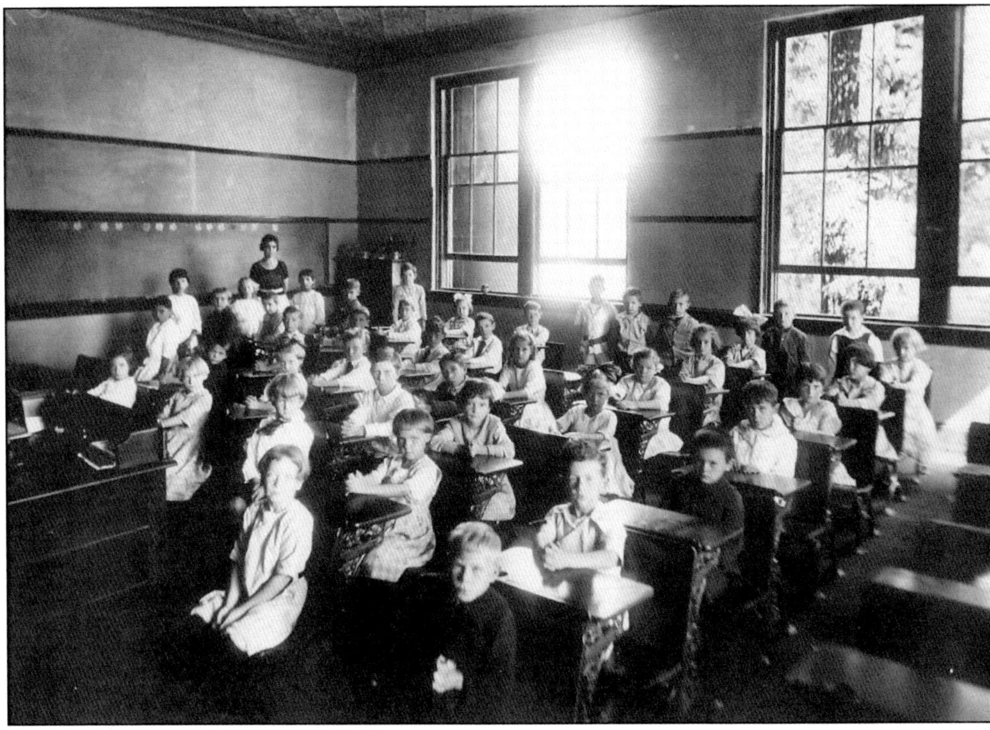

The Interior of Crandall School, c. 1920. Before electricity, the school was lit with gaslights. (Collection of East Brunswick Museum.)

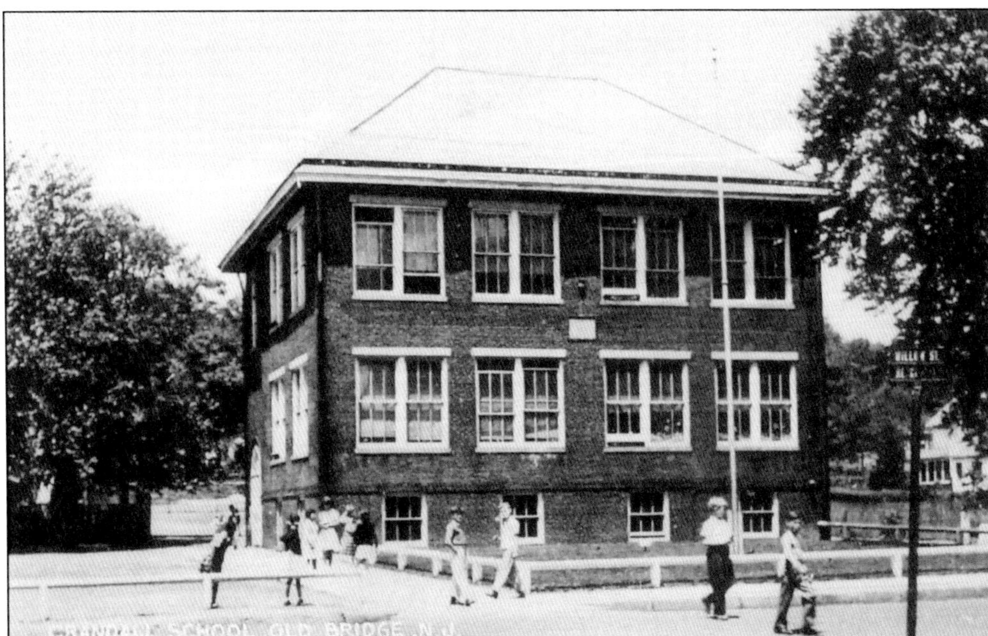

Crandall School, c. 1935. Crandall School still stands today on Kossman Street, in the Old Bridge section. (Collection of Alberta Yuhas.)

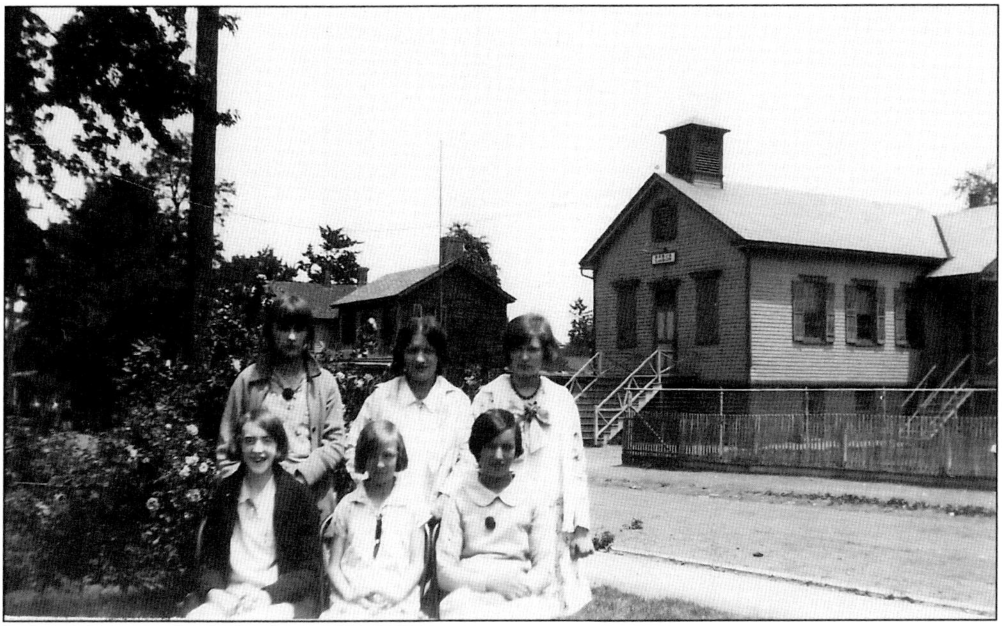

A SCHOOL PHOTOGRAPH. This view shows the old town hall in the background on Kossman Street. (Collection of Alberta Yuhas.)

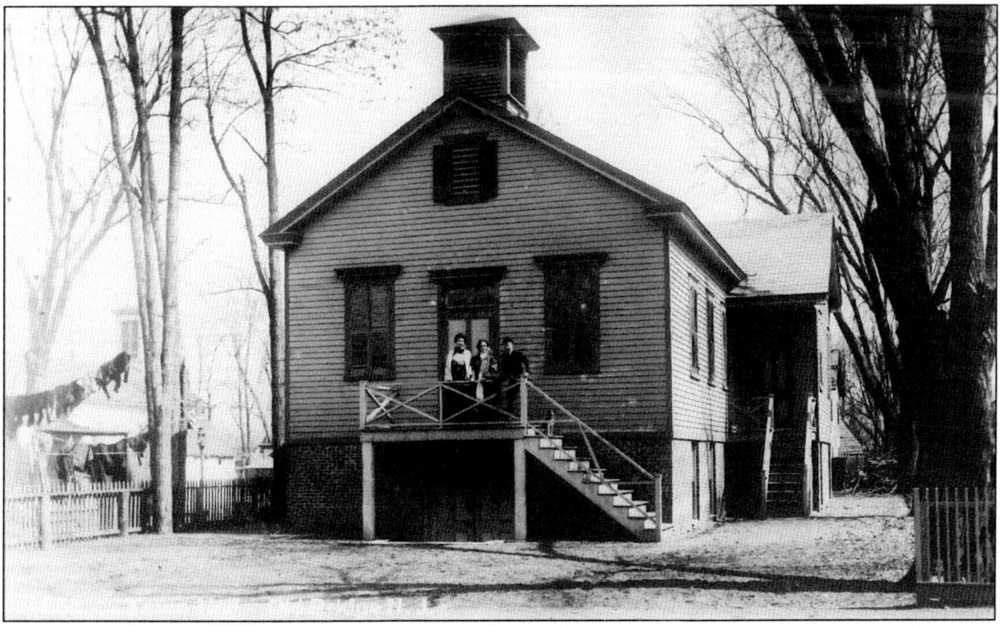

THE TOWN HALL, C. 1915. After the second public school became overcrowded, a new brick schoolhouse was built. The old school was moved across the street and served as the town hall for the Old Bridge section. (Collection of East Brunswick Museum.)

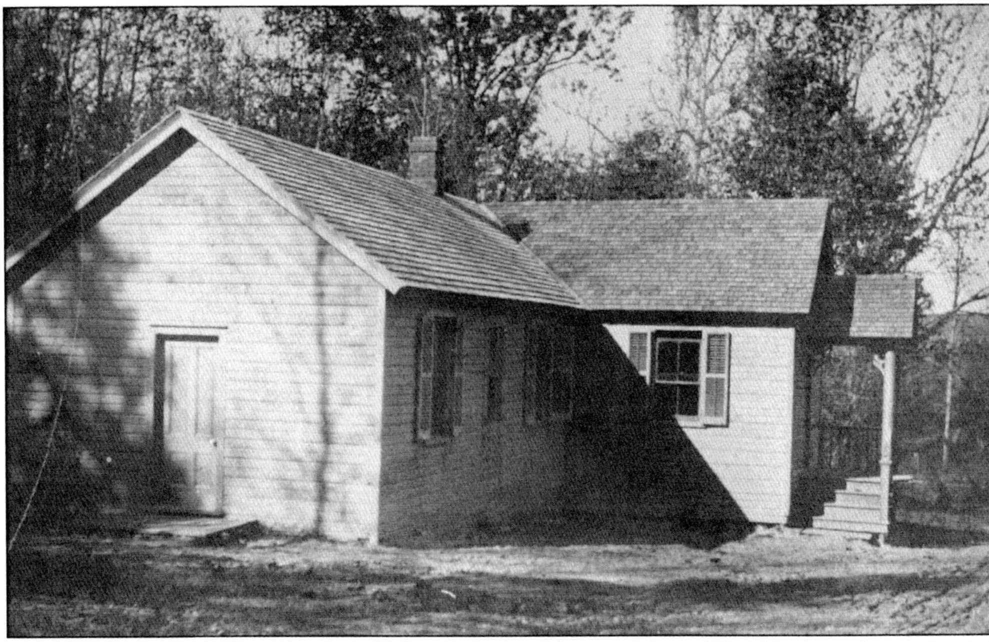

THE SUMMERHILL ROAD SCHOOLHOUSE, C. 1920. The township of East Brunswick was divided into school districts that served children from various sections of the town. This one-room schoolhouse was built in the 1800s and was located near the rear entrance of the Brunswick Square Mall. (Collection of East Brunswick Museum.)

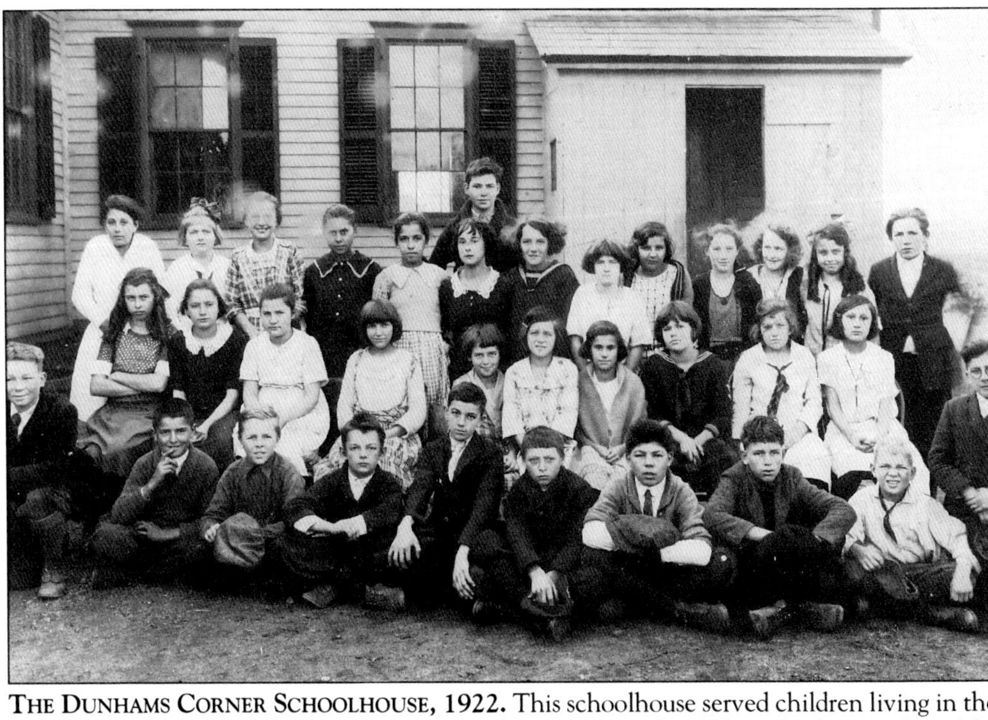

THE DUNHAMS CORNER SCHOOLHOUSE, 1922. This schoolhouse served children living in the Dunhams Corner section of town. Here the sixth, seventh, and eighth grades have gathered for a photograph. (Collection of East Brunswick Museum.)

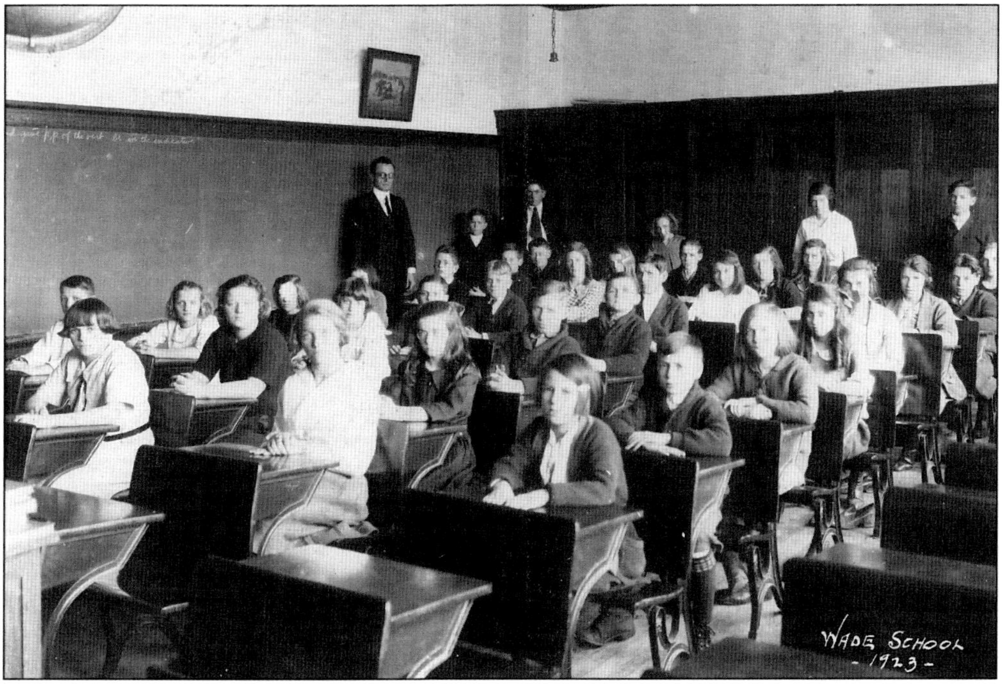

WADE SCHOOL, 1923. The school, located on the Milltown Road, was built in the early 1920s. This interior photograph shows the sixth, seventh, and eighth grades. (Collection of East Brunswick Museum.)

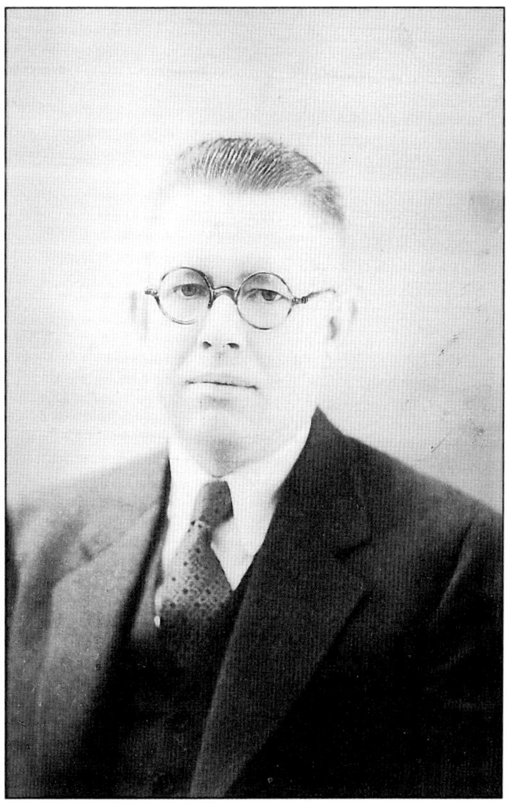

MURRAY CHITTICK, THE SUPERINTENDENT OF SCHOOLS FOR EAST BRUNSWICK. Chittick School, on the Old Bridge Turnpike, is named after him. (Collection of Alberta Yuhas.)

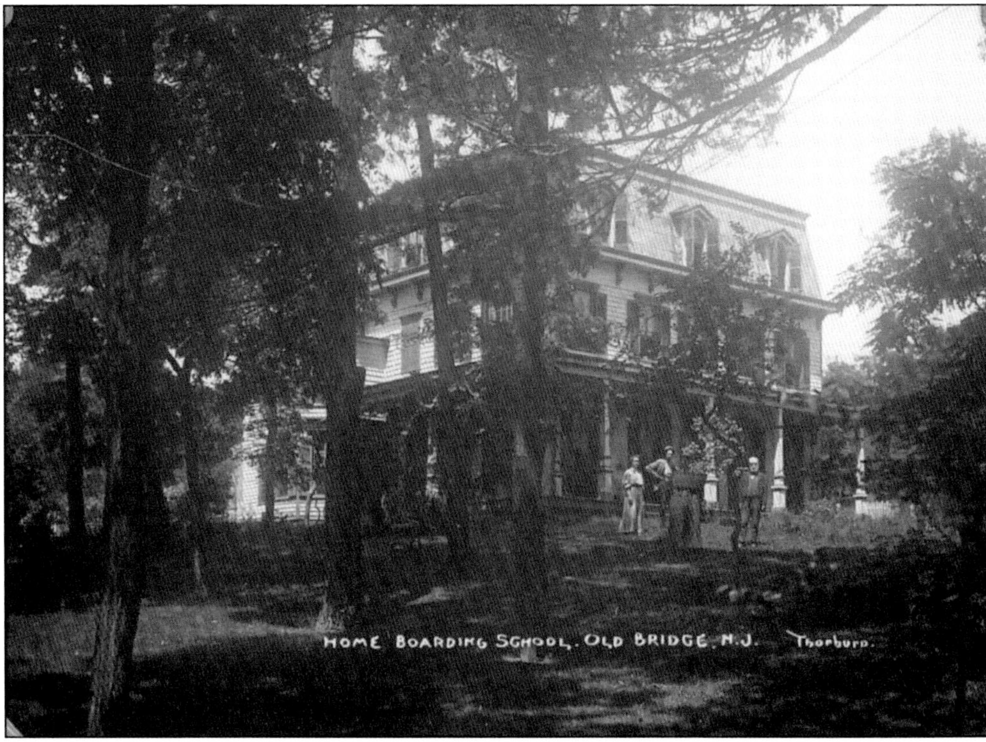

THE HOME BOARDING SCHOOL, C. 1890. A large boarding school was built on River Road in the late 1860s. Local residents, as well as students from other parts of the United States, lived and learned various skills on the property. The building still stands today as a private residence on River Road, but a 1950s fire destroyed the Mansard roof.

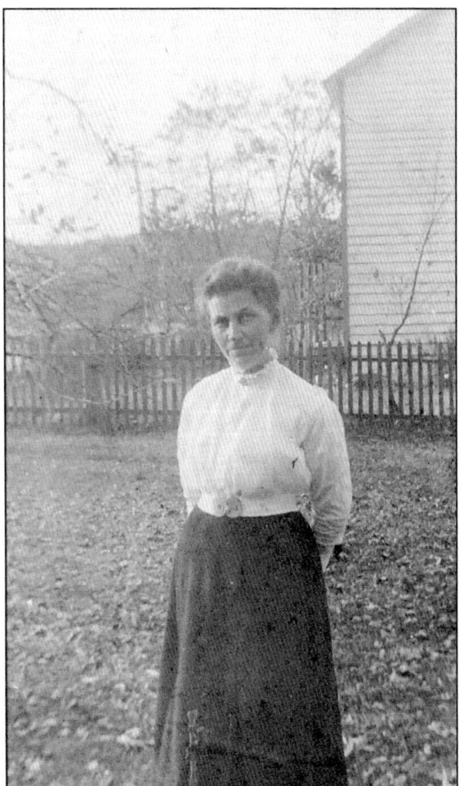

ELLA HAYWARD HOLMES OSBORNE, A TEACHER AT THE HOME BOARDING SCHOOL. Her family also owned considerable property in the Old Bridge section. (Collection of East Brunswick Museum.)

Six

Civic and Public Good

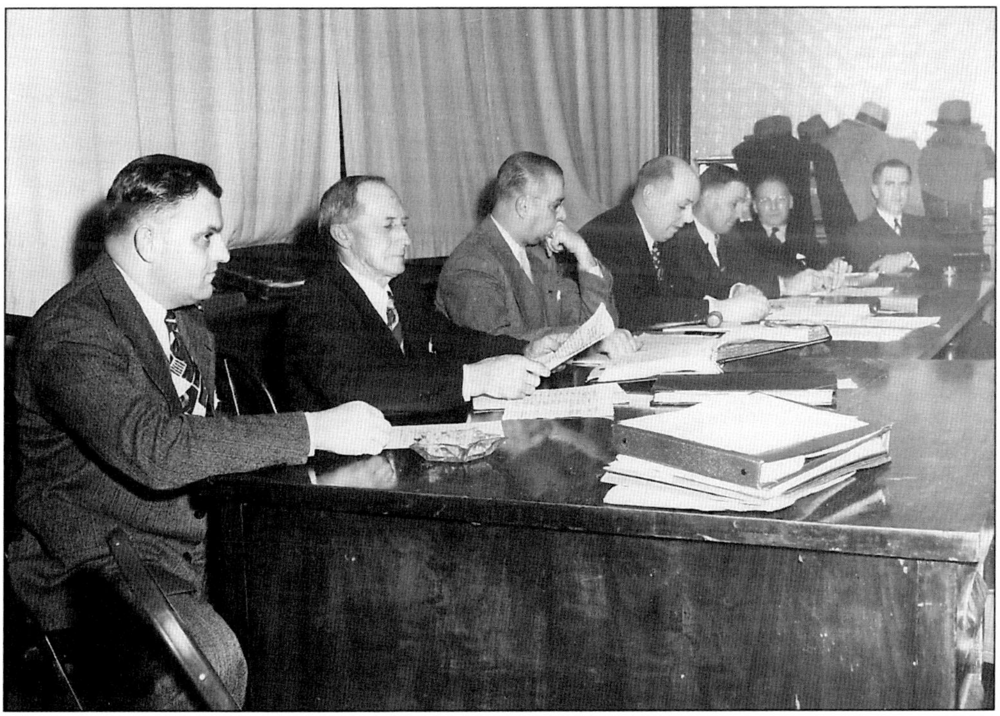

THE TOWNSHIP COMMITTEE, c. 1947. The early governing system of East Brunswick was by committeemen. From left to right are Treasurer Joseph Chapkowski, Clerk Frank Smith, Committeeman Vernon L. Appleby, Chairman Charles Sullivan, Committeeman Charles Skistimas, Attorney Thomas Mitchell, and Tax Assessor Charles Auer. (Collection of East Brunswick Museum.)

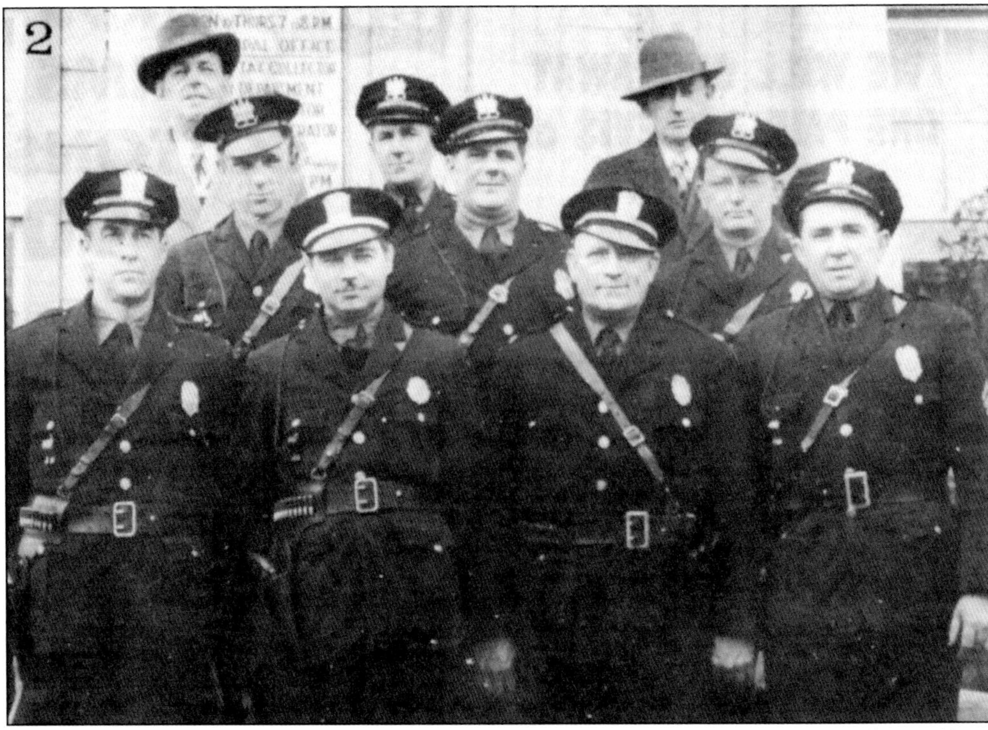

THE EAST BRUNSWICK POLICE FORCE, C. 1945. From left to right are as follows: (front row) Sgt. Miles Kipp, Chief Joseph W. Maslanka, Assistant Chief Stanley Zielinski, and Sgt. Frank Bernath; (middle row) Patrolman Robert Fisher, John Fetyko, John Reese, and Warren Wellman. Mayor Charles Sullivan is at back left, and Judge Walter Grote is at back right. (Collection of Alberta Yuhas.)

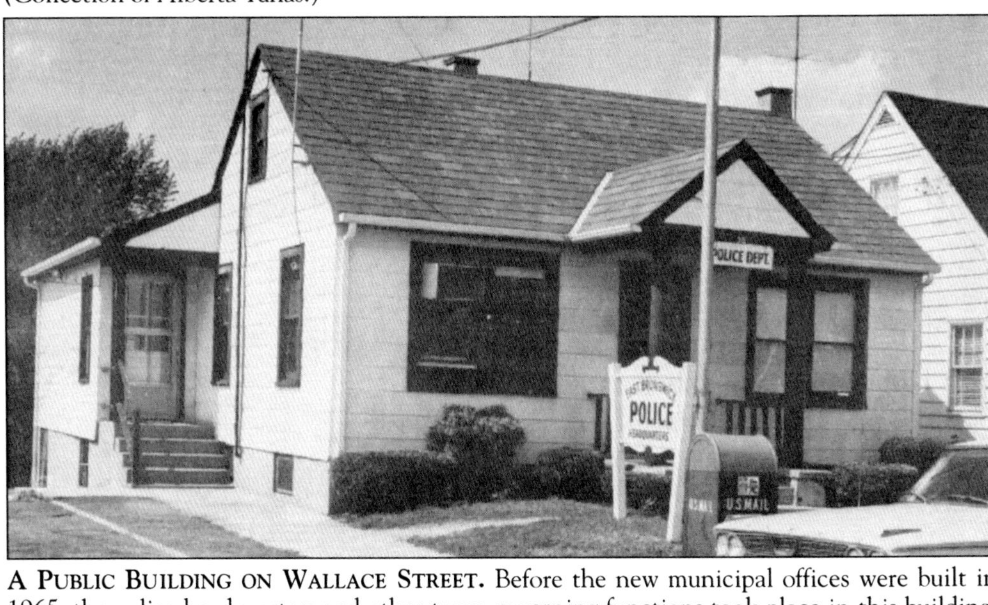

A PUBLIC BUILDING ON WALLACE STREET. Before the new municipal offices were built in 1965, the police headquarters and other town governing functions took place in this building. A second town hall was also located in the Dunhams Corner section. That building still stands today as part of Play House 22. (Collection of East Brunswick Museum.)

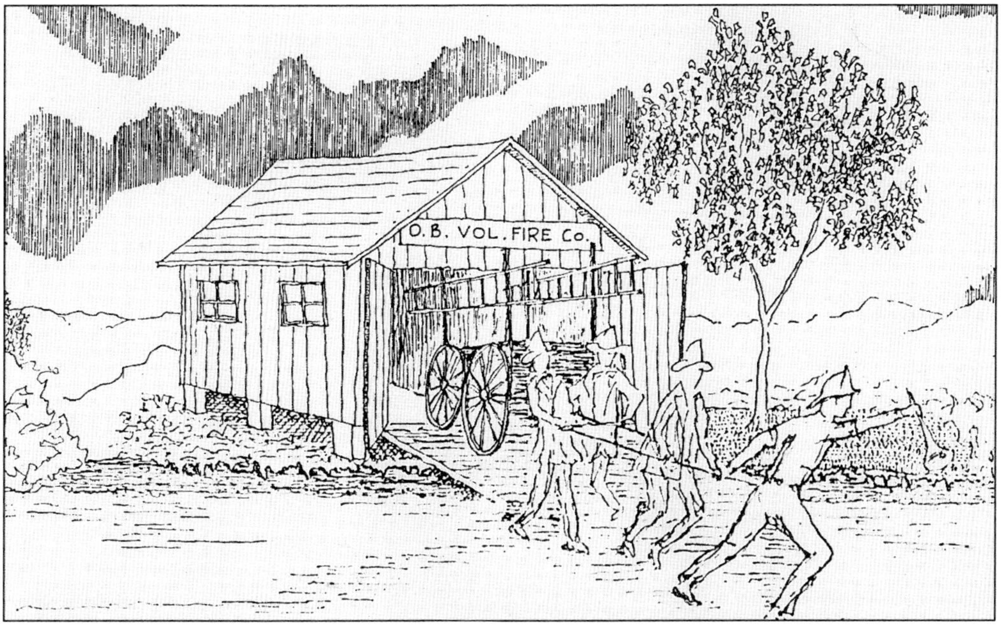

THE FIRST FIREHOUSE, C. 1906. The first firehouse in East Brunswick belonged to the Old Bridge Fire Company. It was located in the Old Bridge section of East Brunswick. A large metal ring donated by the Pennsylvania Railroad was used to alert citizens of a fire. The citizens would then run down to the firehouse, grab hold of the wagon with a water pump, and run with it to the fire scene. The wagon was used in 1912 when local resident William Kraemer and his brother accidentally set their house on fire with bottle rockets. (Collection of William Kraemer.)

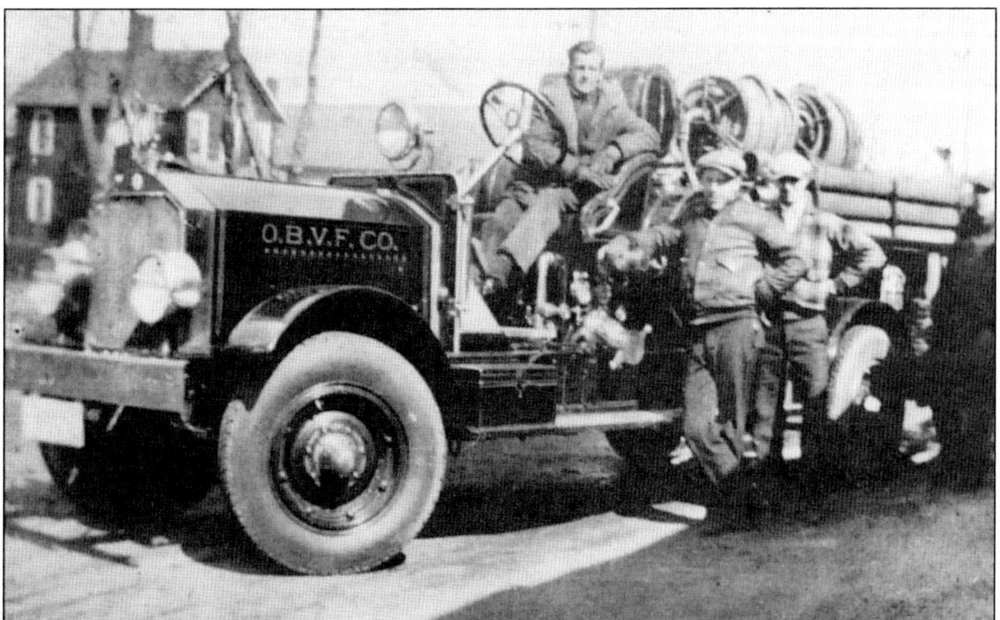

THE OLD BRIDGE FIRE COMPANY'S FIRST MOTORIZED ENGINE, C. 1928. This fire engine was purchased in 1926. (Collection of East Brunswick Museum.)

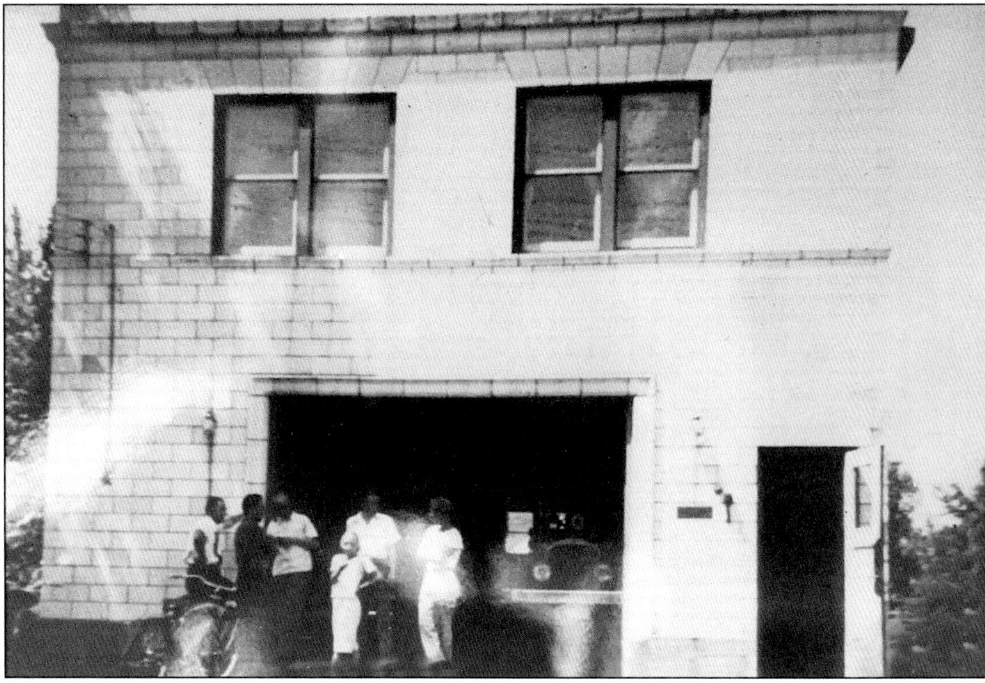

THE PINE STREET FIREHOUSE. The firehouse was built in the early 1920s for the Old Bridge Volunteer Fire Company. Although remodeled, this building still stands today. (Collection of East Brunswick Museum.)

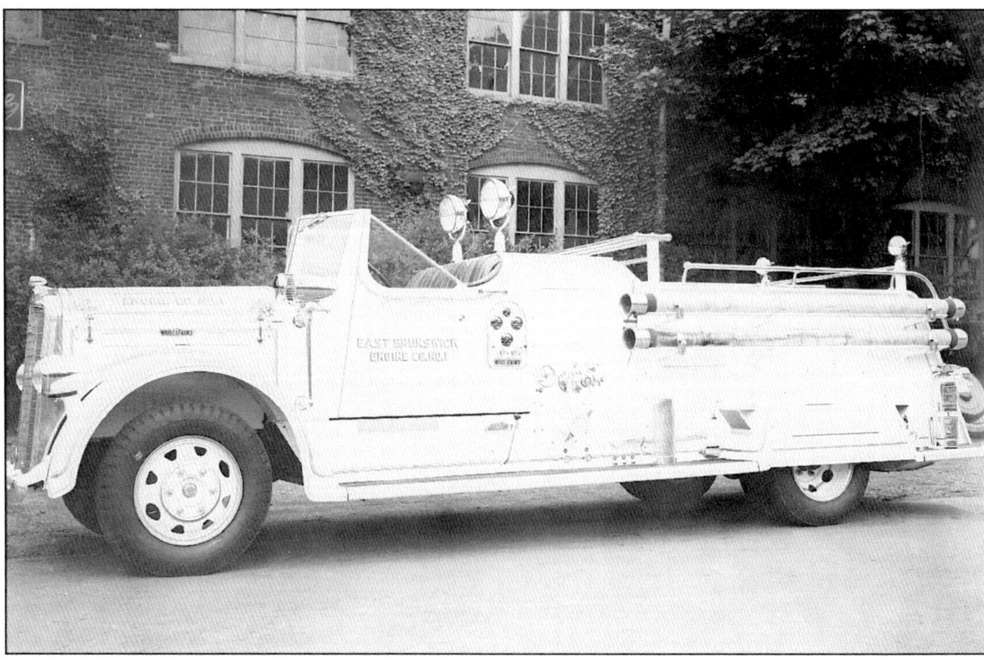

THE "NEW" FIRE TRUCK. In 1938 a second fire department was formed in East Brunswick. A new fire truck was purchased for the company in 1940. This fire engine is still owned today by the East Brunswick Independent Fire Company and is used on special occasions and parades. (Collection of East Brunswick Museum.)

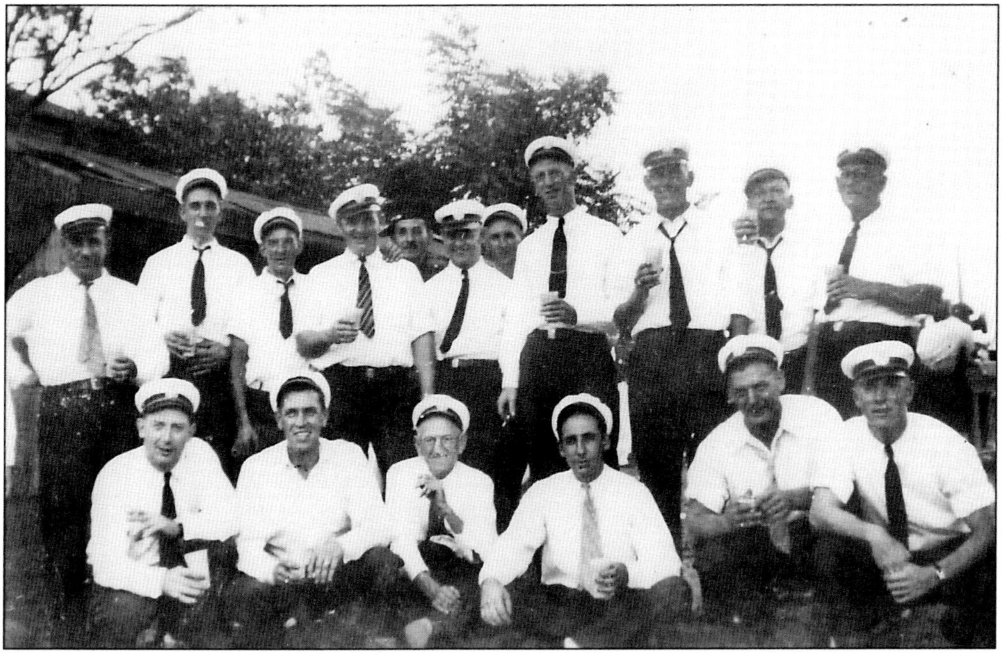

Members of the Old Bridge Fire Company, c. 1936. From left to right are as follows: (front row) Gus Rastag, Ed Hoff, James Barber, Bill Kraemer, Carlton Burket, and Donald Treat; (back row) Frank Heitzman, Tom O Halleran, Charles Morvac, Bill Mount, "Larry Walter Matawan," Pete Buesamy, Joe Smith, Willis Treat, Joe Berdell, Fred Wellman, and Raymond Treat. (Collection of East Brunswick Museum.)

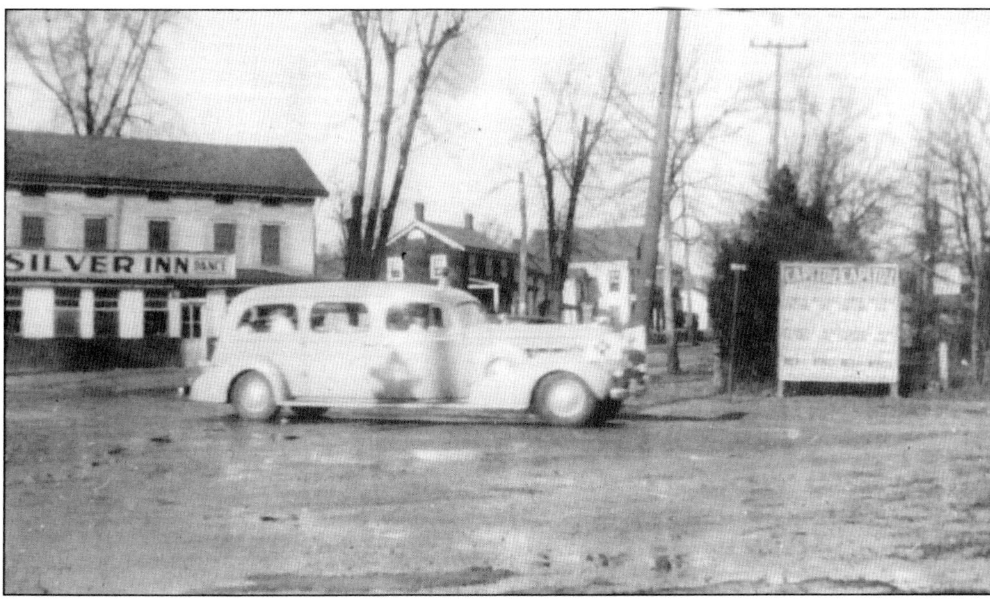

An Old Ambulance, South River. Before East Brunswick had a rescue squad, local residents had to rely on South River. The ambulance is seen around the corner, near the intersection of the Old Bridge Turnpike and Main Street, in the late 1930s. The billboard in the background advertises the new movies playing at the Capital Theater in South River. (Collection of East Brunswick Museum.)

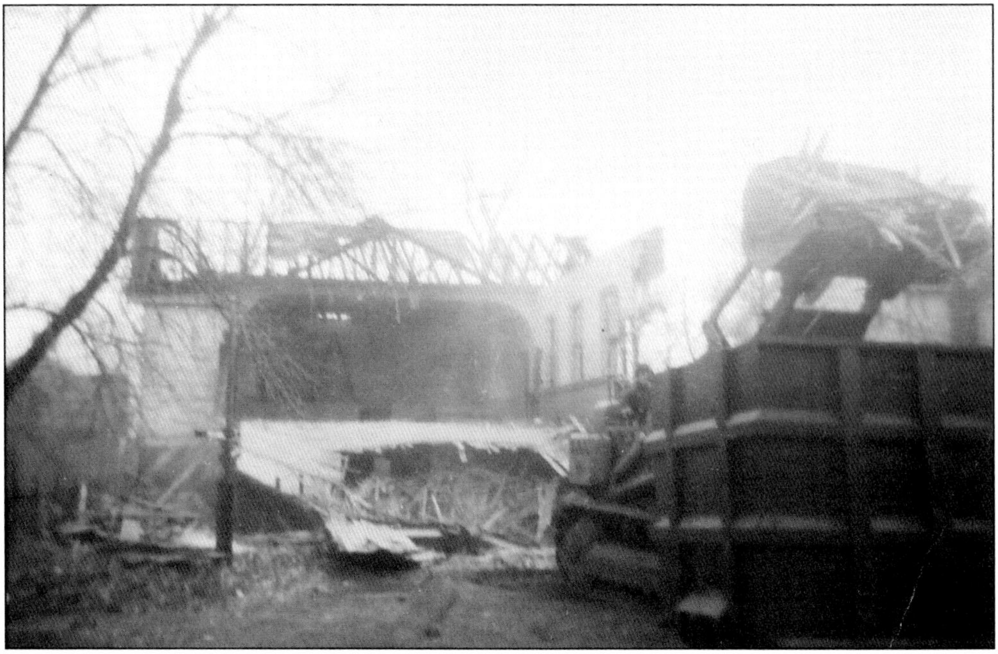

THE DEMOLITION OF THE OLD TOWN HALL, 1969. Originally built as a schoolhouse, the building was moved across the street around 1907 to serve as the town hall. The building stood for many years until it was demolished. (Collection of Alberta Yuhas.)

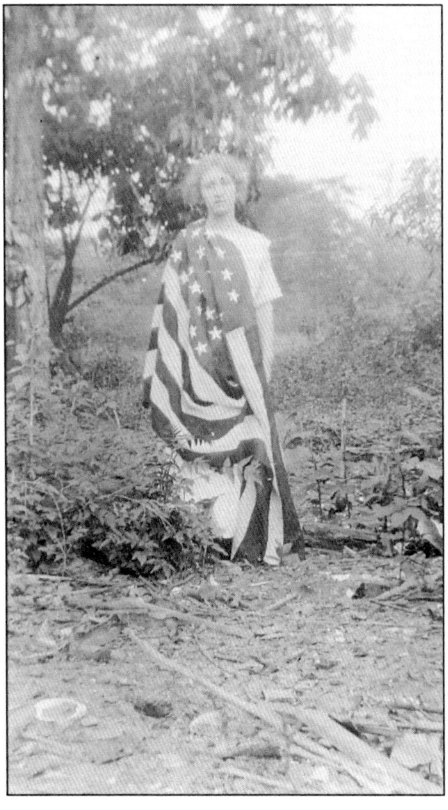

EDNA OSBORNE, A RESIDENT OF THE OLD BRIDGE SECTION. Edna is shown here around 1910 as a patriotic Camp Fire Girl. (Collection of East Brunswick Museum.)

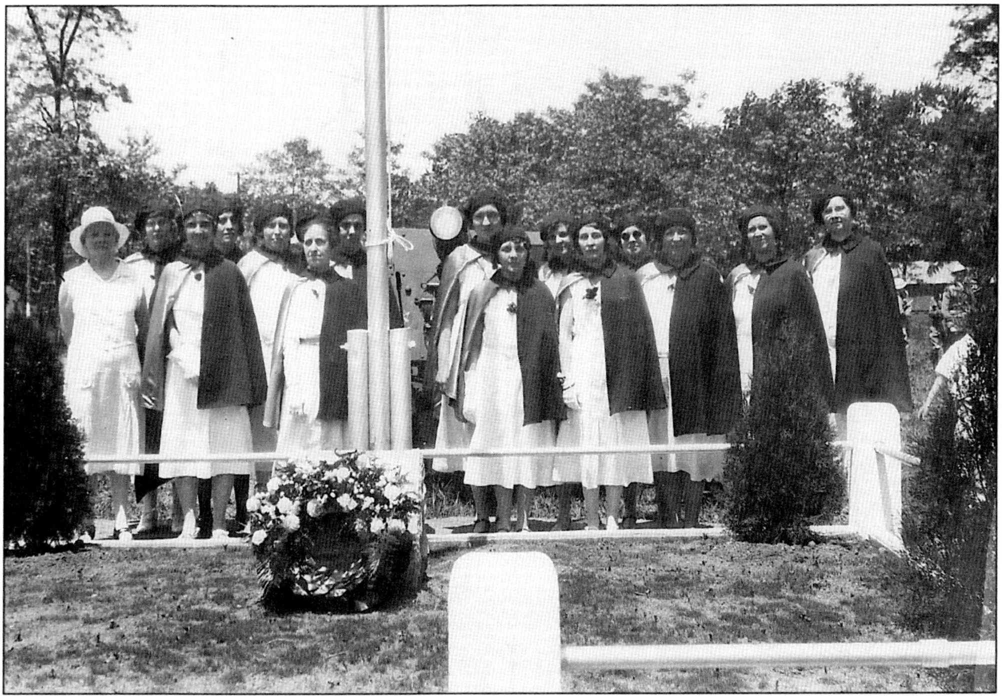

WOMEN'S AUXILIARY, C. 1930. These women gathered in front of the war memorial on the site of what would later become the local Veterans of Foreign Wars building, on the corner of Emerson and Matawan Road. (Collection of Alberta Yuhas.)

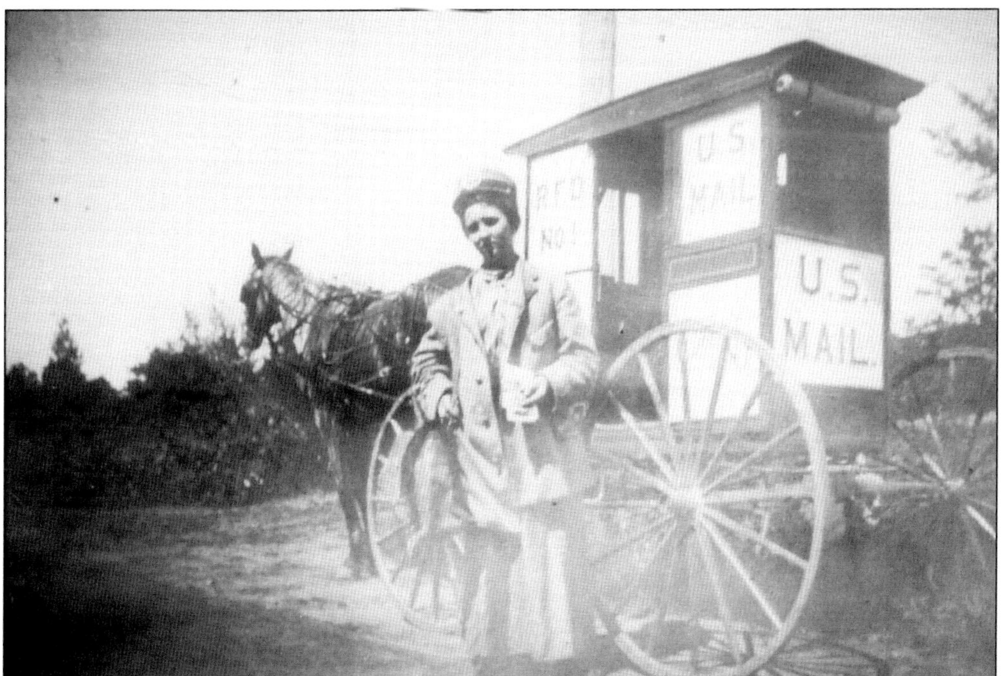

THE MAIL WAGON, C. 1900. Louela Jolly poses wearing the mailman's hat and jacket. (Collection of East Brunswick Museum.)

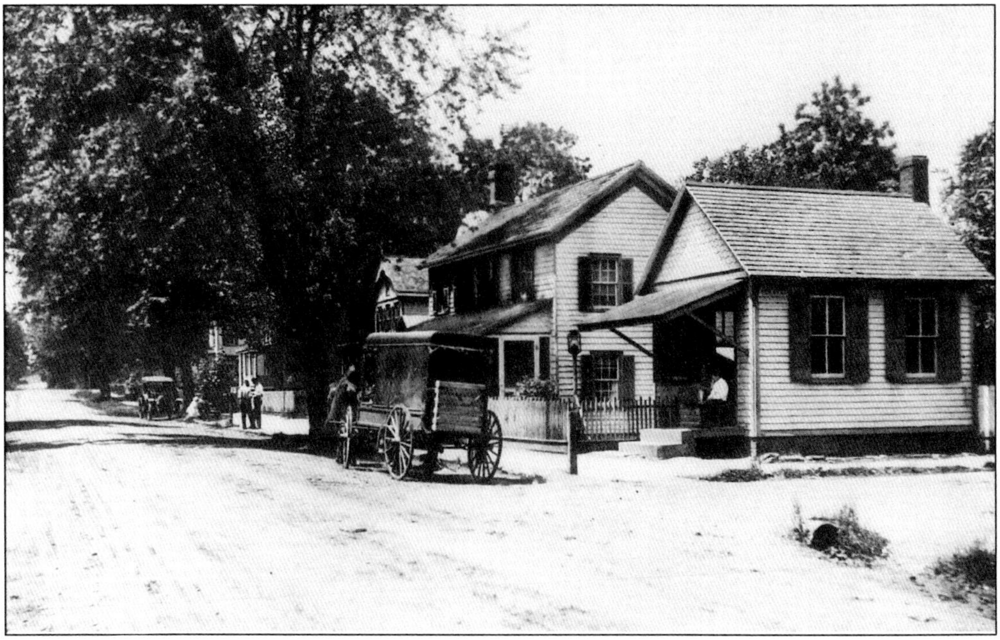

The Post Office, Main Street. The post office was located next to the Appleby house on Main Street in the Old Bridge section. Here, a wagon bringing the mail has arrived out front. (Collection of East Brunswick Museum.)

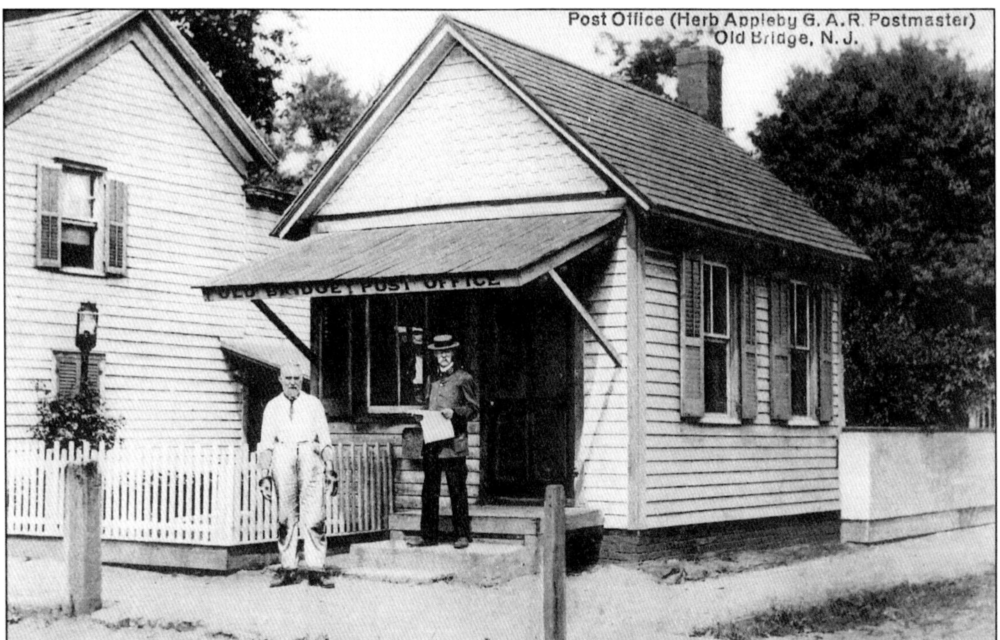

The Small Post Office near the Appleby Home. This post office was built around the turn of the century. The man standing to the left is Postmaster Herb Appleby, a veteran of the Civil War. Herb lived in the home next to the post office, and died in the house in 1921. He liked to garden and is shown here wearing his gardening clothes. (Collection of East Brunswick Museum.)

The Cement Block Post Office, c. 1910. This post office was built out of cement on the other side of the Appleby home, after the old post office was converted into a store. Both buildings were torn down in 1944 when the homestead was donated to the town. The cement foundation is still visible next to the house today. (Collection of East Brunswick Museum.)

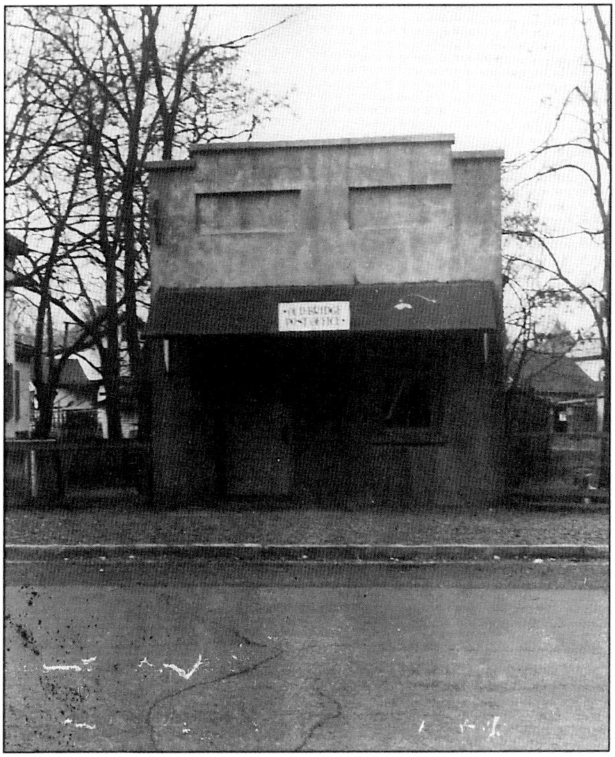

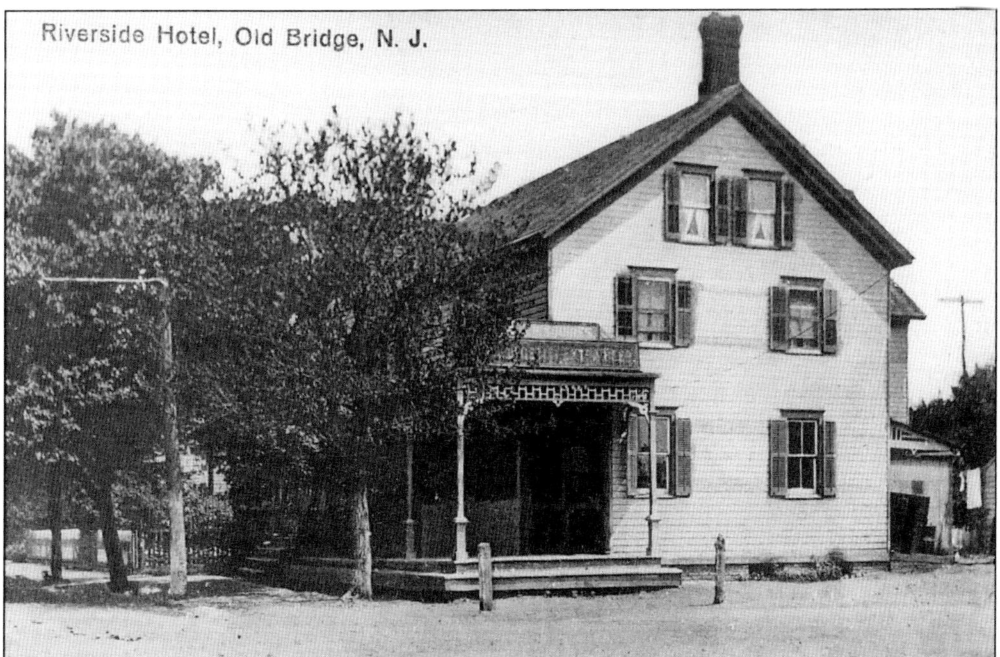

The Riverside Hotel, c. 1910. This hotel was operated by the Squires family. The building is still standing on Emerson Street. (Collection of East Brunswick Museum.)

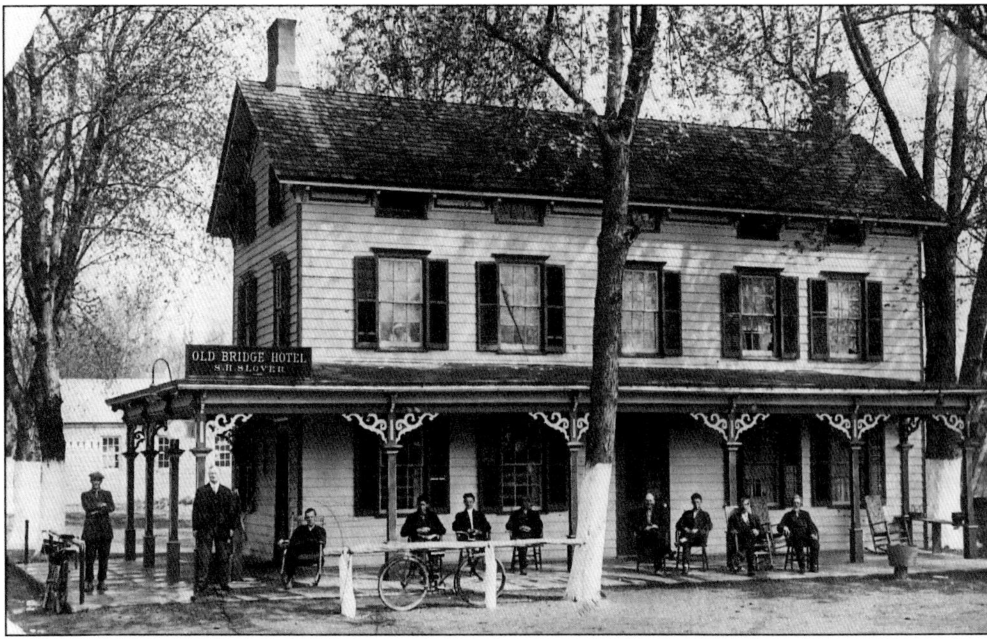

THE OLD BRIDGE HOTEL, C. 1890. This building stood on the corner of Kossman Street and the Old Bridge Turnpike. It was a stopping place for travelers on stage lines between New Brunswick and the shore. (Collection of East Brunswick Museum.)

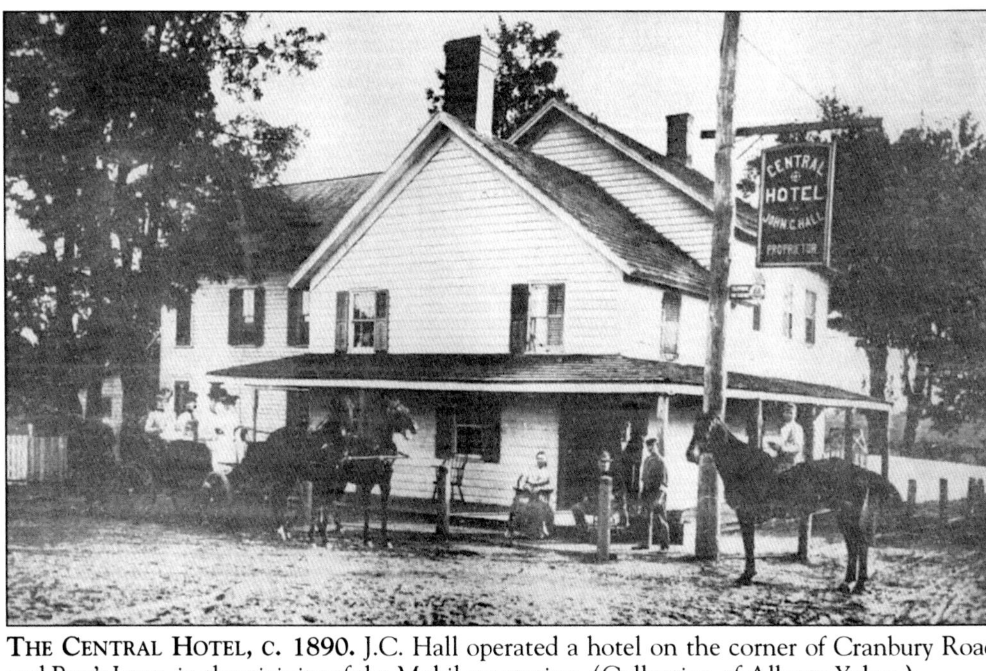

THE CENTRAL HOTEL, C. 1890. J.C. Hall operated a hotel on the corner of Cranbury Road and Rue's Lane, in the vicinity of the Mobil gas station. (Collection of Alberta Yuhas.)

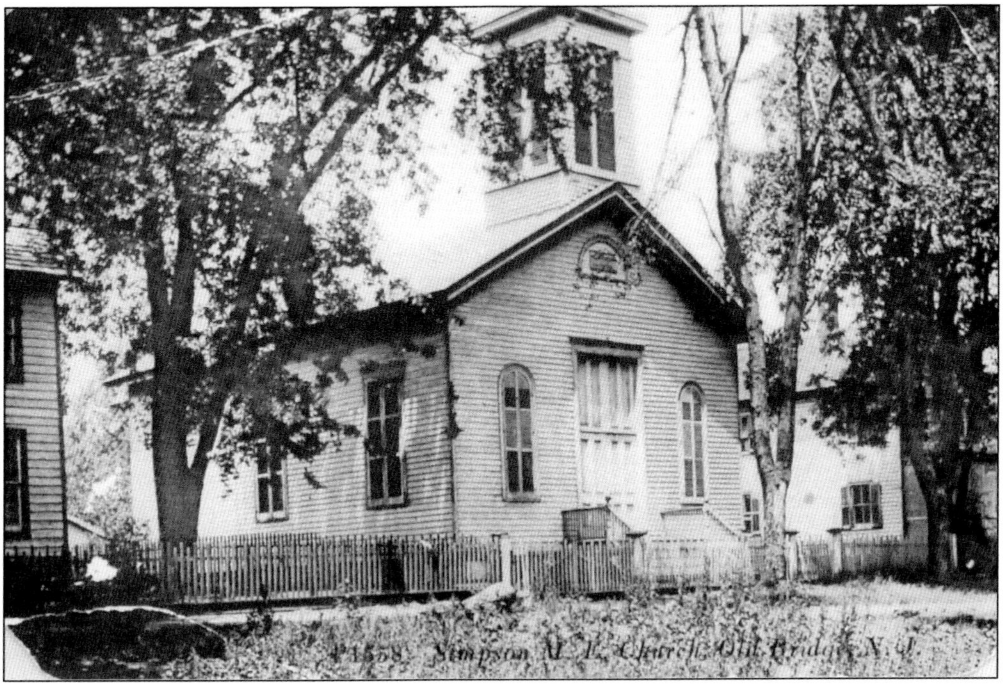

THE SIMPSON METHODIST CHURCH, 1890. This church was built in 1862. The congregation later moved to Madison Township. The township eventually purchased the building, and in 1980 it was opened as the East Brunswick Museum. (Collection of East Brunswick Museum.)

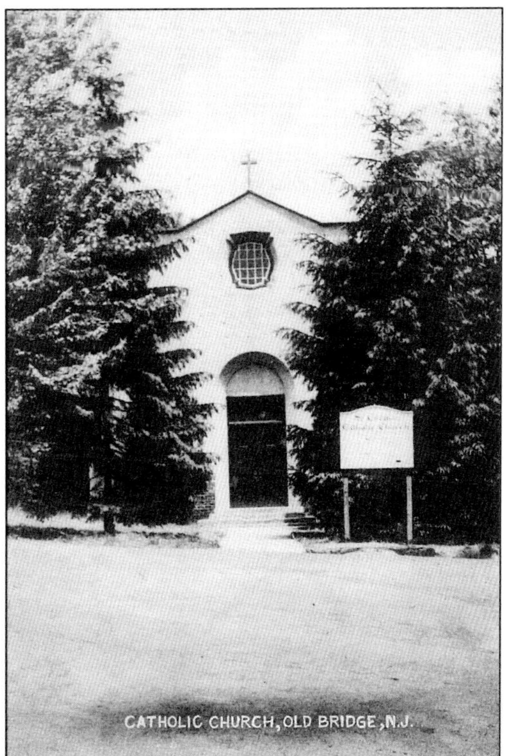

THE ST. THOMAS CATHOLIC CHURCH, BUILT IN 1921. This mission-style building still stands on the corner of Chestnut Street and the Old Bridge Turnpike. (Collection of East Brunswick Museum.)

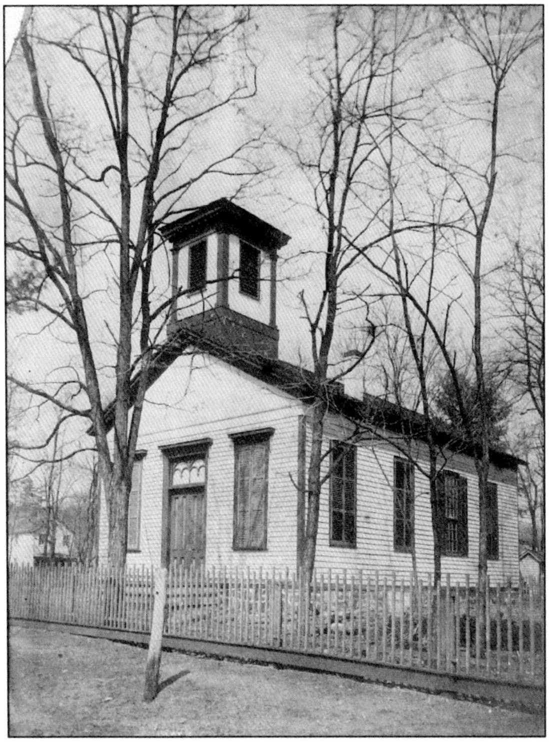

THE OLD BRIDGE BAPTIST CHURCH, C. 1880. This congregation was founded by some members of the old congregation from South River who wanted the right to play music in church. The new congregation built this church in 1844. (Collection of East Brunswick Museum.)

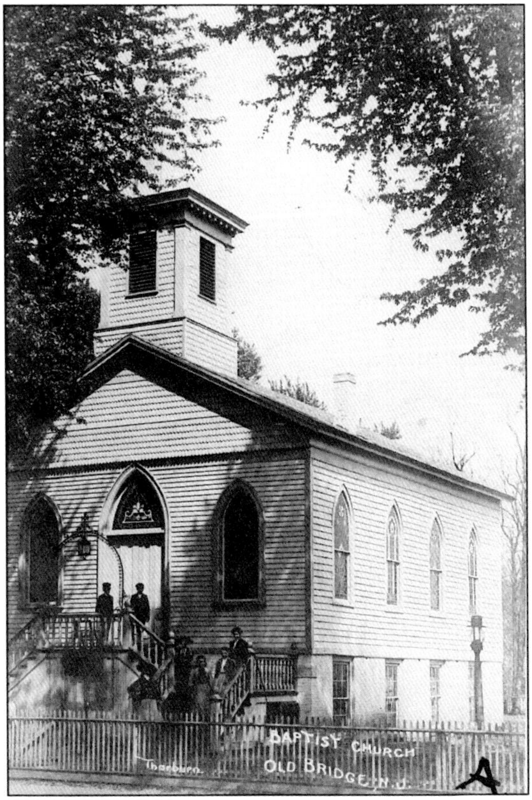

THE OLD BRIDGE BAPTIST CHURCH. In 1894, as legend has it, the church was moved 90 degrees to face a different direction because church-goers disliked the smell emanating from a pig sty across the street from the old entrance. The church was placed on a larger foundation made with stone cut by prisoners at the Sing Sing Prison in New York and shipped to the church by barge. (Collection of East Brunswick Museum.)

Seven

Farms

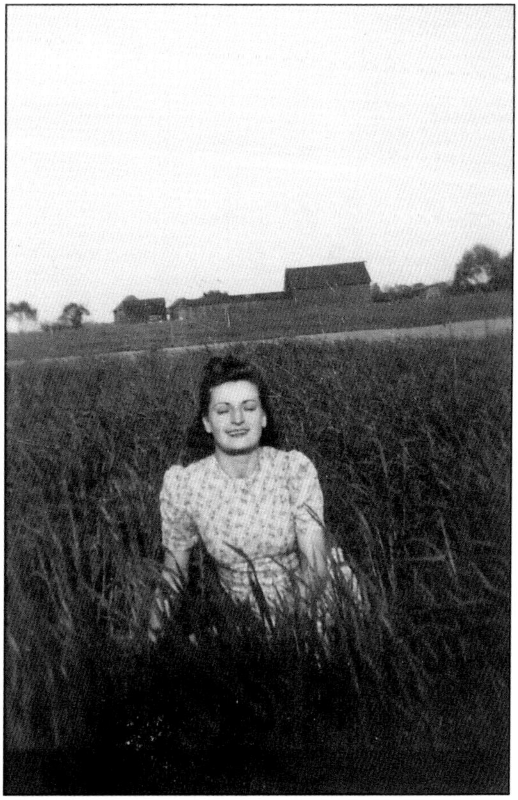

HELEN ZDANOWICH IN THE VAST FARM FIELDS ALONG RUE'S LANE, C. 1940. (Collection of Arciszewski Family.)

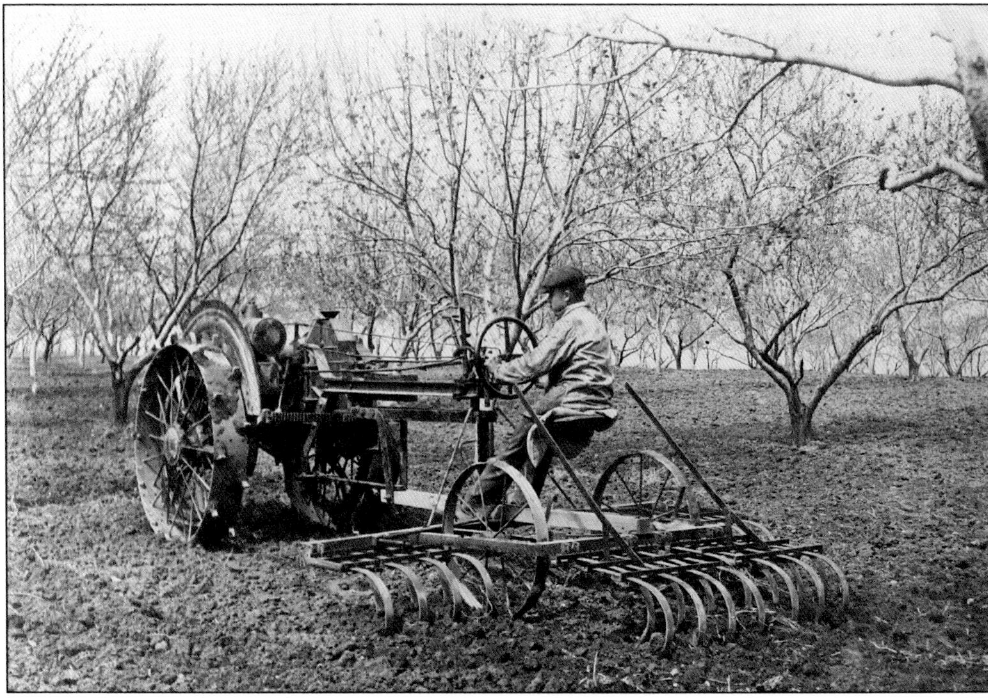

An early Tractor Making Its Way through the Apple Orchards on the Smith Farm, Milltown Road, c. 1915. (Collection of the Smith Family.)

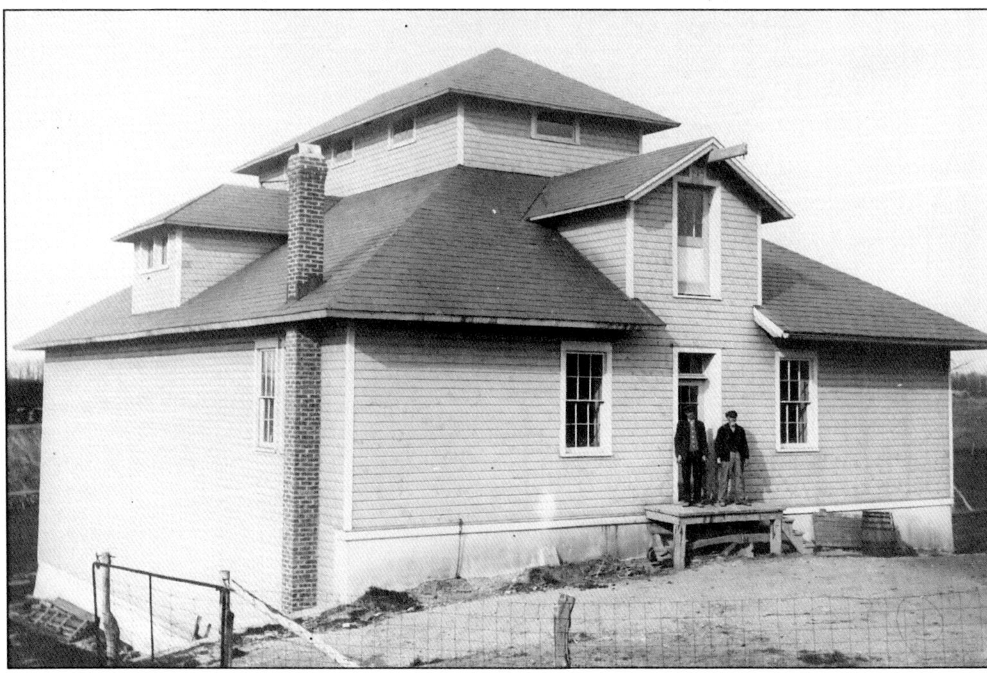

The Cold Storage Building on the Smith Farm. In 1911 the Smith family built one of the first cold storage buildings in the state. Apples could be placed into cold storage, making them available after the harvest season. Unfortunately, a fire in later years destroyed the building. (Collection of the Smith Family.)

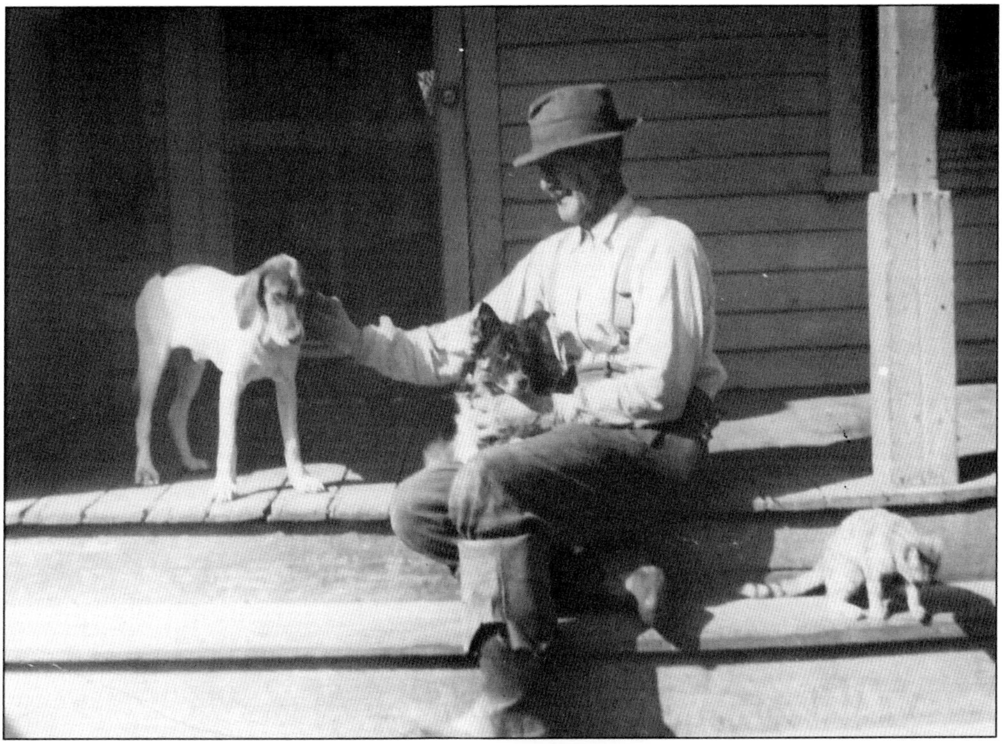

HENRY WARNSDORFER. Henry is sitting on the steps of his home in the Dunhams Corner section of town. (Collection of East Brunswick Museum.)

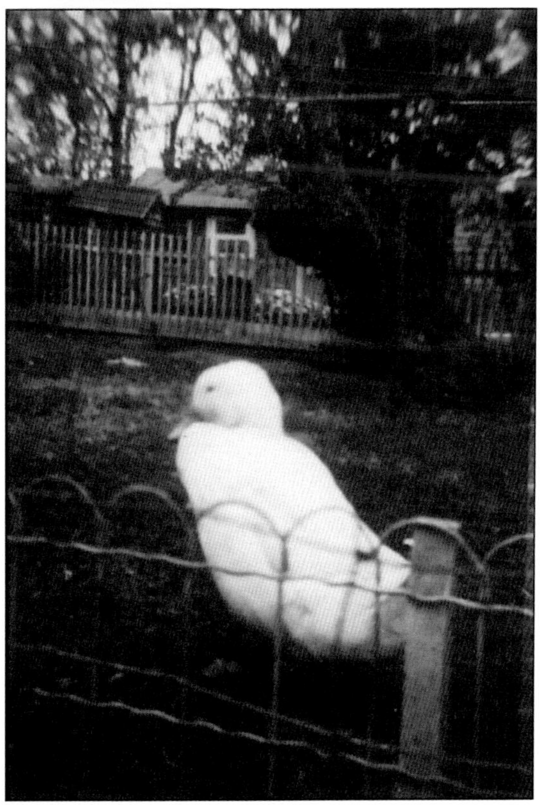

A HAPPY DUCK ON A FARM IN THE OLD BRIDGE SECTION, c. 1930. (Collection of East Brunswick Museum.)

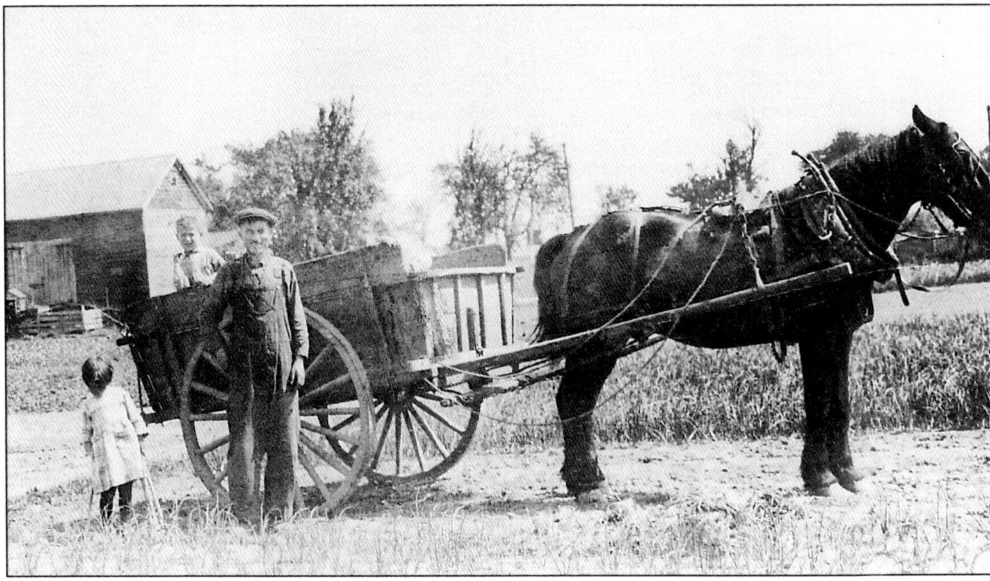

MEMBERS OF THE GIAMERESE FAMILY POSING NEAR A HORSE-DRAWN CART, C. 1900. The Giamerese family has a long tradition of farming in East Brunswick. Horse-drawn carts were for many years the best mode of transportation available to people. (Collection of Giamerese Family.)

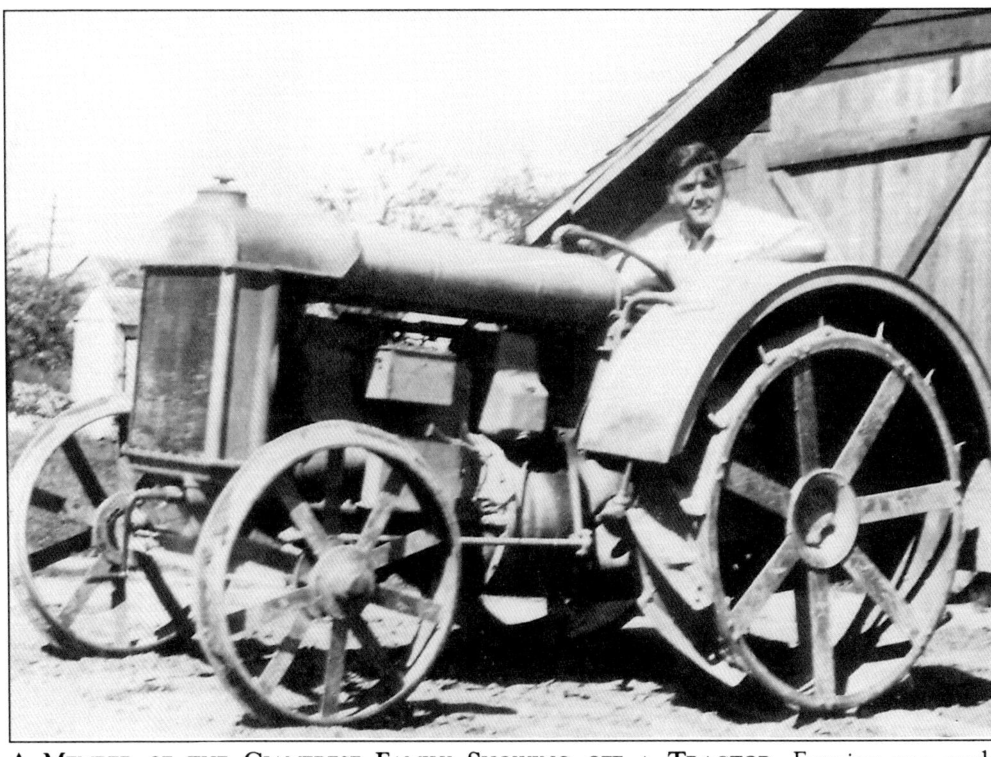

A MEMBER OF THE GIAMERESE FAMILY SHOWING OFF A TRACTOR. Farming was made easier and more efficient with the advent of motorized farm equipment. (Collection of the Giamerese Family.)

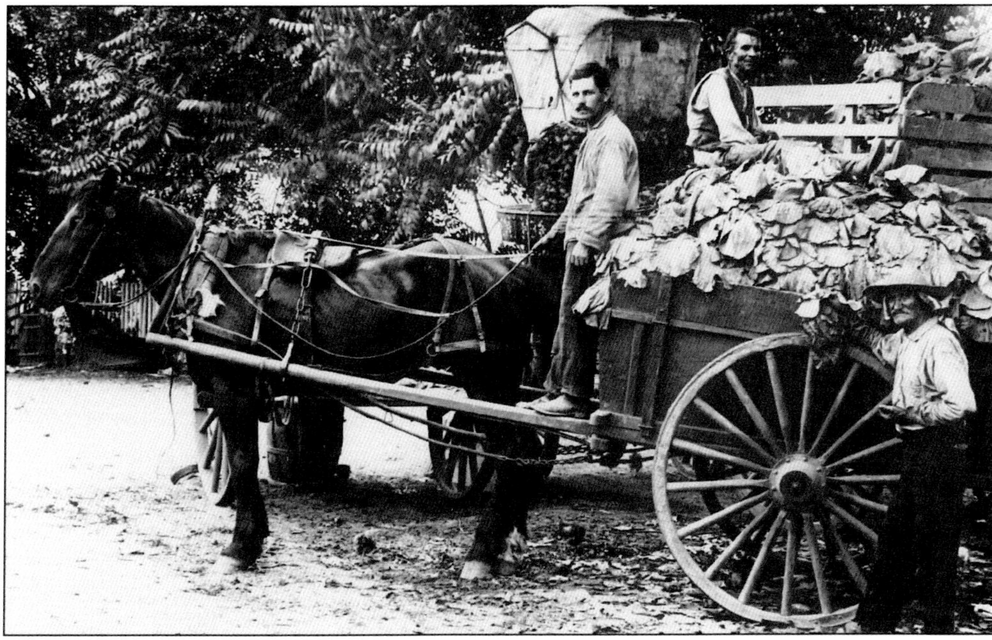

MEMBERS OF THE GIAMERESE FAMILY POSE WITH WITH A HORSE CART FULL OF CABBAGES. In the early part of the 20th century an influx of new immigrants came to East Brunswick and the neighboring communities. They brought with them the farming skills practiced in their home county. (Collection of the Giamerese Family.)

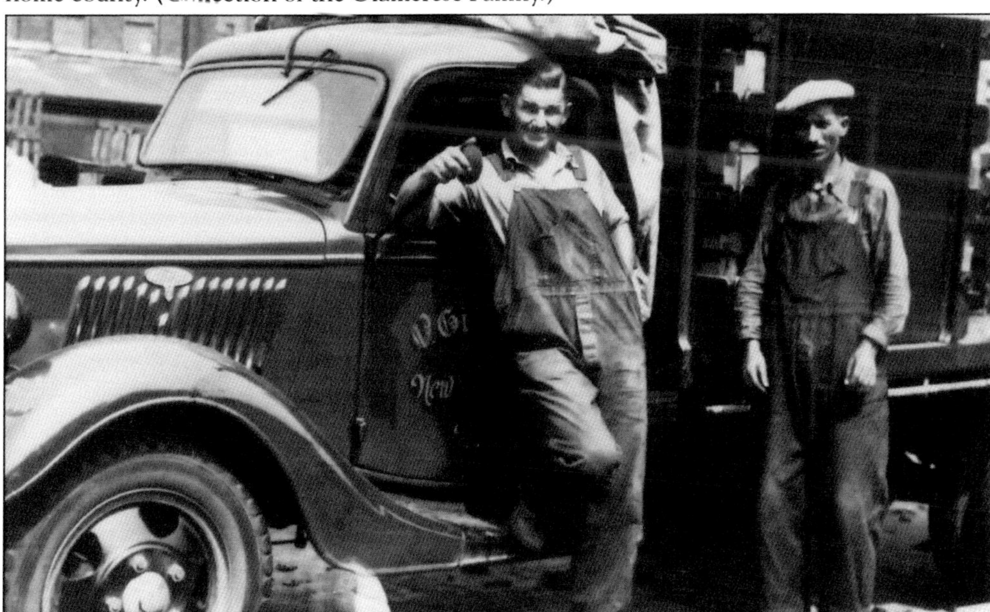

A C. 1937 PHOTOGRAPH OF MEMBERS OF THE GIAMERESE FAMILY AND ONE OF THEIR TRUCKS. The Giamerese family, along with other area farmers, sold their crops at city markets. In the 19th century much of the produce was shipped to New York City. By the time this photograph was taken, many of the local families were trucking their own produce to markets in Newark. (Collection of the Giamerese Family.)

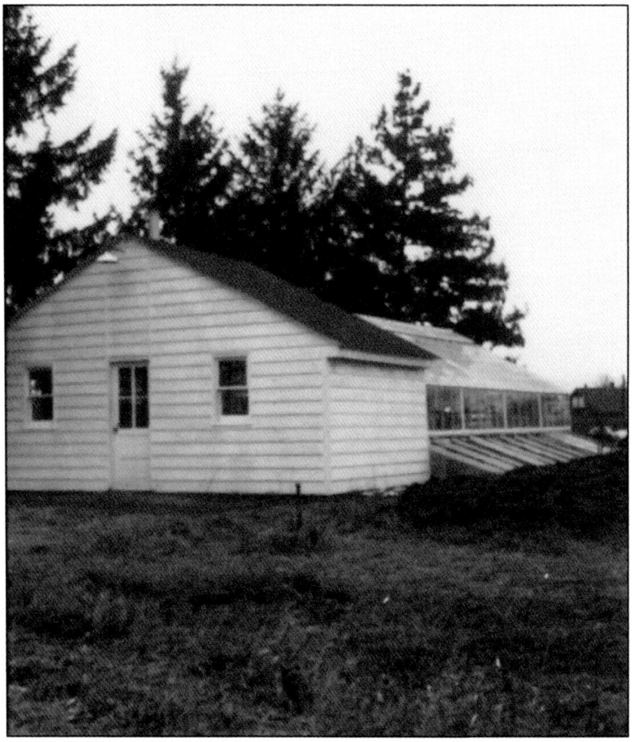

THE GREENHOUSE ON THE AUER FARM, C. 1960. This building still stands on Cranbury Road behind the old Smith-Auer farmhouse. It was built in the 1960s. (Both photographs from the Collection of the East Brunswick Museum.)

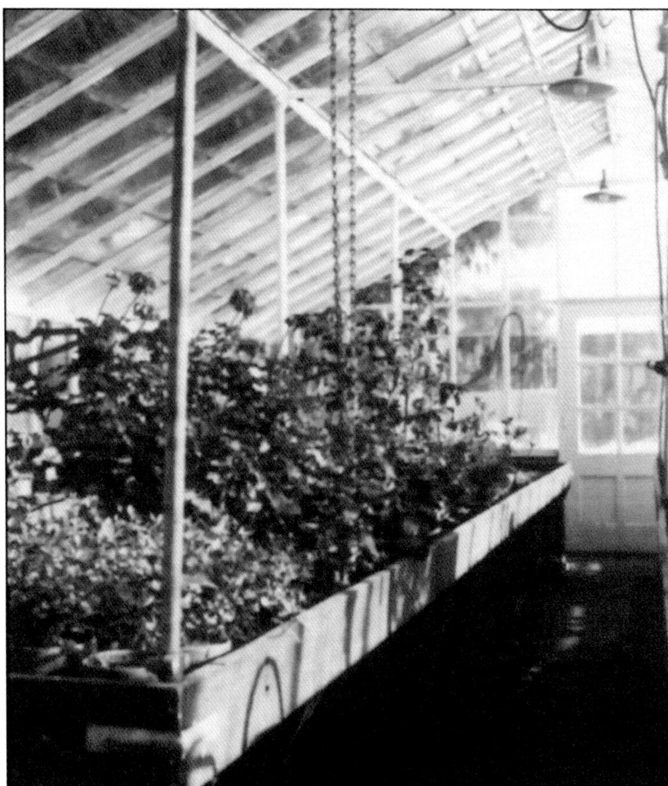

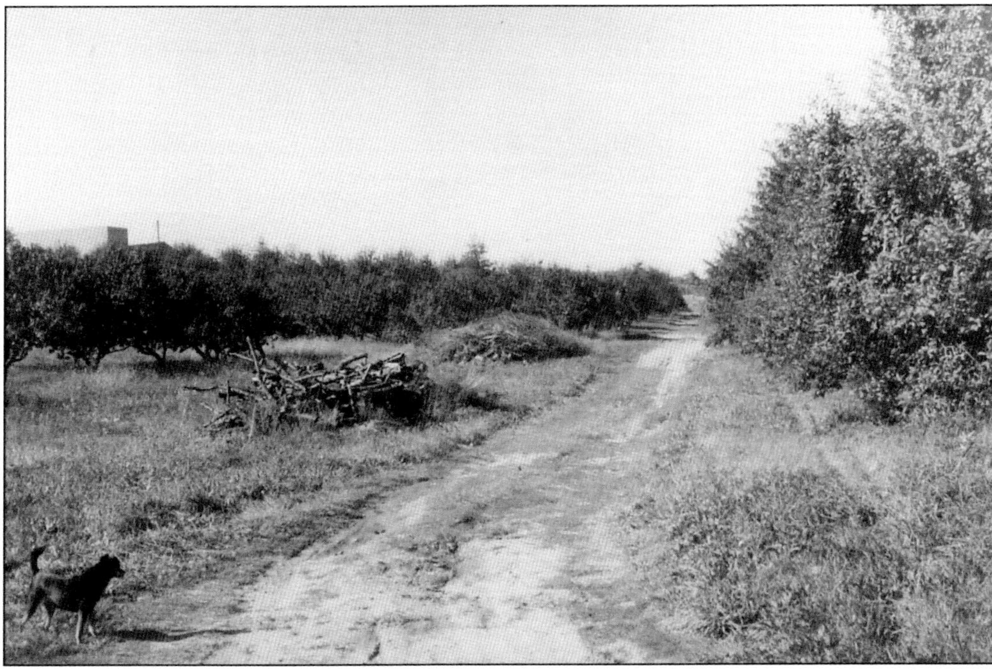

The Apple Orchard on the Smith Farm, c. 1960. Remnants of the apple orchard are still around today in the lower fields by the East Brunswick High School. (Collection of East Brunswick Museum.)

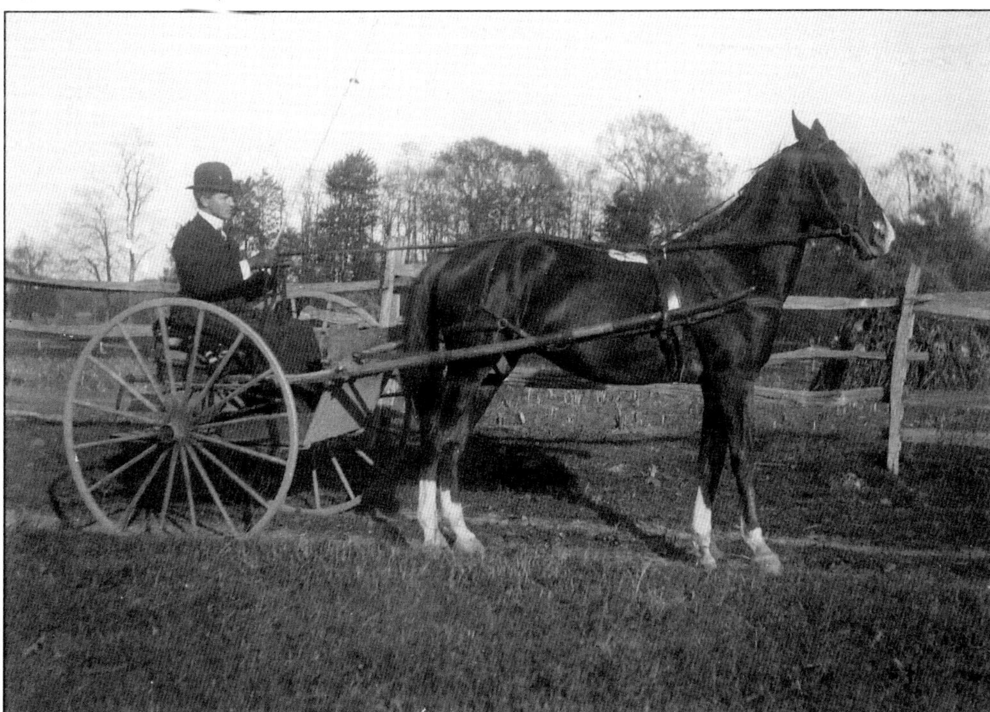

John Smith, c. 1900. John Smith lived on a farm where the present-day East Brunswick High School is located. (Collection of Grace Auer.)

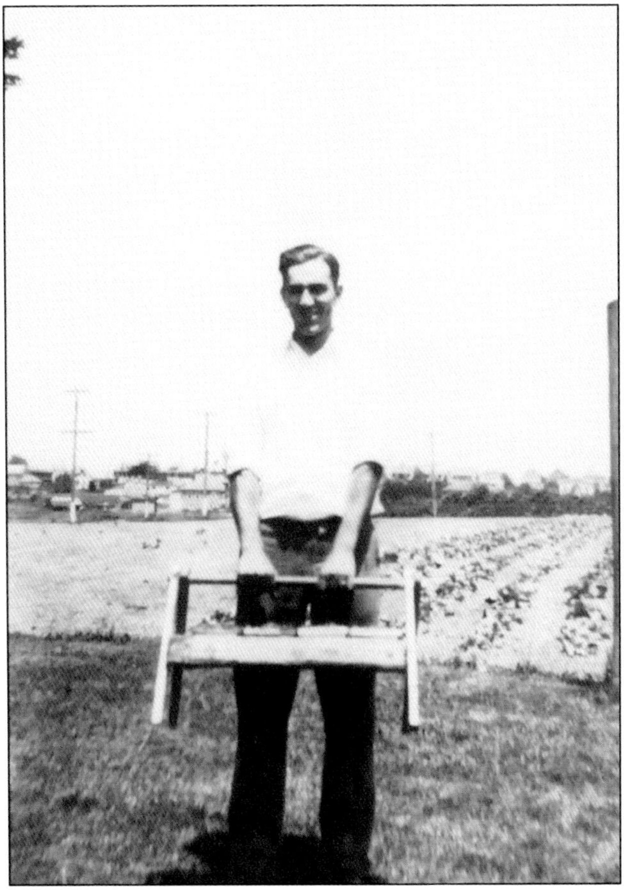

Charles Auer and Some Freshly Picked Berries from His Farm on Cranbury Road. (Collection of East Brunswick Museum.)

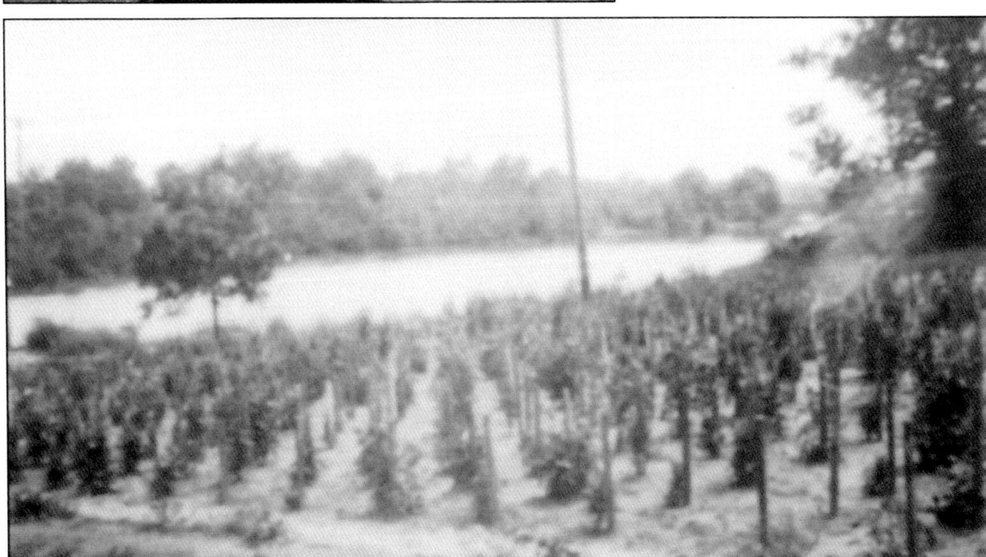

Charles Reid's Dahlia Garden. Charles was a factory worker at the Old Bridge Enamel Brick and Tile Company and raised prize-winning dahlias at his home on 36 River Road. (Collection of Alberta Yuhas.)

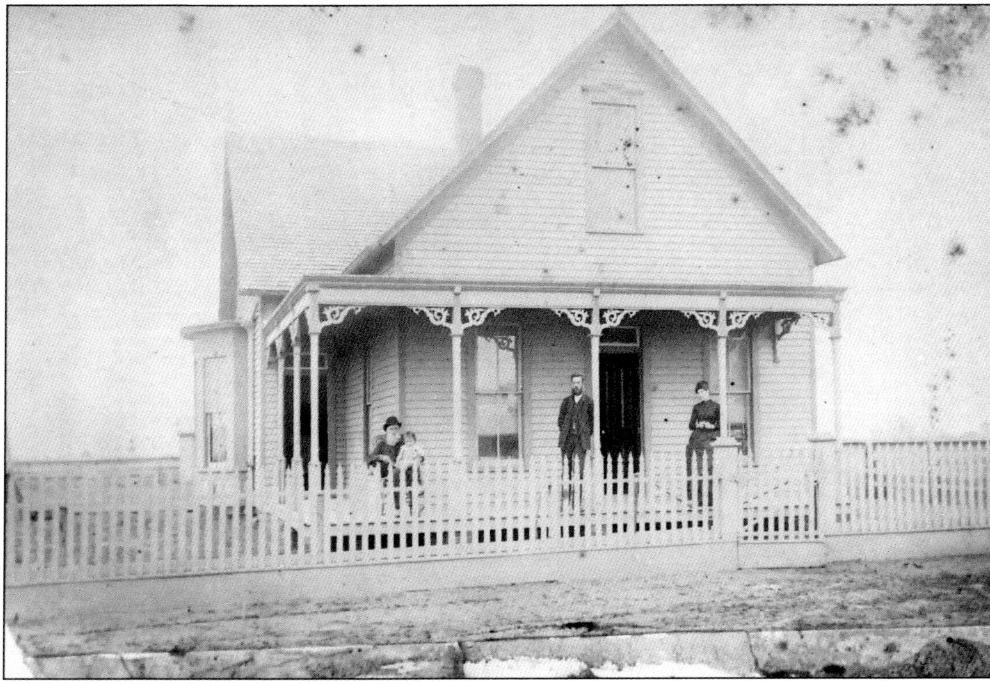

A FARM ON THE OLD STAGE ROAD, C. 1900. This little cottage farmhouse was demolished in later years for the construction of a 1960s housing development. (Collection of East Brunswick Museum.)

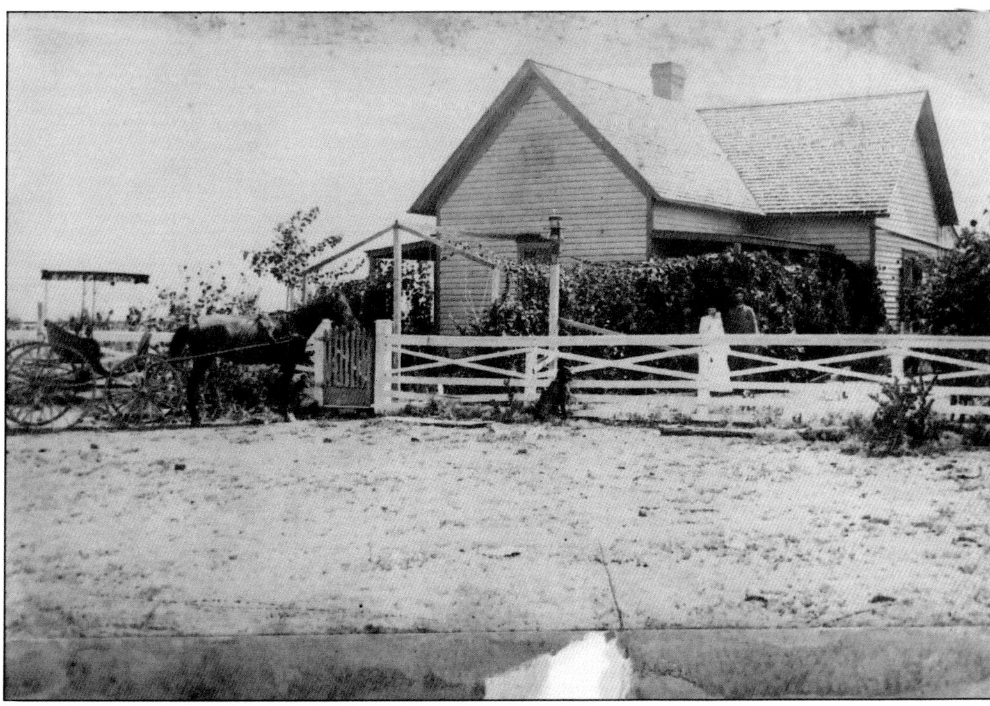

ANOTHER VIEW OF THE FARM COTTAGE, C. 1900. (Collection of East Brunswick Museum.)

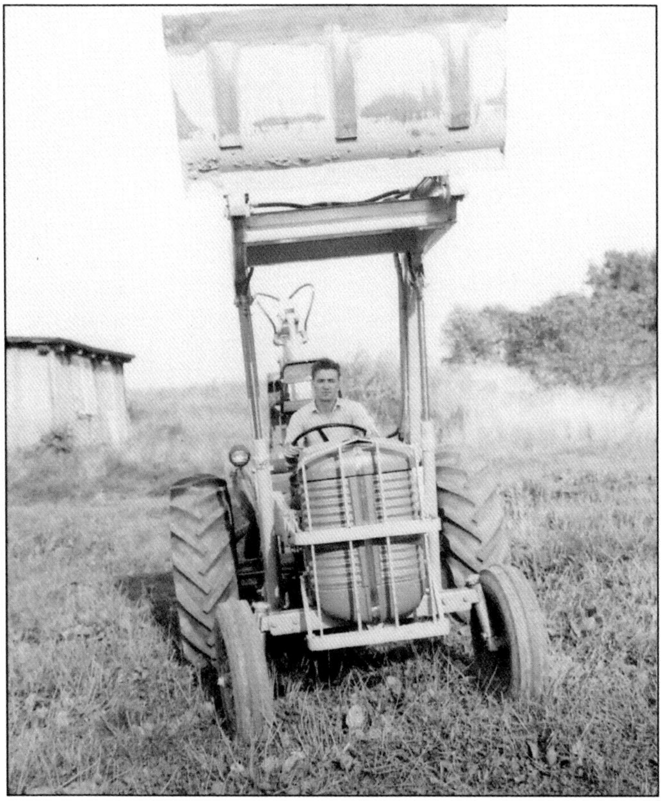

ALEX ZDANOWICH. Alex is shown here trying out his tractor on the Zdanowich Farm on Rue's Lane, *c.* 1950. The farmhouse still stands on the corner of Rue's Lane and Mercer Road. (Collection of Arciszewski Family.)

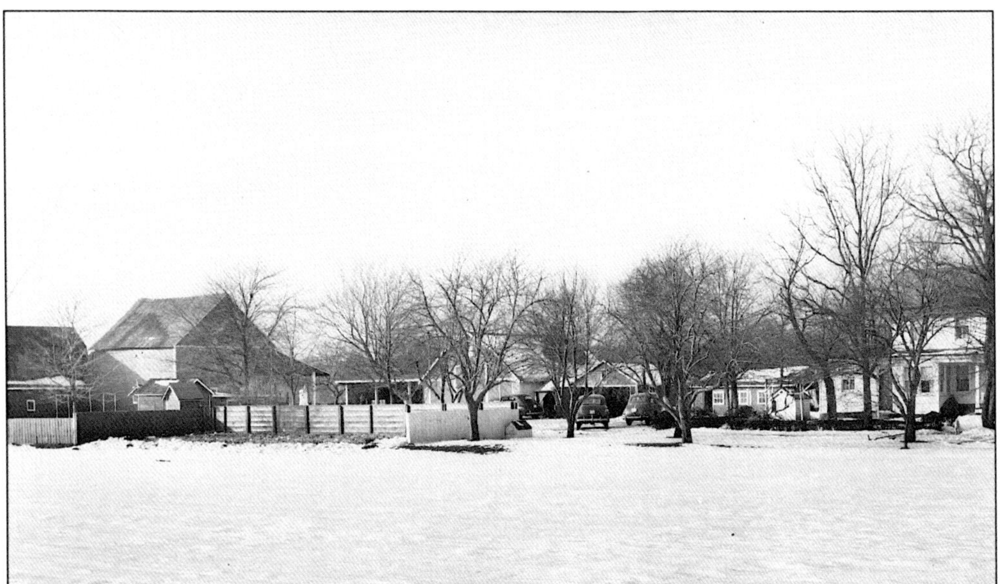

THE DOUGLAS FARM, SUMMERHILL ROAD, C. 1945. Although all the outbuildings are gone, this home still stands, surrounded by a housing development on the corner of Deerfield Avenue and Summerhill Road. (Collection of East Brunswick Museum.)

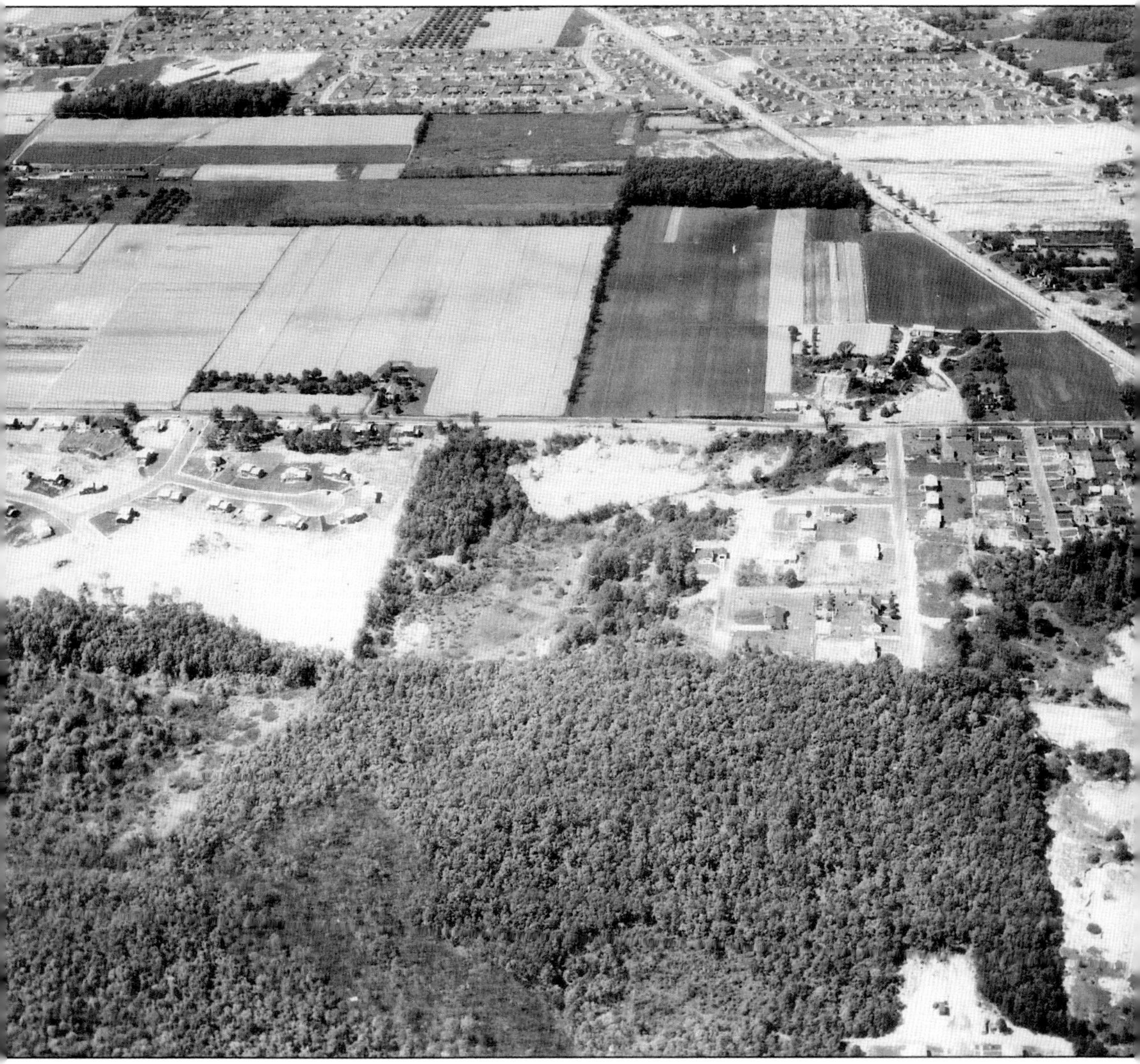

A c. 1955 Aerial Photograph of East Brunswick on the Cusp of Suburban Development. Route 18 runs from the top to the bottom right of the photograph. The farms along Rue's Lane would make way for housing developments and a county vocational school. Irwin School is visible to the top left of the photograph. The apple orchard in the top middle of the photograph is where Path Mark and Rickels are today, on Race Track Road. Previously, a horse racing tack was located there. (Collection of East Brunswick Museum.)

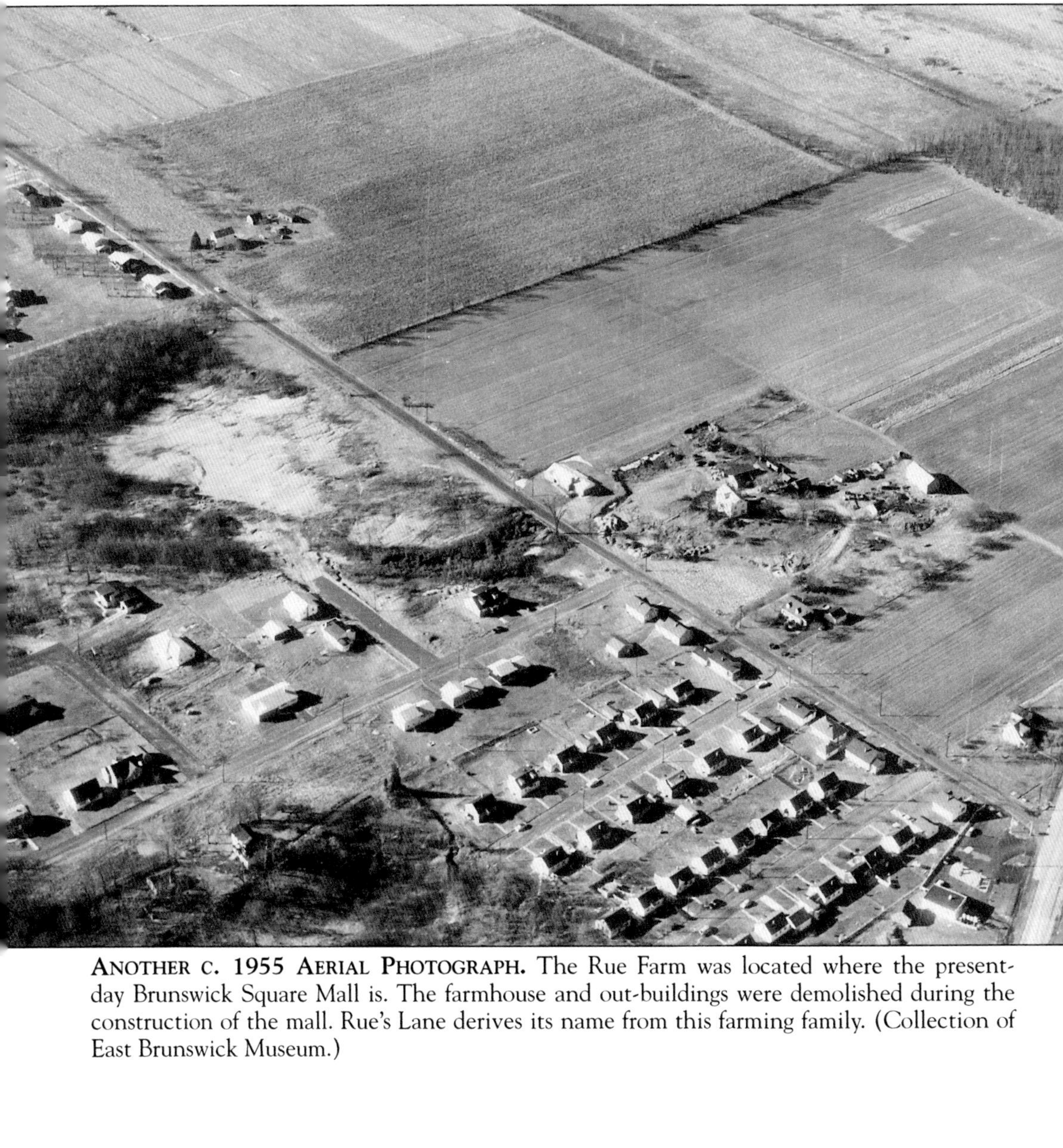

ANOTHER C. 1955 AERIAL PHOTOGRAPH. The Rue Farm was located where the present-day Brunswick Square Mall is. The farmhouse and out-buildings were demolished during the construction of the mall. Rue's Lane derives its name from this farming family. (Collection of East Brunswick Museum.)

Eight

Industry

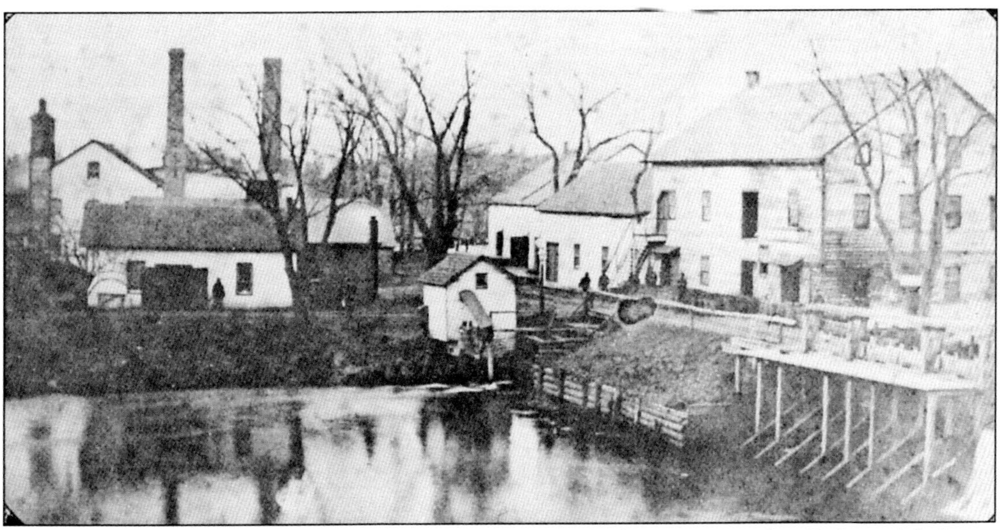

THE LICORICE MILL, C. 1880. This mill was located where present-day Duhernal Lake is. The factory originally opened as a gunpowder mill in the early 1800s. (Collection of East Brunswick Museum.)

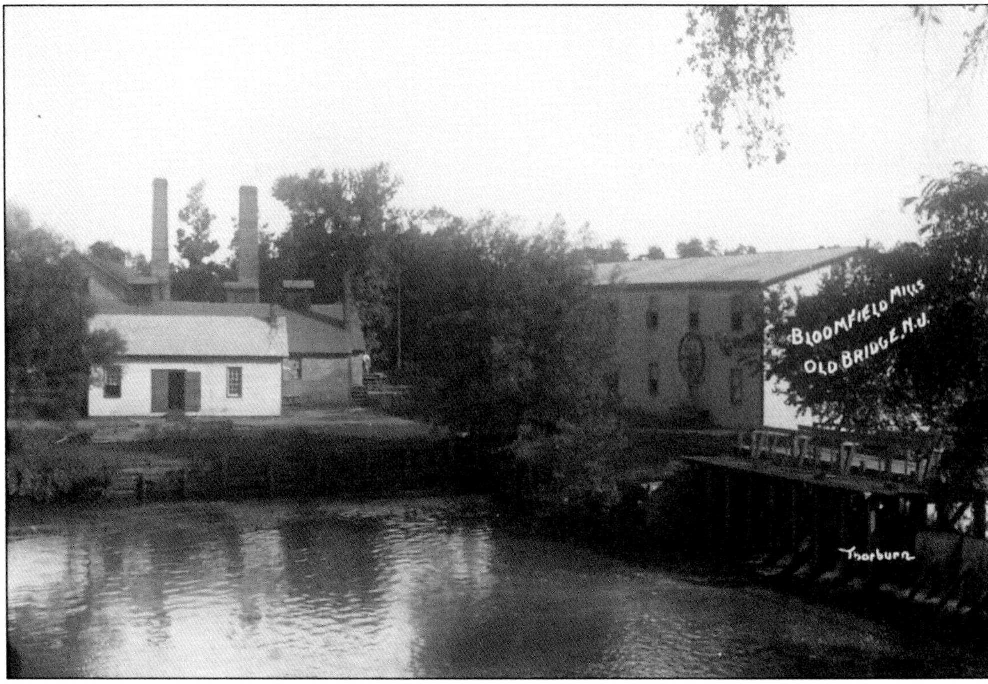

BLOOMFIELD MILLS, C. 1900. Located on a site now beneath the waters of Duhernal Lake, this factory was demolished in the 1930s when a dam was built for industrial purposes. Duhernal Lake gets its name from three factories: Duponts, Hercules, and National Lead. (Collection of East Brunswick Museum.)

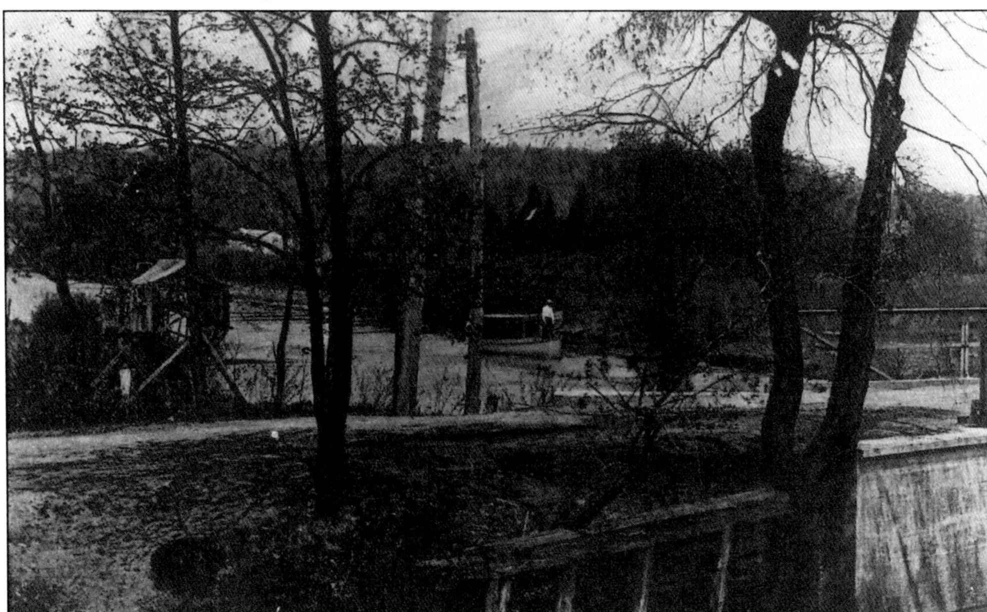

THE BRIDGE THAT CROSSES OVER THE SOUTH RIVER, CONNECTING MAIN STREET TO SAYREVILLE, C. 1900. A fisherman has hung his net on a revolving rack on the bank of the river to dry and repair it. The South River and Raritan Bay provided fishermen from the East Brunswick area with extra income. (Collection of East Brunswick Museum.)

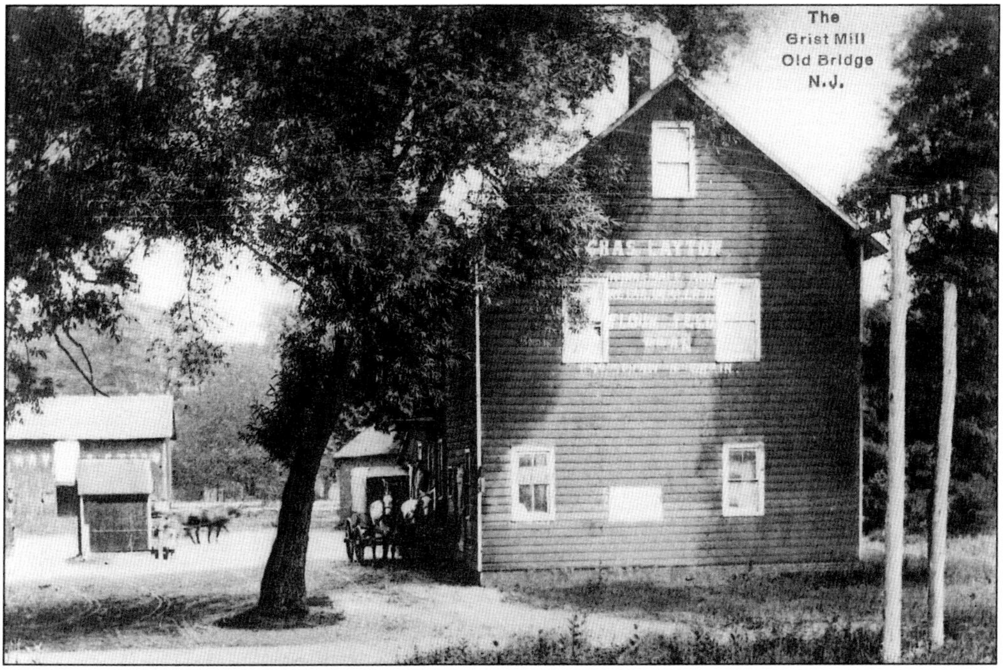

LAYTON'S GRISTMILL, C. 1890. Charles Layton operated a gristmill on the corner of River Road and Main Street in the Old Bridge section. (Collection of East Brunswick Museum.)

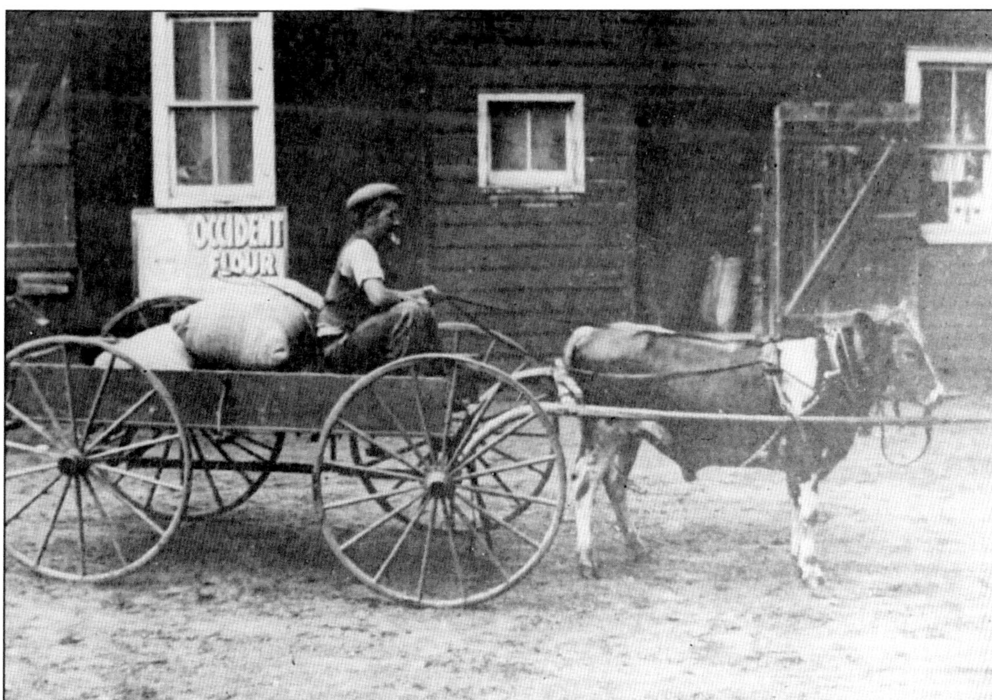

AN OX CART, C. 1900. The local gristmill in the Old Bridge section had an ox cart to carry freshly ground flour to its customers. (Collection of East Brunswick Museum.)

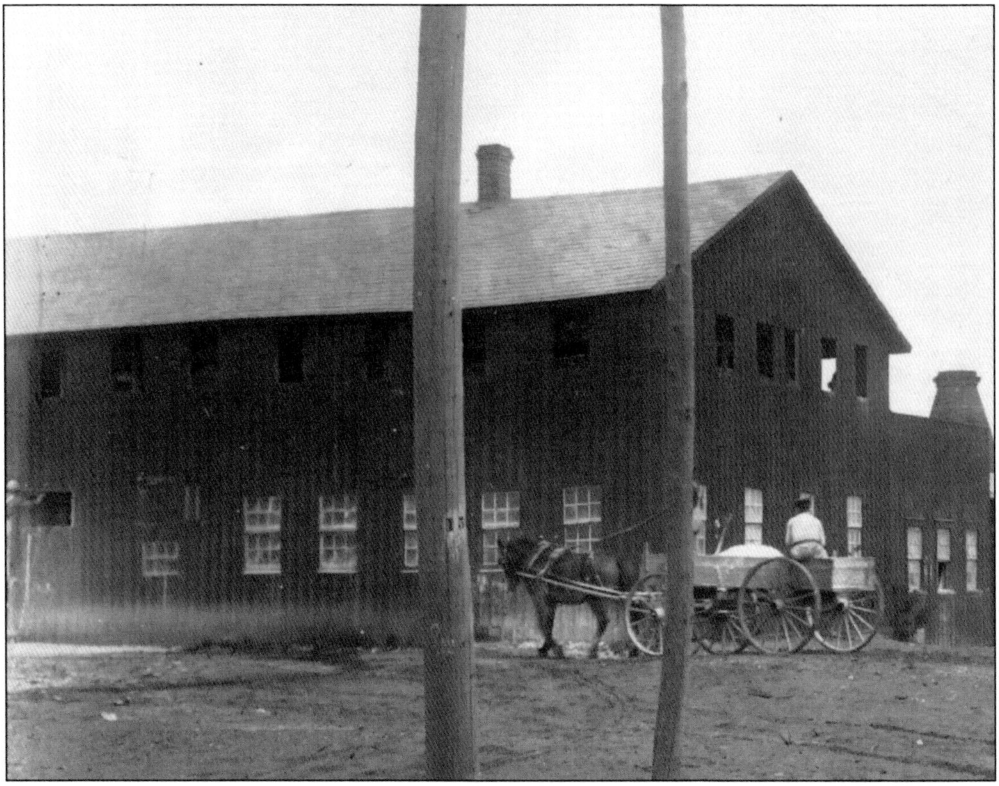

The Old Bridge Brick and Tile Company, c. 1900. Parts of this factory today are located on Bordentown Avenue in Sayreville. Many East Brunswick residents worked for this company making tile for the Holland Tunnel and large hotels in New York City. Two hundred people lost their jobs when the factory closed in 1929. (Collection of East Brunswick Museum.)

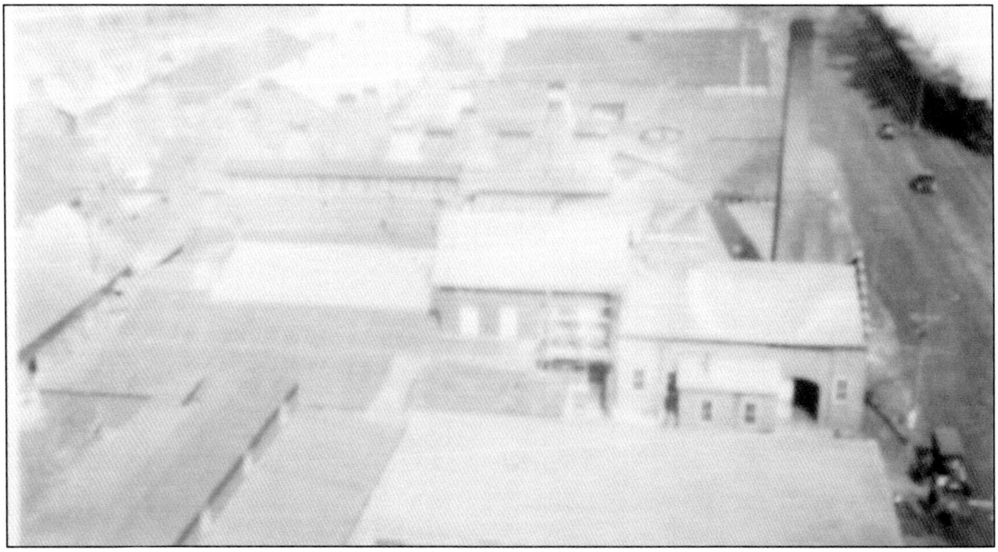

A c. 1910 View of the Old Bridge Enamel Brick and Tile Company from the Company's Water Tower. The construction of the water tower saved the factory money on its insurance policy. (Collection of Alberta Yuhas.)

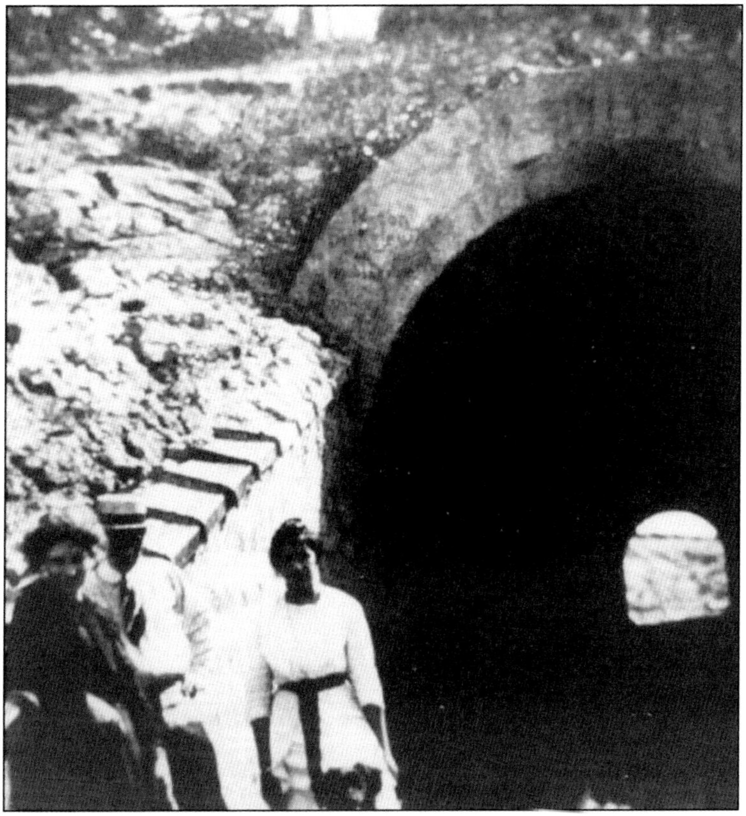

THE TRAIN TUNNEL C. 1900. East Brunswick is part of the Raritan Valley Clay District. Rich deposits of this clay were mined for the production of bricks and other ceramics. American Enamel operated a clay mine where the present-day Route 18 Flea Market is. A train then brought the clay through a tunnel underneath the Old Bridge Turnpike to the factory. The tunnel collapsed in later years. It was located near the back commuter parking lot by the Route 18 Flea Market. (Collection of Ann Alverez.)

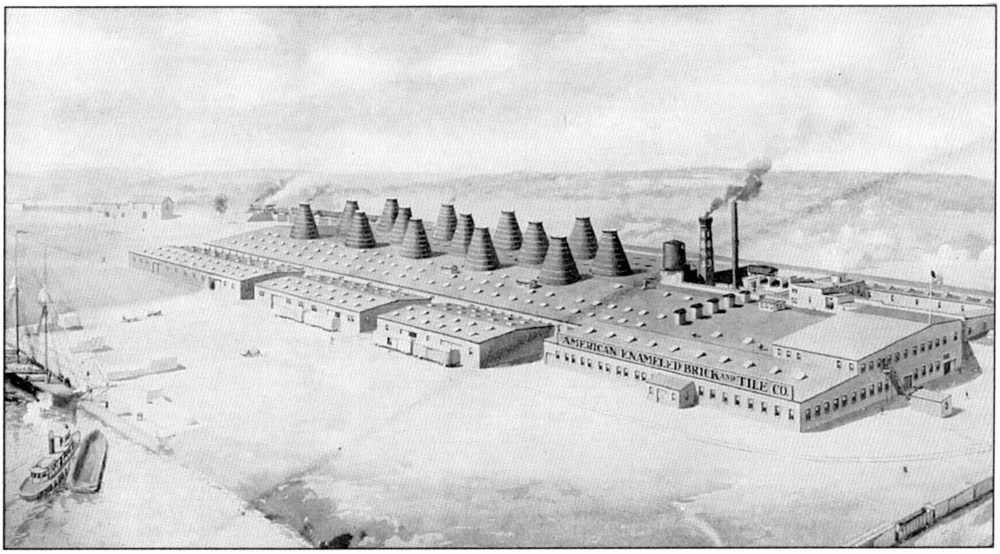

THE AMERICAN ENAMEL BRICK FACTORY. The American Enamel Brick Factory operated from the early 1900s until the 1920s off of Edgeboro Road on Brick Plant Road. The company made a special enamel brick for building facades, and owned a clay pit where the Route 18 Flea Market stands today. Today, many of these old clay pits have been examined by archaeologists, who have discovered deposits of amber dating back 94 million years ago. (Collection of Mark Nonestied.)

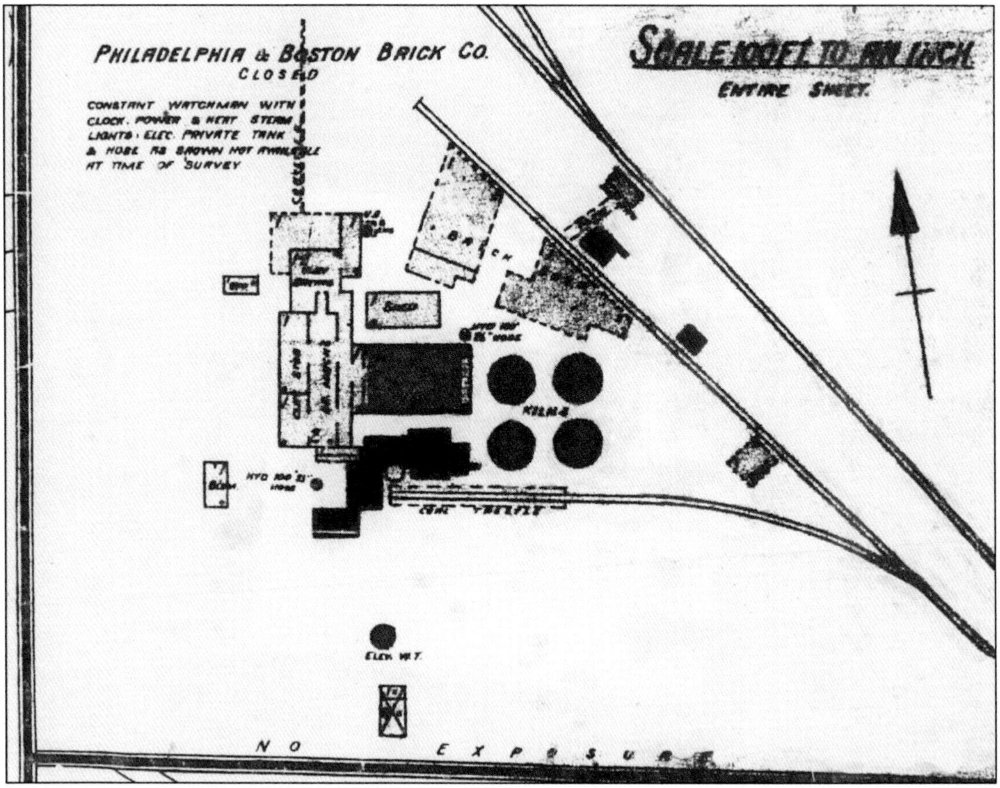

A 1924 SANBORN FIRE INSURANCE MAP. The Boston and Philadelphia Face Brick Company operated in East Brunswick in the early part of the 20th century. Located along the Raritan River Railroad, the company employed 60 people in 1912. Today the remnants of the factory are located off of Stratford Road.

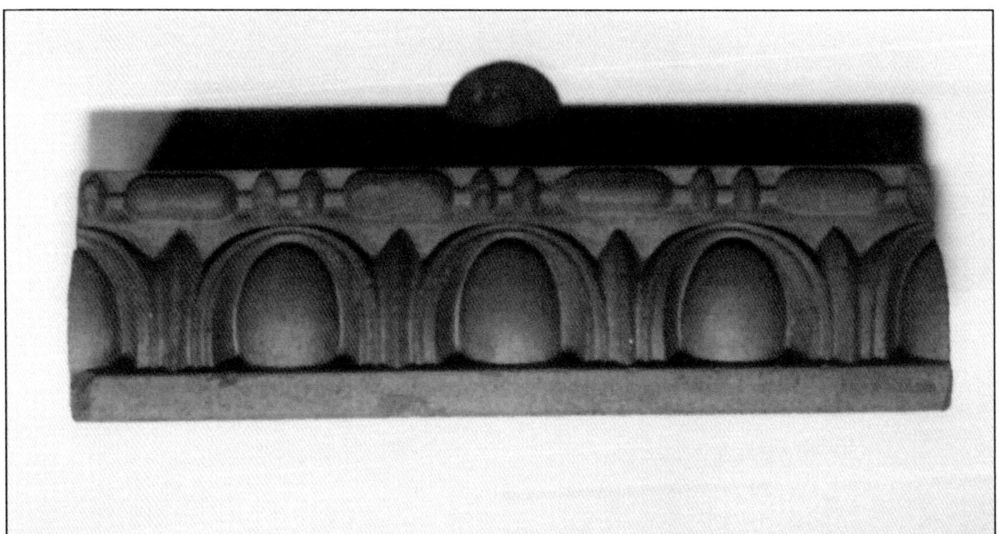

A PRESSED BRICK, 1900. The Boston and Philadelphia Face Brick Company made fancy pressed brick for building facades. Clay was mined from local clay pits and transported to the factory by rail for processing into bricks. (Collection of Mark Nonestied.)

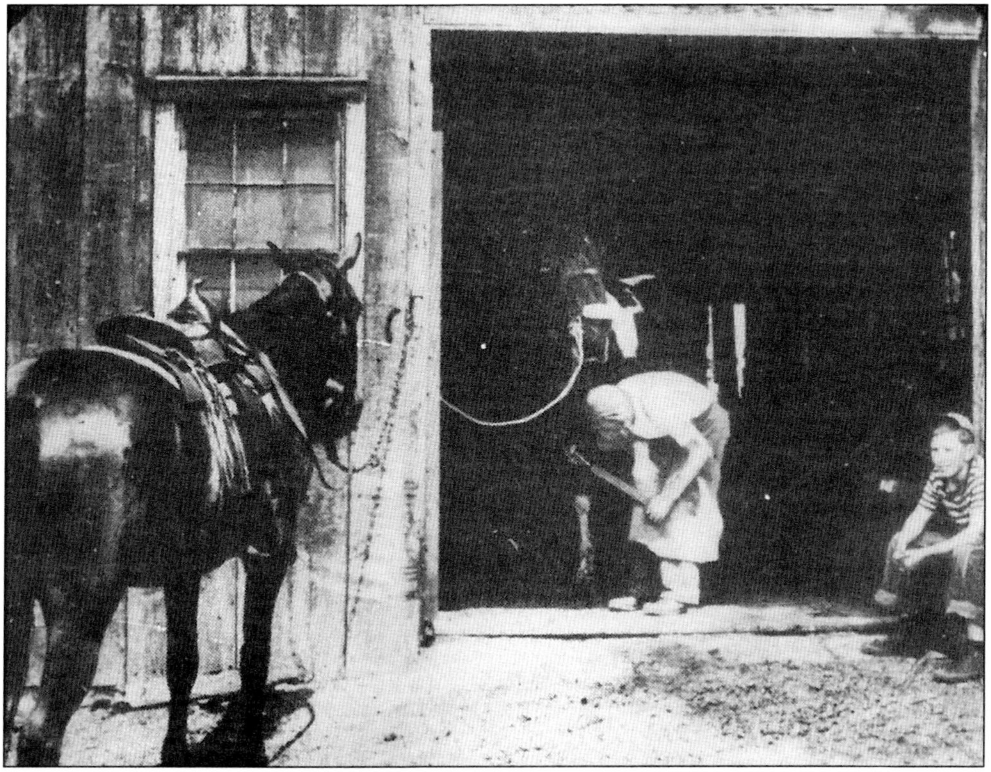

J.K. DILL'S BLACKSMITH SHOP, c. 1900. Local residents knew that the banging of metal meant J.K. Dill was at work. (Collection of East Brunswick Museum.)

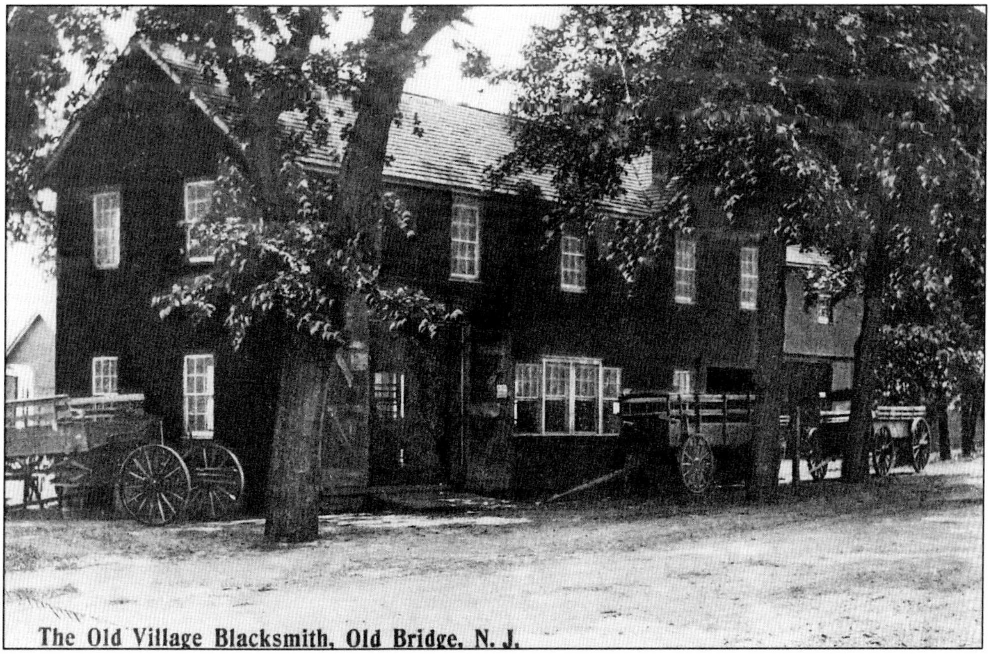

J.K. DILL'S BLACKSMITH SHOP, c. 1900. The first fire engine for the town, a wagon with a pump, was made here in 1906. (Collection of East Brunswick Museum.)

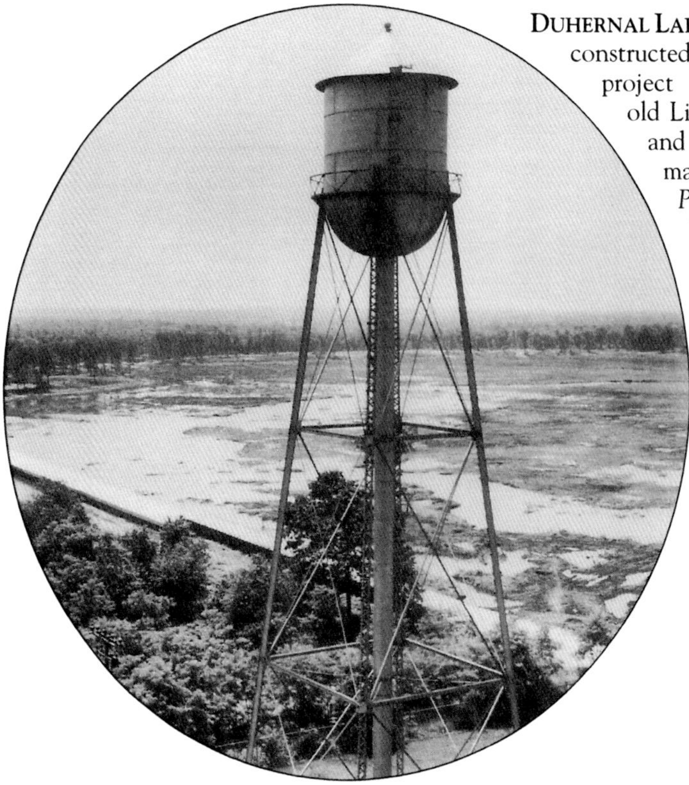

DUHERNAL LAKE, 1939. Duhernal Lake was constructed in the 1930s as an industrial project for several factories. The old Licorice Mill was demolished and flooded when the lake was made. (From *Middlesex County Pictorial 1939*; collection of East Brunswick Museum.)

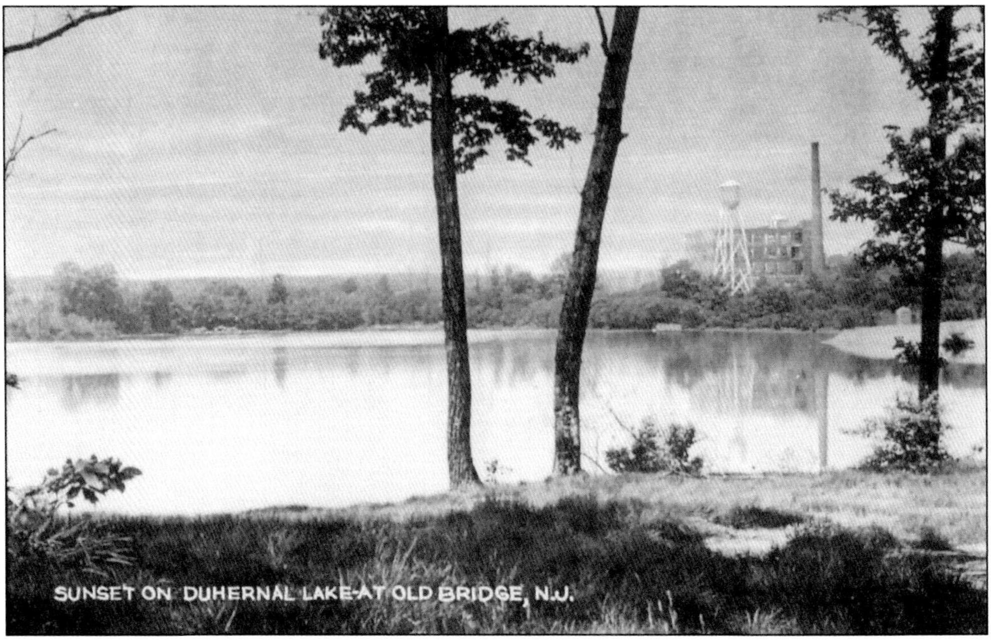

DUHERNAL LAKE AT SUNSET, C. 1935. Duhernal Lake was man-made in the 1930s by the construction of a dam along the South River. The Anheuser-Busch Factory is visible in the background. (Collection of Alberta Yuhas.)

Nine

Transportation Routes

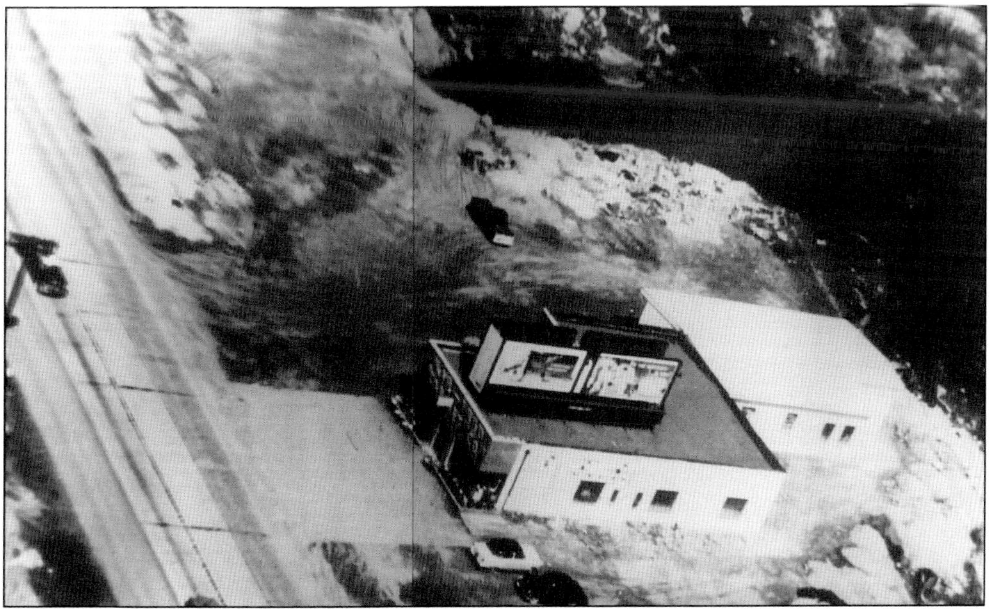

ROUTE 18, 1953. This aerial photograph shows Marfred Cabinets. The store was located near the present-day Route 18 Flea Market and Sam's Club. The large depressions in the rear are old clay pits. Route 18 was a two-lane cement highway. A third lane, used for passing cars, was added at a later date. (Collection of East Brunswick Museum.)

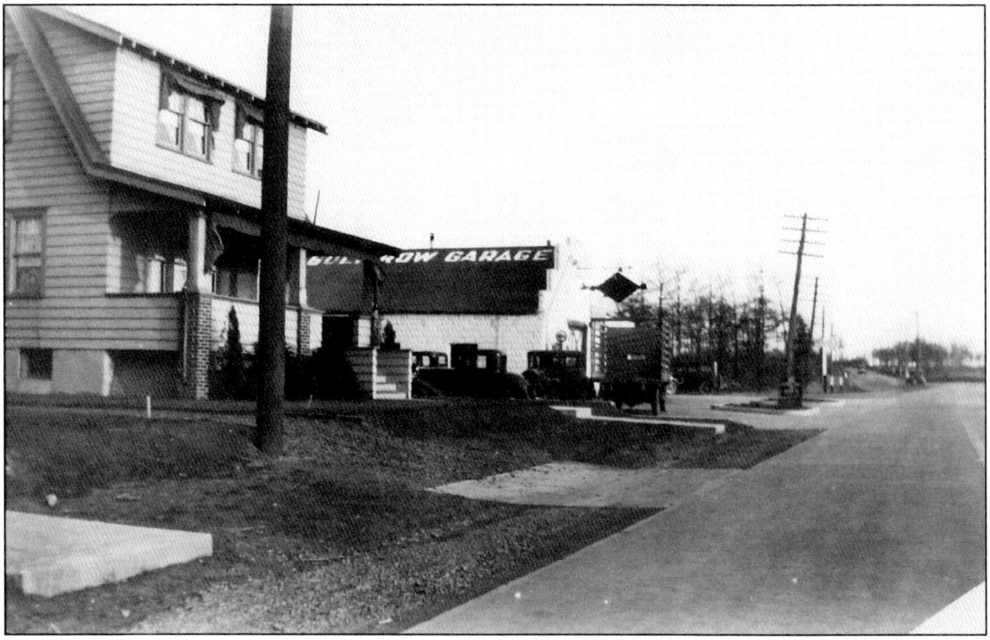

ROUTE 18, C. 1933. The road to the left is the Old Bridge Turnpike as it merges with Route 18 near Edgeboro Road. The Sunoco gas station that at one time was owned by the Warnsdorfer family is still in use on Route 18 North. The home was later turned into a store that burned down several years ago. (Collection of East Brunswick Museum.)

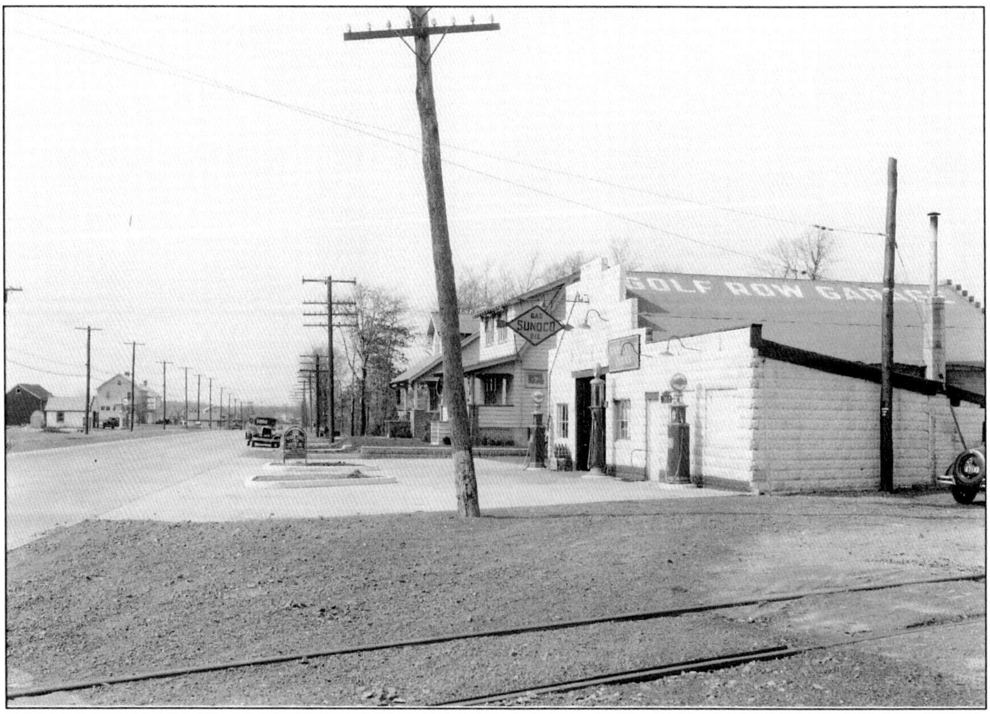

ROUTE 18 LOOKING NORTH, C. 1933. This view shows Route 18 North, just past Edgeboro Road and the Old Bridge Turnpike intersection. (Collection of East Brunswick Museum.)

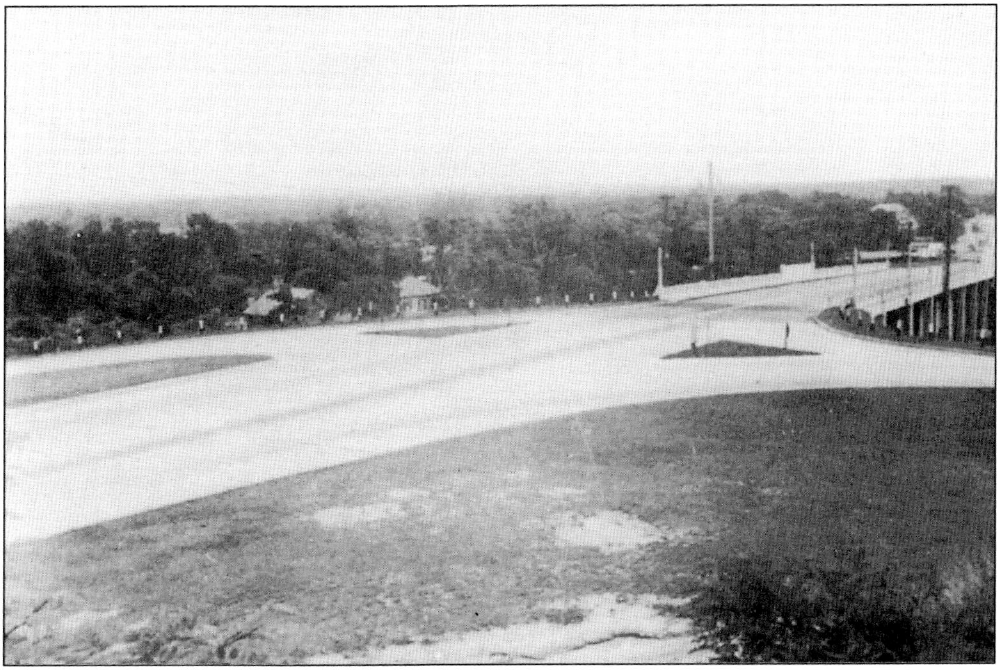

ROUTE 18 SOUTH, C. 1938. The Route 18 bridge crossing over Main Street is visible in the background, and the exit for Main Street is to the right. (From *Middlesex County Pictorial 1938*; collection of East Brunswick Museum.)

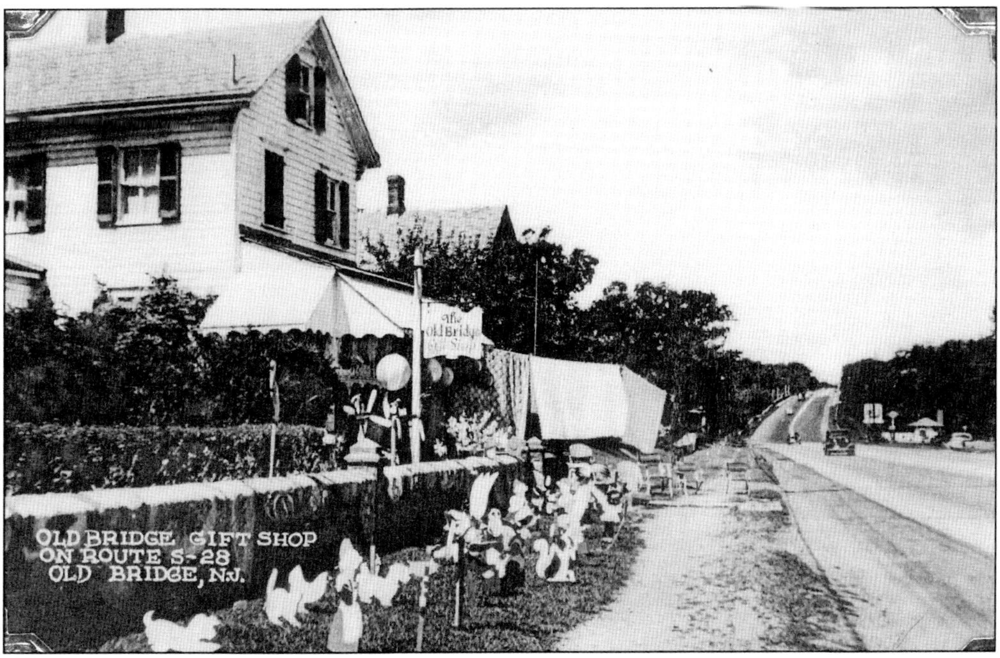

ROUTE 18 LOOKING NORTH, C. 1935. Route 18 was originally a two-lane highway named S-28. The bridge crossing over Main Street is visible in the background. (Collection of East Brunswick Museum.)

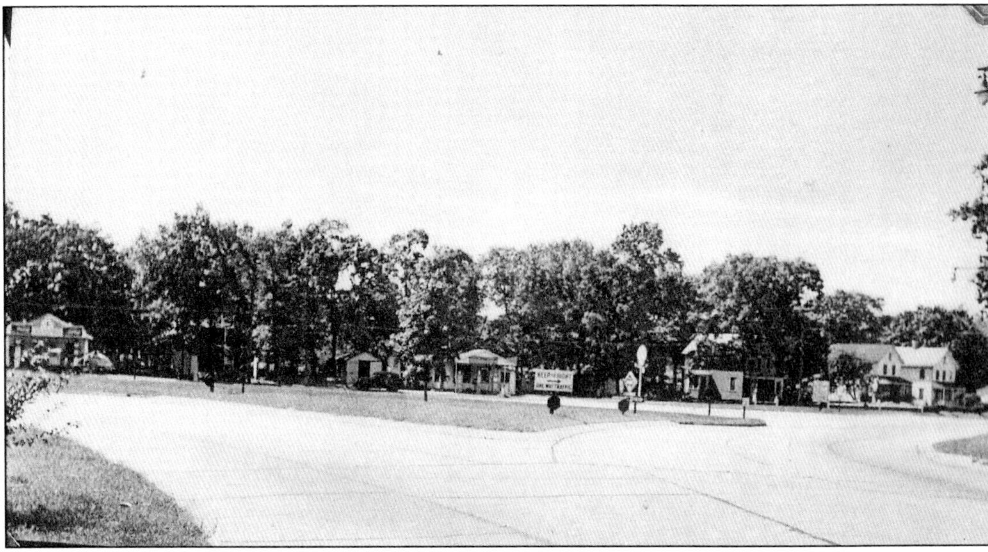

ROUTE 18. Originally, Route 18 South ended at a traffic circle near the Englishtown Road exit, after crossing over Main Street into Madison Township. (Collection of East Brunswick Museum.)

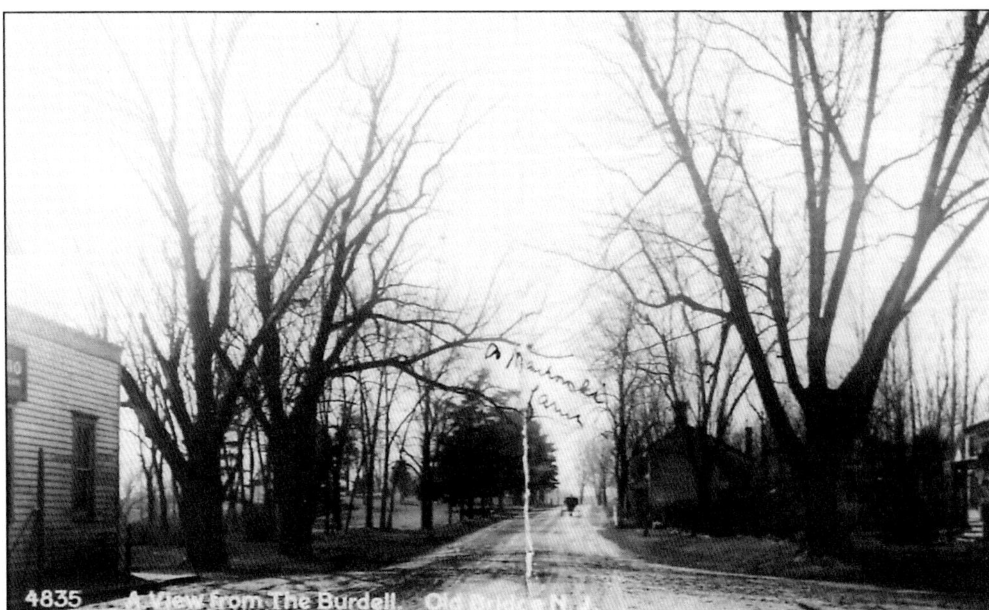

MAIN STREET, LOOKING TOWARD SPOTSWOOD, C. 1900. Today Route 18 crosses over this spot. The house to the right was owned by the Van Wickle family and was demolished for the construction of the Route 18 bridge over Main Street. (Collection of East Brunswick Museum.)

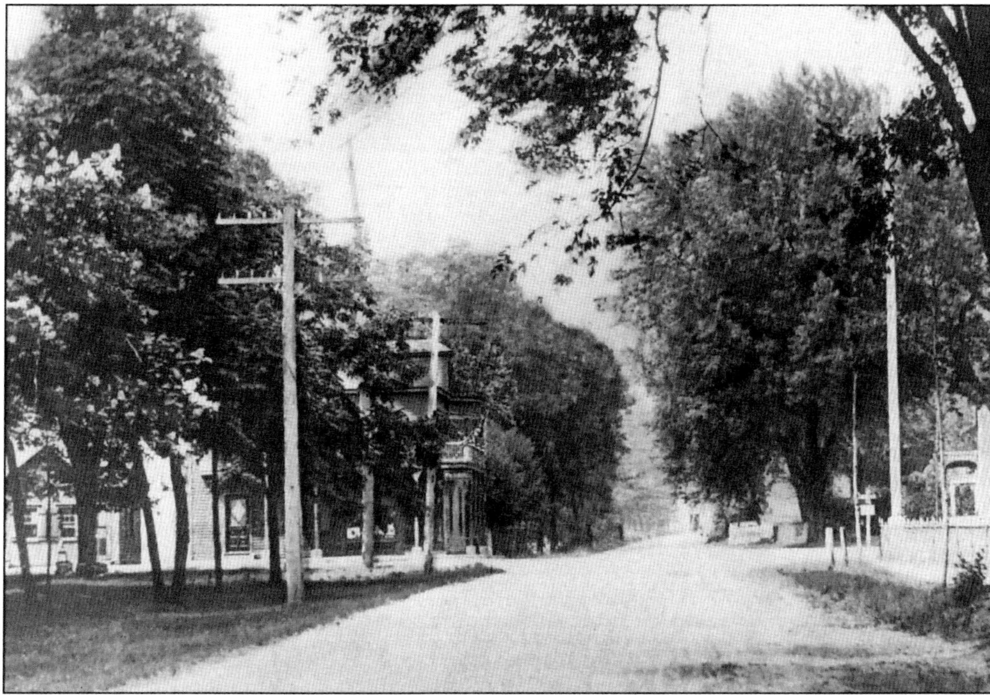

The Intersection of the Old Bridge Turnpike and Main Street, c. 1900. The building on the left of the intersection still stands as a barbershop. Today, Route 18 crosses Main Street near the center of the photograph. (Collection of East Brunswick Museum.)

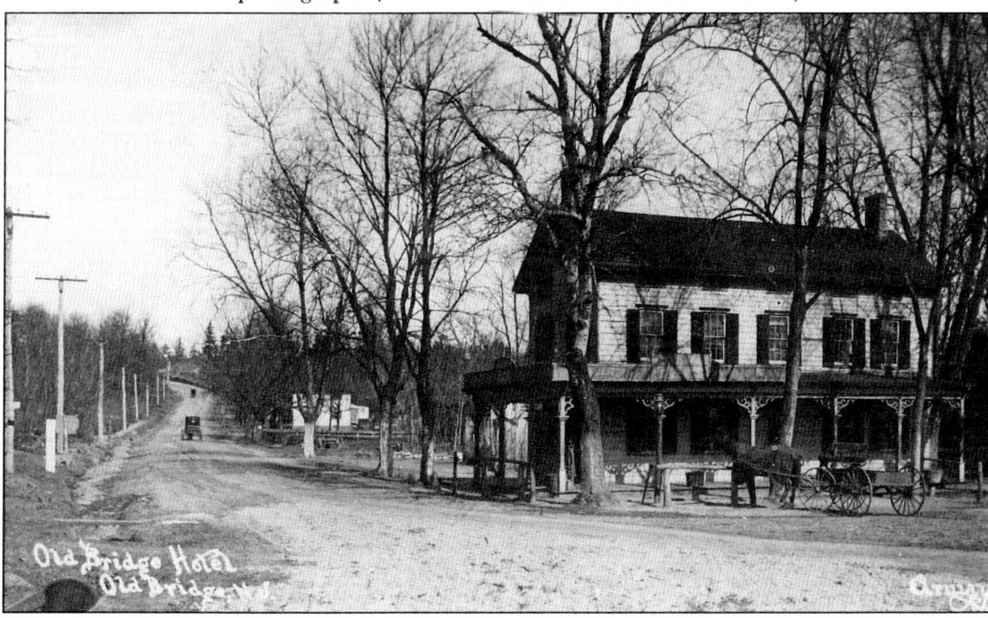

The Old Bridge Turnpike Looking North, c. 1900. The stone wall on the Old Bridge Turnpike and the Chestnut Hill Cemetery are located to the top right of the photograph. This route was originally laid out in the early 1800s as a toll road. Several tollbooths were established to collect 3¢ for people traveling by horse or 1¢ for those wishing to walk on the turnpike. (Collection of East Brunswick Museum.)

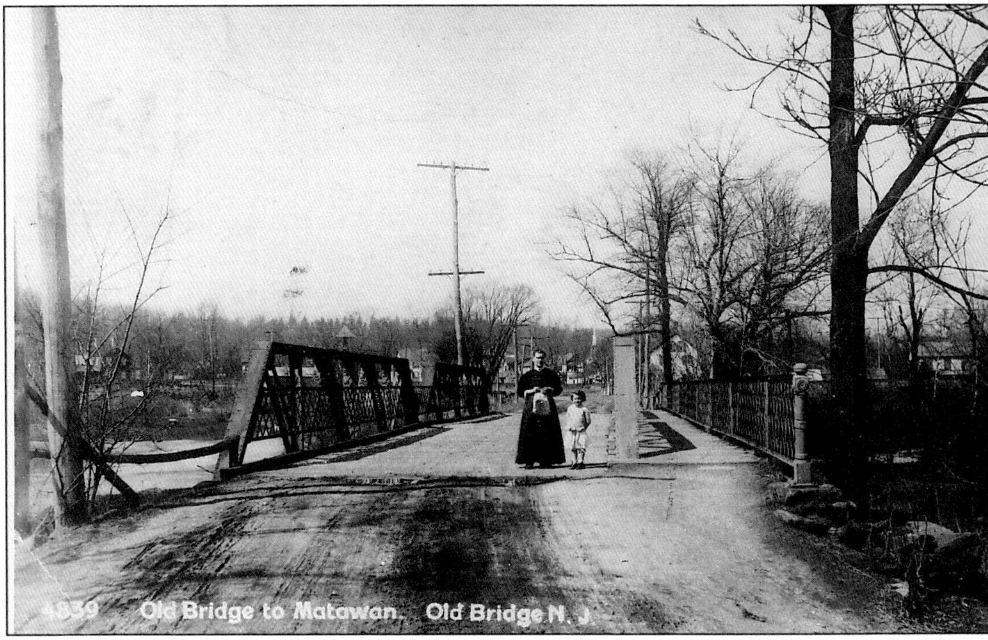

THE MATAWAN ROAD BRIDGE, C. 1900. The Historic District of Old Bridge is located in the background of the photograph . (Collection of East Brunswick Museum.)

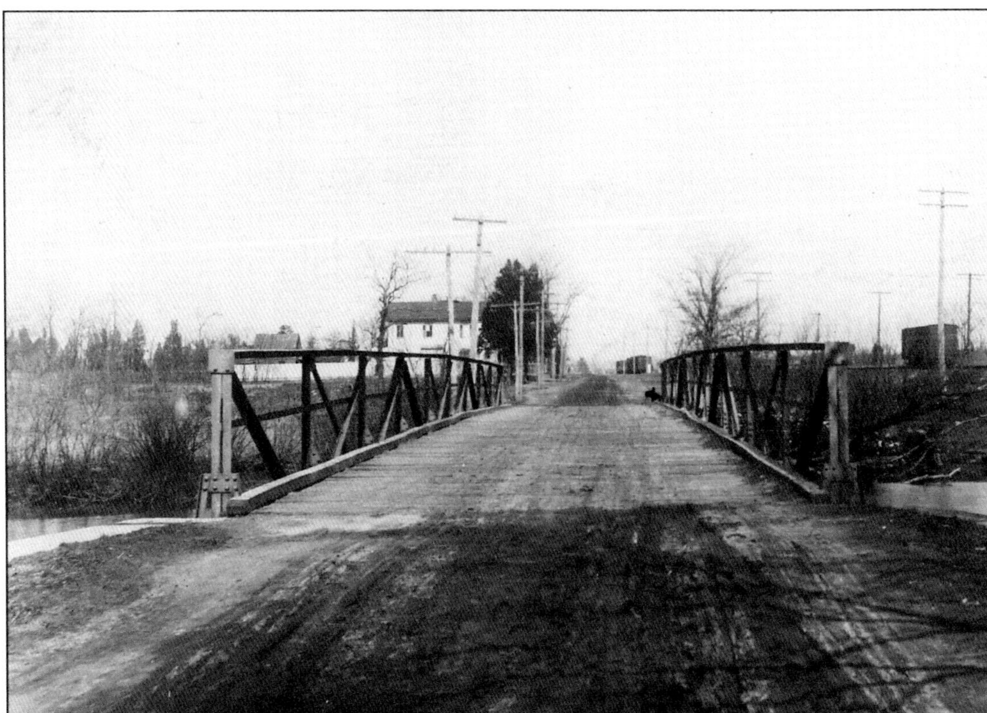

LOOKING DOWN MAIN STREET OVER THE BRIDGE INTO SAYREVILLE, C. 1900. (Collection of East Brunswick Museum.)

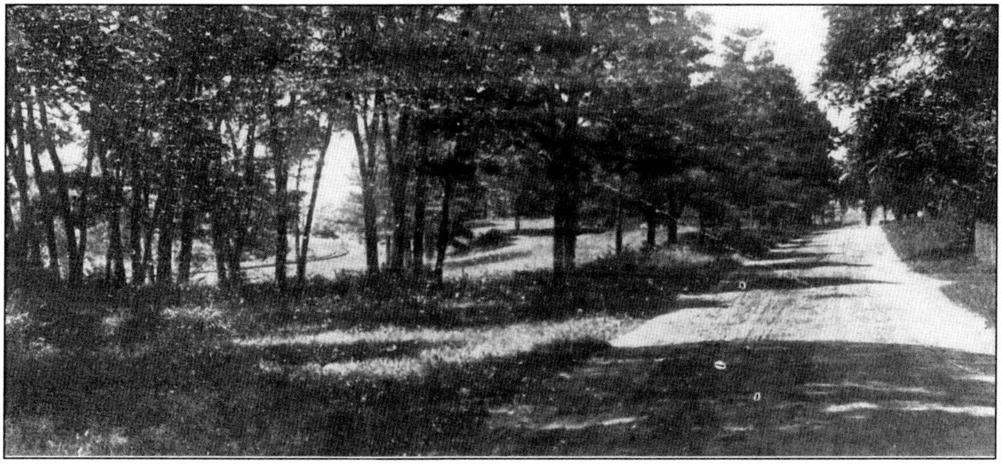

A View of Main Street Looking toward Old Stage Road, c. 1890. The Bowne Munro School was built on the tract of land to the top right of the photograph. (Collection of East Brunswick Museum.)

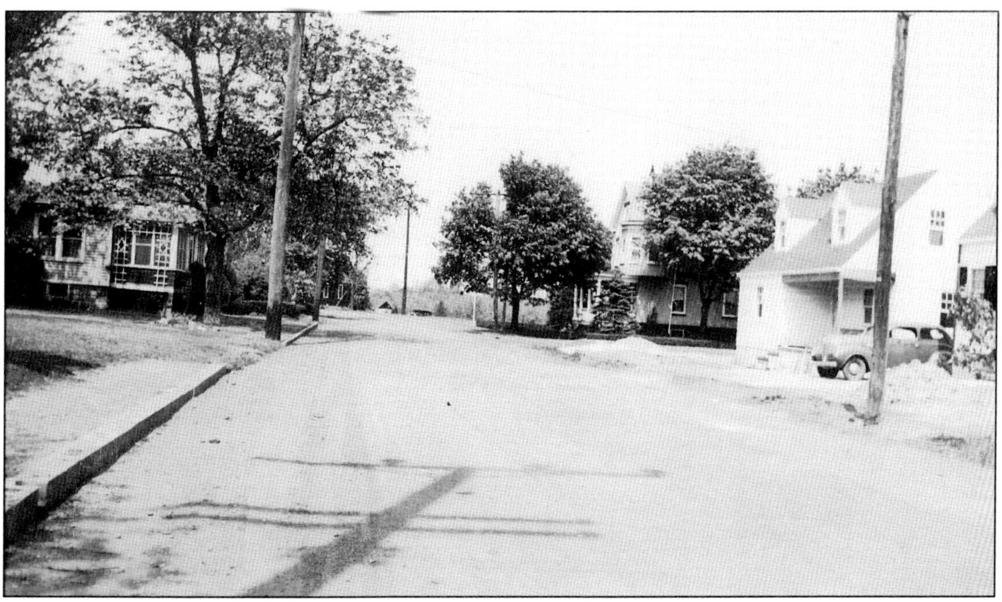

Kossman Street Looking toward River Road, c. 1948. (Collection of Florence Mount.)

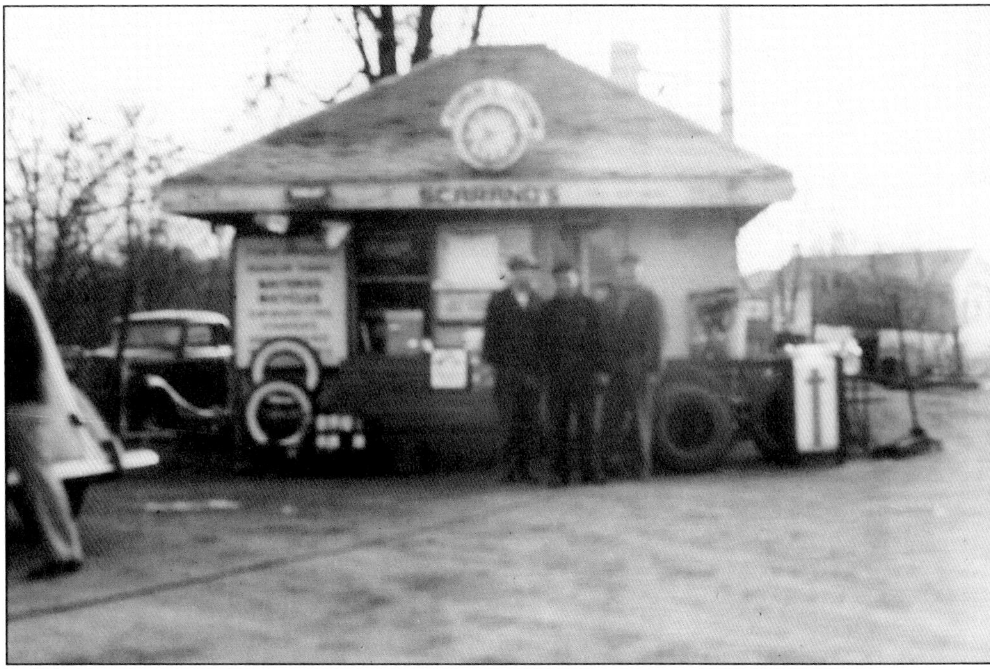

Scarano's Garage, 1954. Scarano's was located on the corner of the Old Bridge Turnpike and Main Street, where the Village Deli is today. (Collection of Alberta Yuhas.)

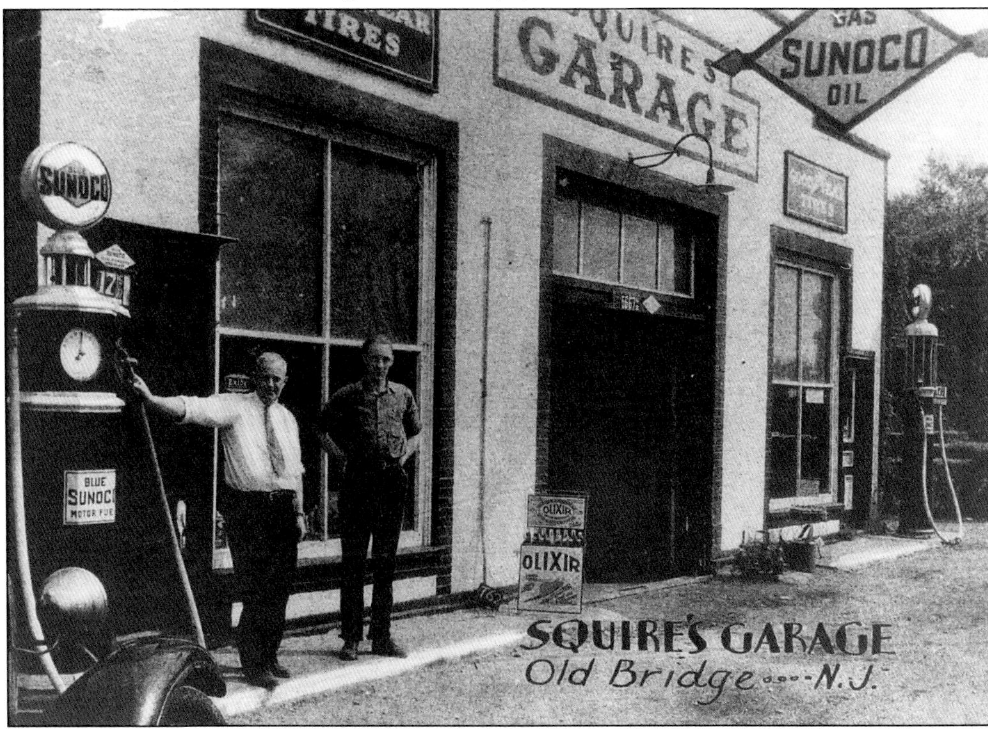

Squire's Garage, c. 1930. This was an early gas station located on Matawan Road, before the bridge that crossed into Madison Township. The building still stands as the Route 18 Glass Store. (Collection of East Brunswick Museum.)

OLGA ZDANOWICH, ALONG RUE'S LANE, C. 1945. The field to the left is where Great Oak Park and Winton Road are today. (Collection of Arciszewski Family.)

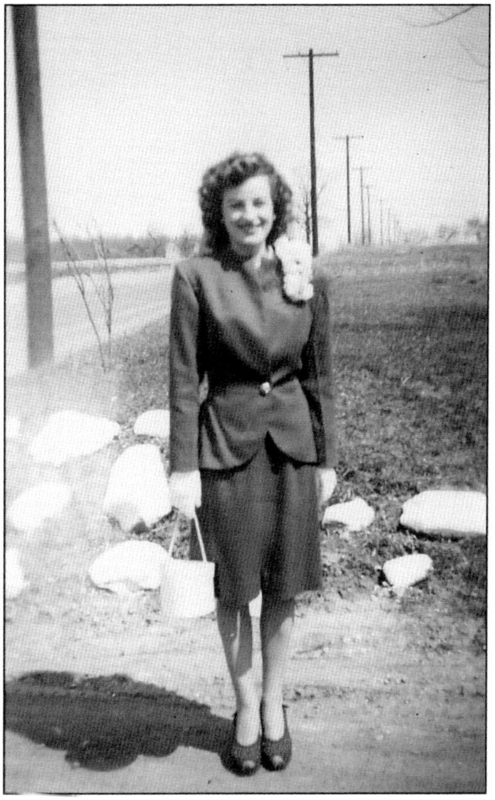

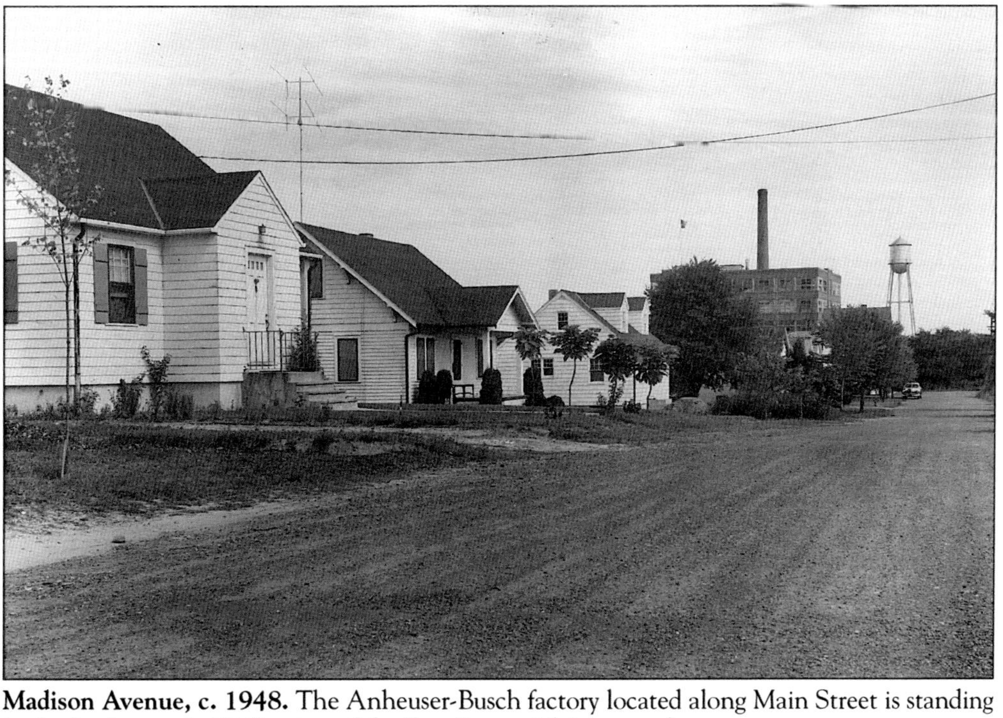

Madison Avenue, c. 1948. The Anheuser-Busch factory located along Main Street is standing in the background. (Collection of the East Brunswick Museum.)

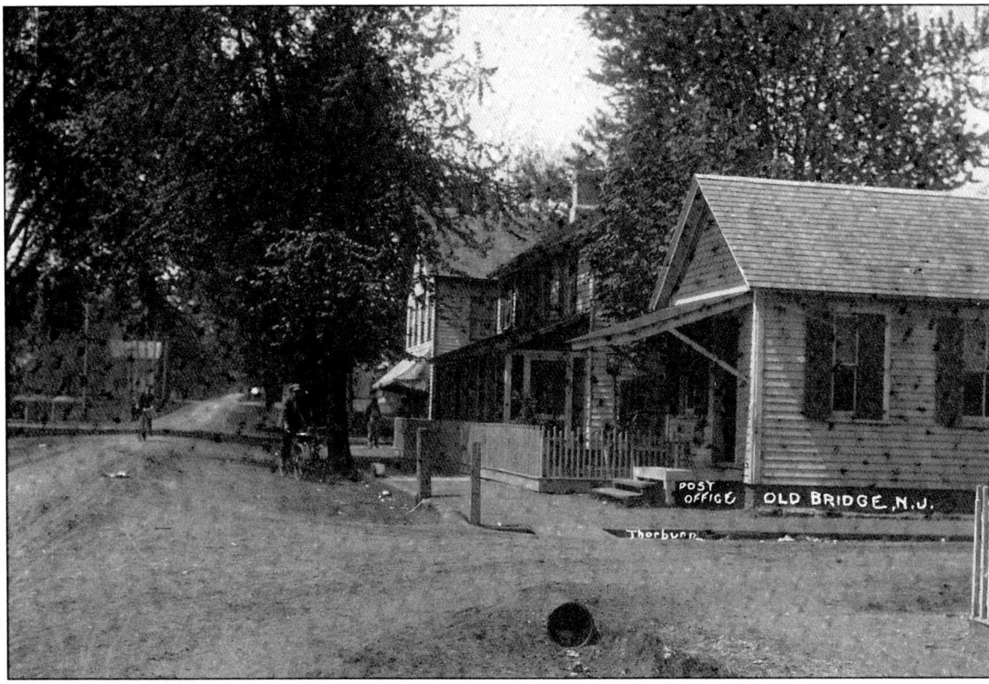

MAIN STREET, LOOKING NEAR THE CORNER OF THE OLD BRIDGE TURNPIKE, C. 1890. (Collection of East Brunswick Museum.)

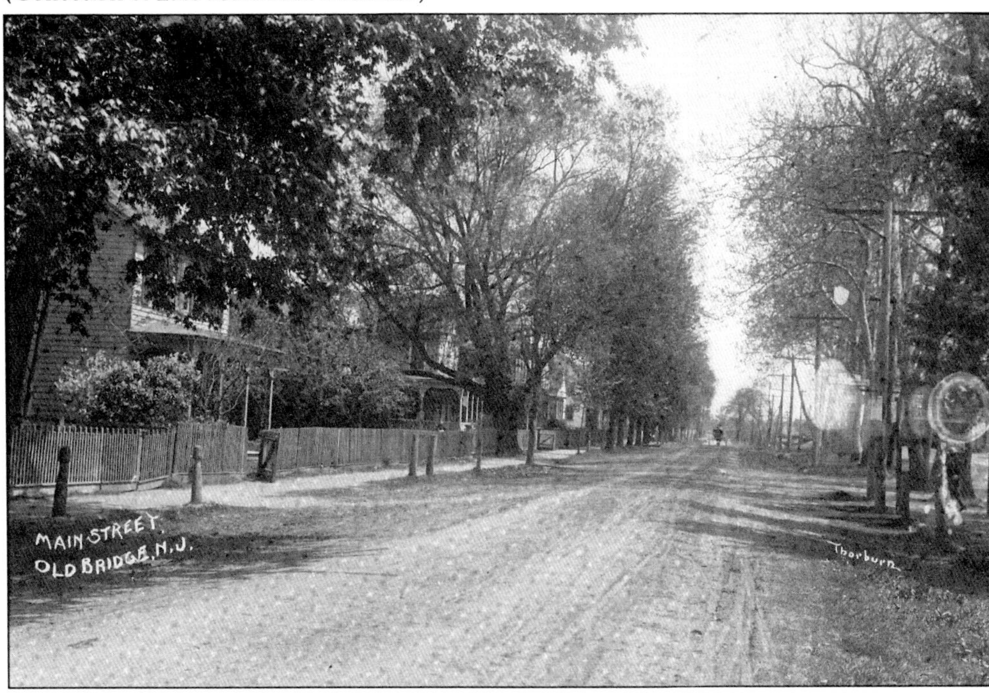

MAIN STREET, LOOKING INTO SAYREVILLE, C. 1900. The Old Bridge section was very picturesque at the turn of the century. It attracted German photographer Thorburn, who took photographs of the area and had them reproduced onto postcards. (Collection of East Brunswick Museum.)

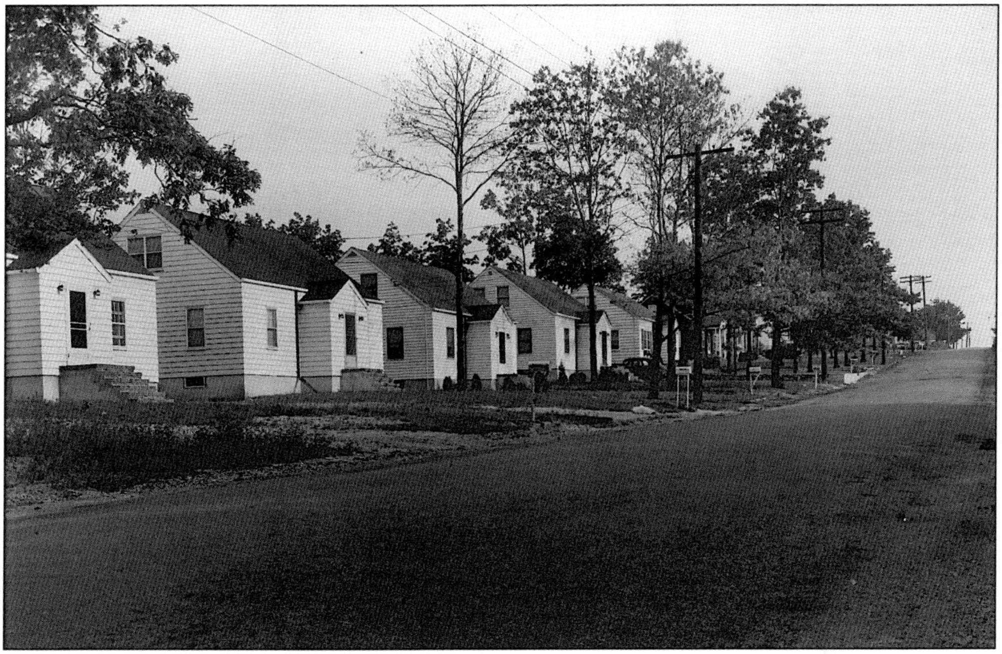

Ryders Lane Looking Toward the Intersection of Milltown Road, c. 1948. (Collection of the East Brunswick Museum.)

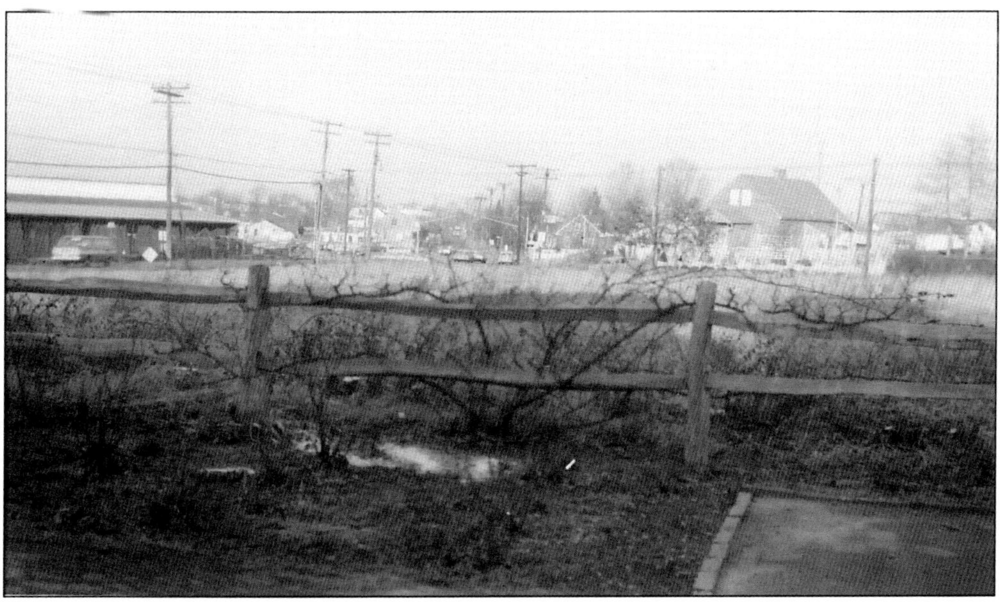

The Intersection of Cranbury Road and Route 18, c. 1968. This photograph was taken prior to the construction of the overpass. (Collection of East Brunswick Museum.)

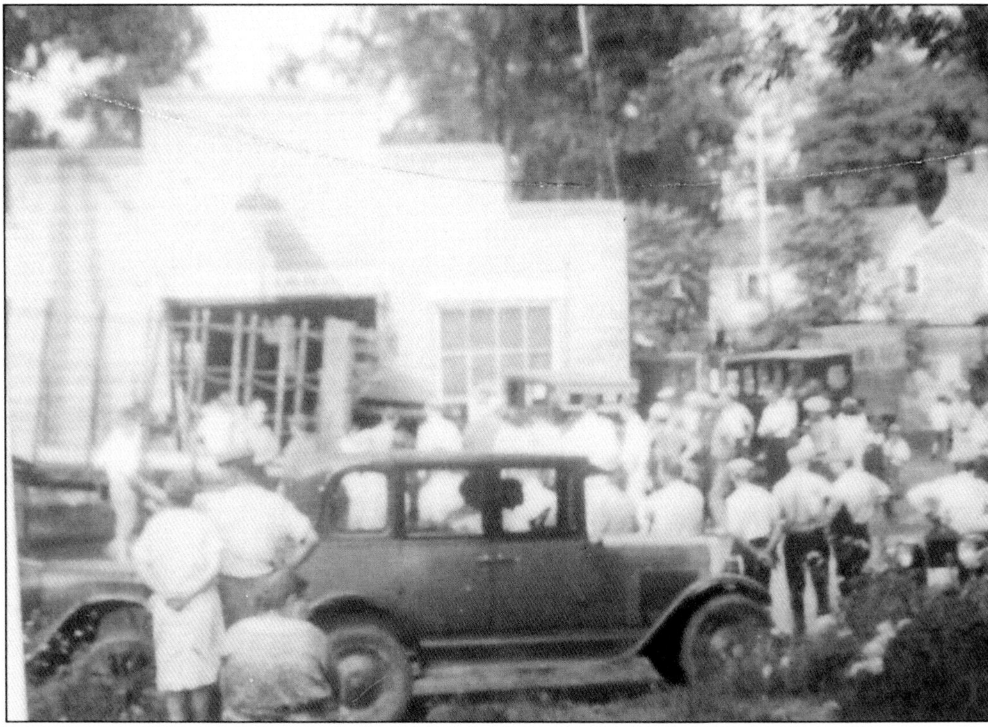

A Truck Accident, c. 1930. Residents of the Old Bridge section gathered around a truck that lost its brakes going up the hill on the Old Bridge Turnpike. The garage in the background was located on the corner of Pine Street and the Old Bridge Turnpike. (Collection of Alberta Yuhas.)

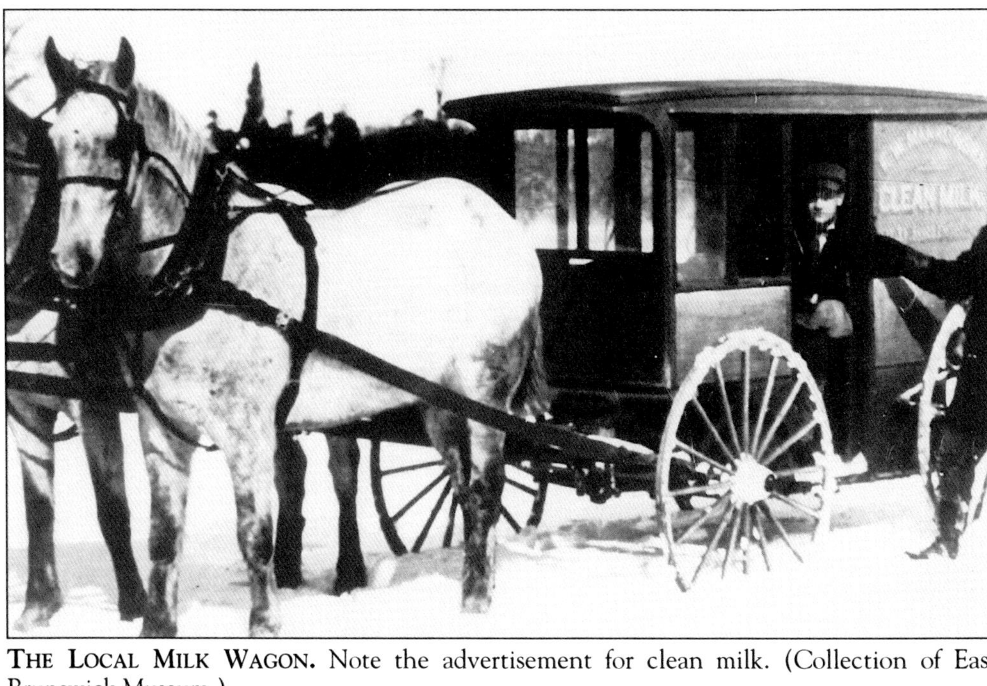

The Local Milk Wagon. Note the advertisement for clean milk. (Collection of East Brunswick Museum.)

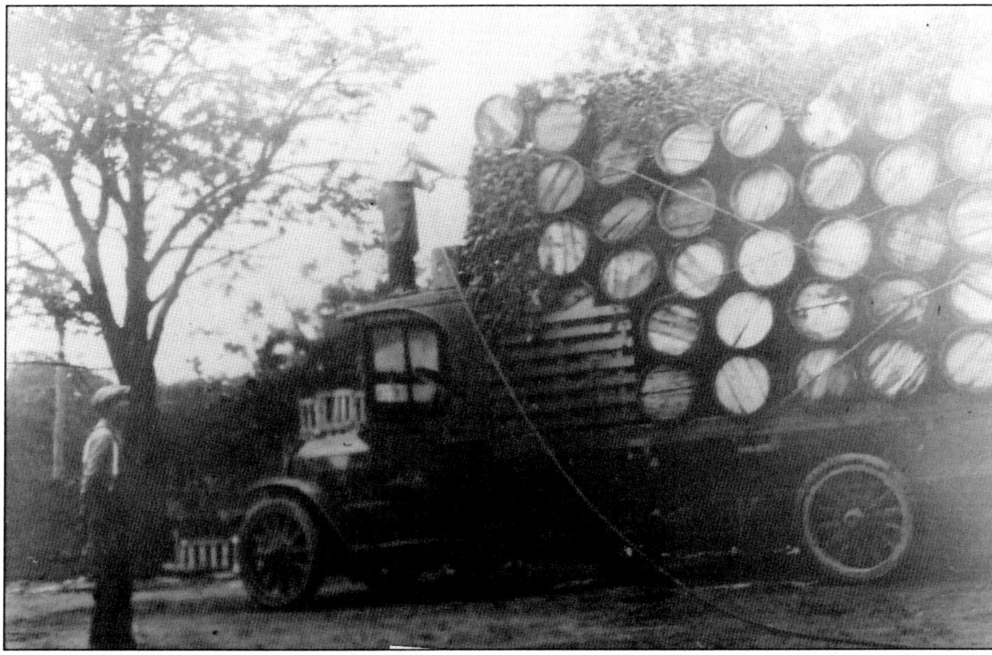

A Market Truck, c. 1920. This truck has been packed beyond capacity with produce bound for local markets. In the 19th century, the quickest means of transporting produce to markets was by river. In later years, railroads would surpass river transportation, and in turn be surpassed by trucks, which benefited from the construction of a better road system. (Collection of the Giamerese Family.)

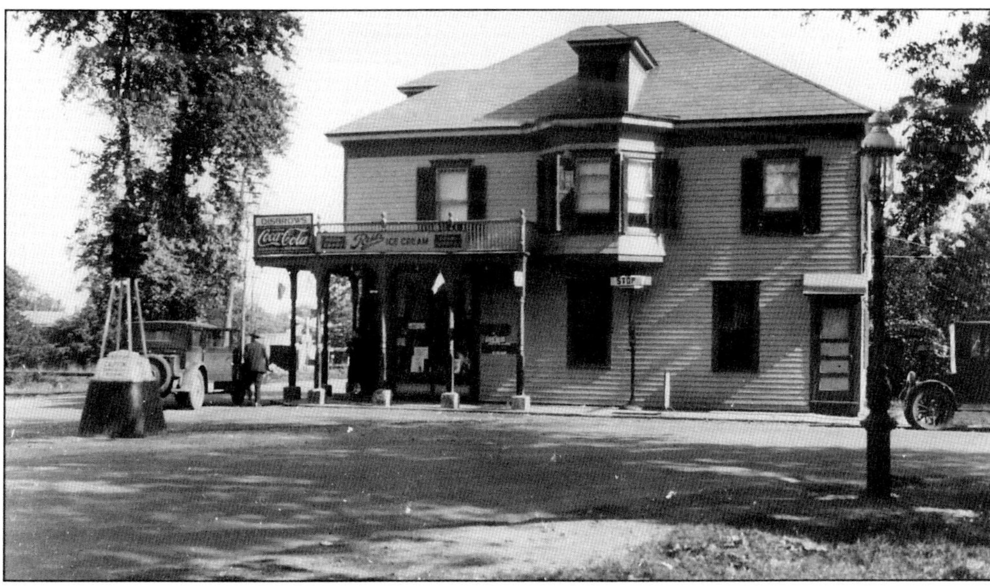

The Intersection of the Old Bridge Turnpike and Main Street, c. 1930. The traffic light was installed in 1927 and is still in the possession of the township. A gas light can be seen to the right of the photograph. In the early days of motor cars, automobiles would sometime turn the corner too sharp and knock the columns off the ice cream store. This building still stands as a barber shop. (Collection of East Brunswick Museum.)

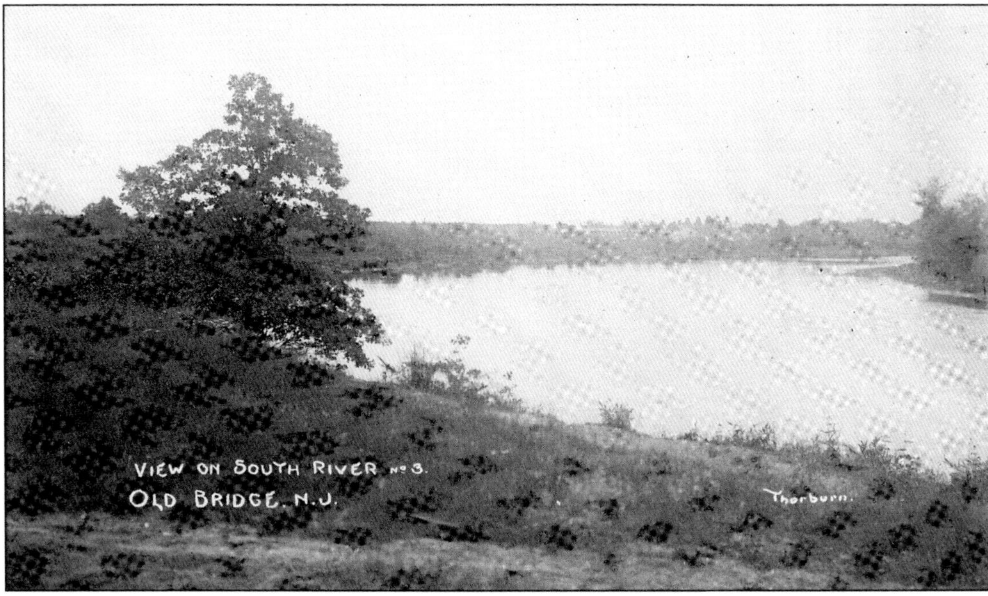

A View on the South River, c. 1900. The head of navigation for the South River was at Old Bridge. This section of town flourished as a trading center between farmers in the interior of the town and markets in New York City. (Collection of East Brunswick Museum.)

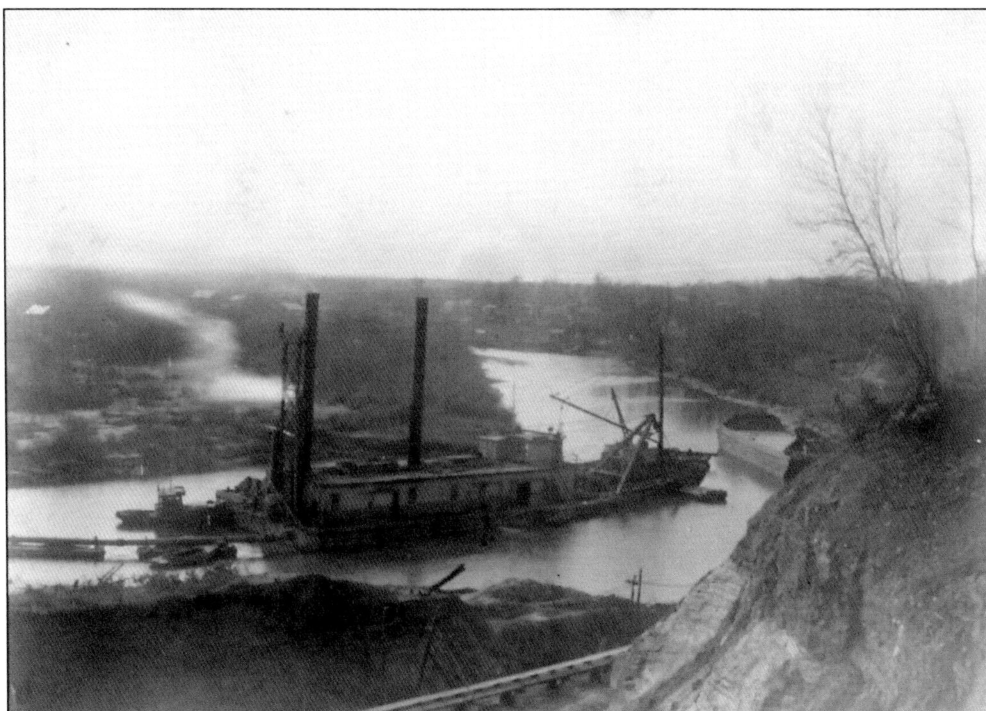

A South River Scene. Until the 1920s, large boats would come up the South River, and periodically the river had to be dredged to accommodate the larger vessels. This view was taken from the hill on River Road, where the Marcus Wright Sand Company used to be. Today, a development is being built here. (Collection of Alberta Yuhas.)

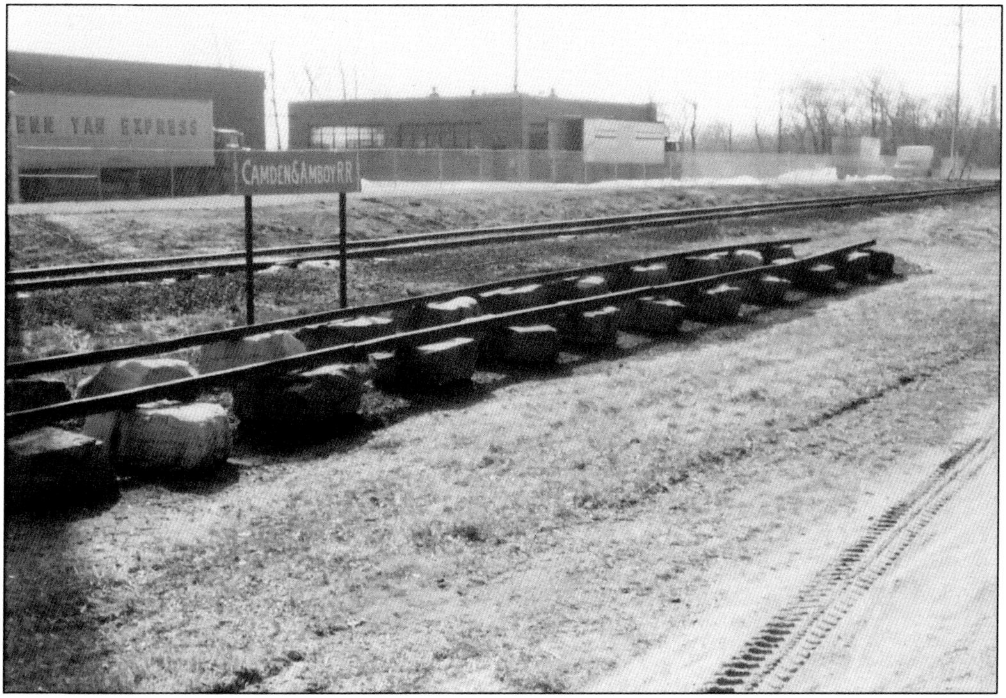

The Original Tracks of the Camden and Amboy Railroad, 1832. The rails sat on top of stone blocks that were cut at the Sing Sing Prison in New York. When the shipment of stone blocks became too slow, workers began using trees, a practice that led to the wooden railroad ties we have today. The Camden and Amboy Railroad was New Jersey's first rail line. (Collection of East Brunswick Museum.)

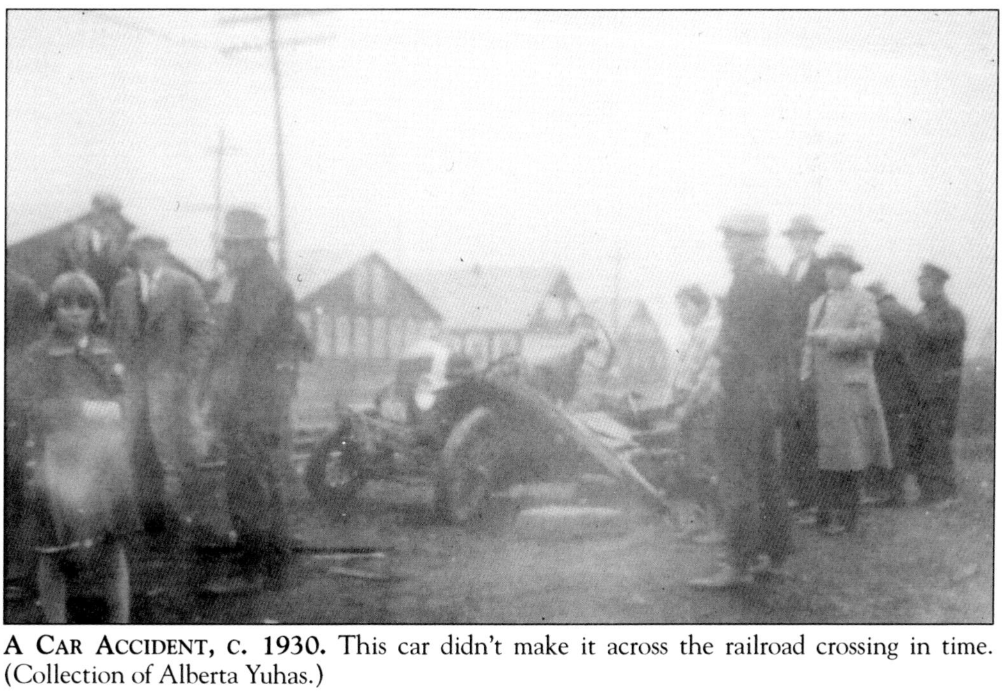

A Car Accident, c. 1930. This car didn't make it across the railroad crossing in time. (Collection of Alberta Yuhas.)

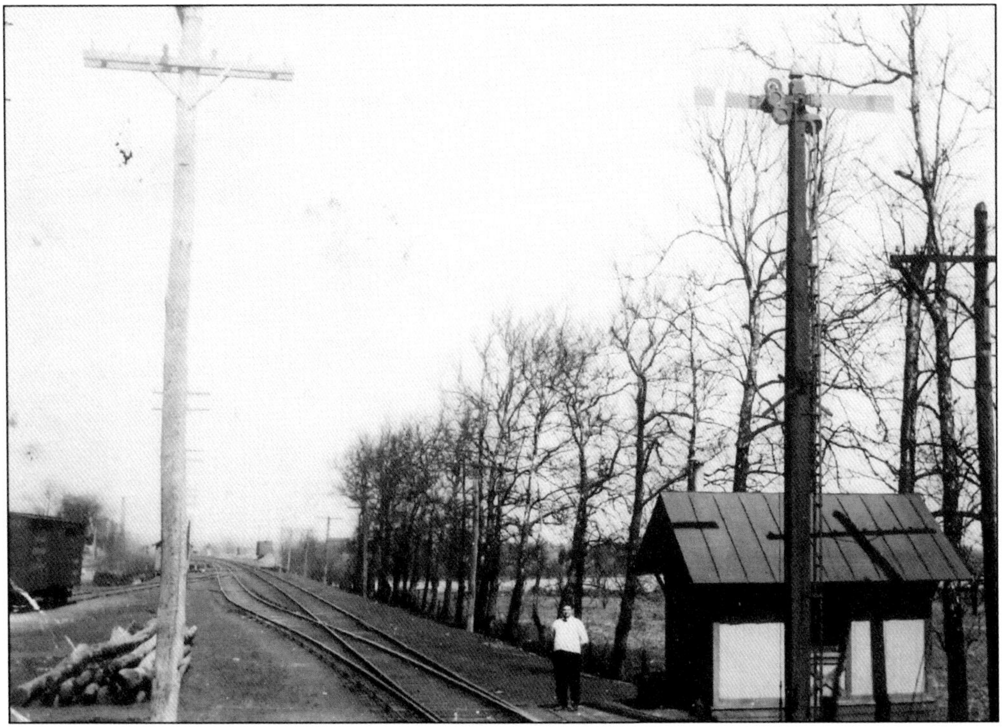

TRAIN TRACKS INTO SAYREVILLE, C. 1890. The building to the right was a telegraph office for the station in the Old Bridge section. (Collection of East Brunswick Museum.)

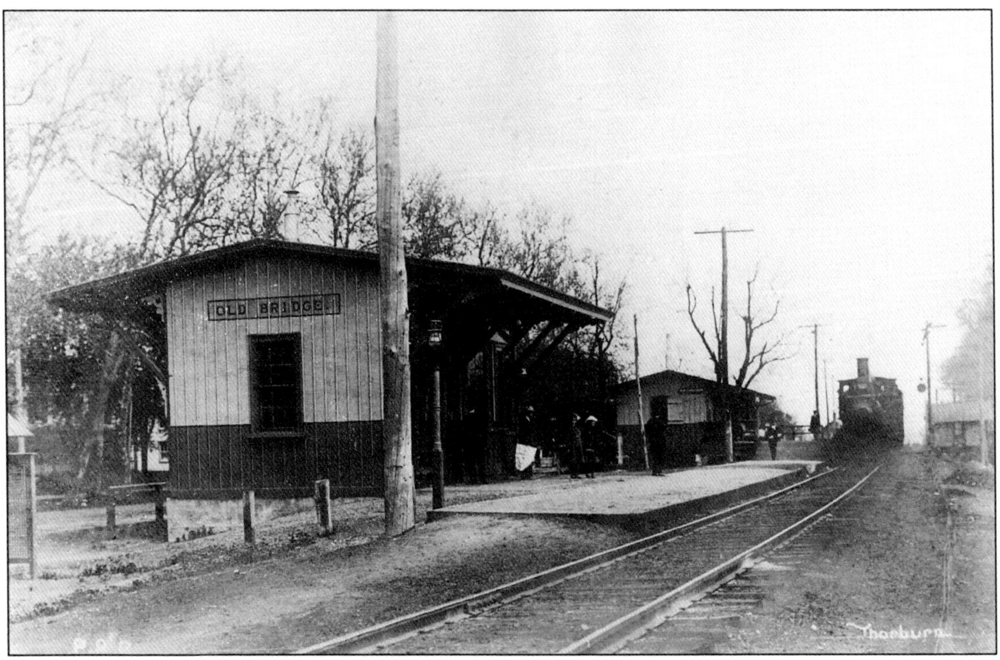

THE OLD BRIDGE TRAIN STATION, C. 1910. Two stations were located in the Old Bridge section—one was for passengers, while the other was for freight. (Collection of East Brunswick Museum.)

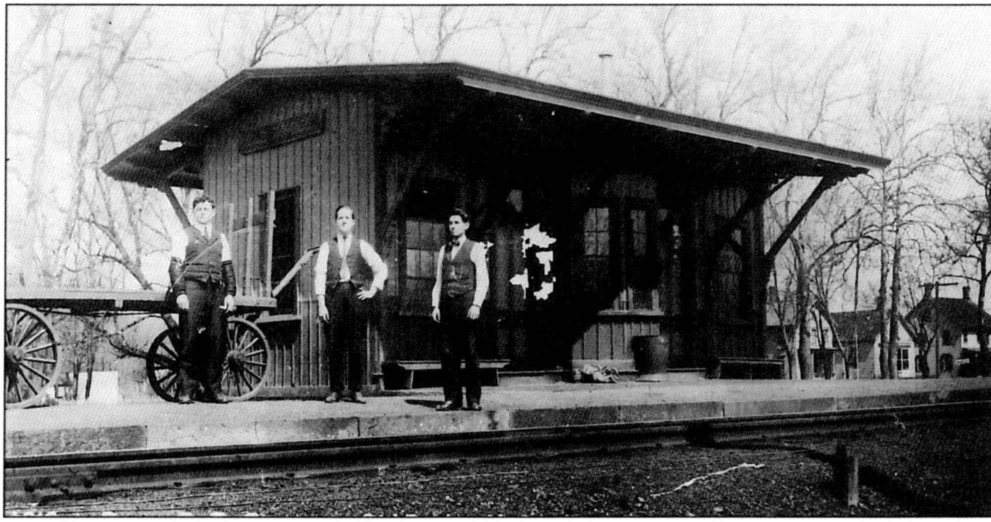

THE FREIGHT STATION, C. 1910. Passengers as well as freight traveled on the railroad. Originally the Camden and Amboy Railroad, it later would become the Pennsylvania Railroad, and today it is used by Conrail. Boxcars filled with strawberries bound for New York markets left the station during the harvest season. (Collection of East Brunswick Museum.)

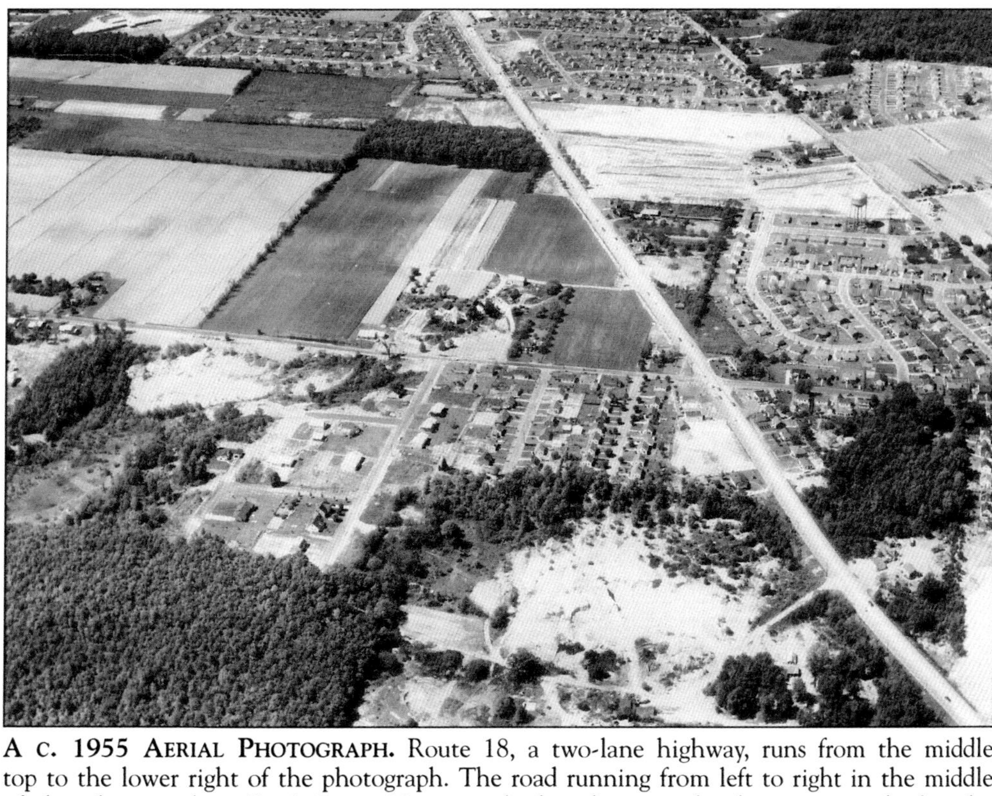

A C. 1955 AERIAL PHOTOGRAPH. Route 18, a two-lane highway, runs from the middle top to the lower right of the photograph. The road running from left to right in the middle of the photograph is Rue's Lane. Various suburban housing developments on both sides of the highway were starting to take their toll on the local farms by the time this photograph was taken. (Collection of East Brunswick Museum.)

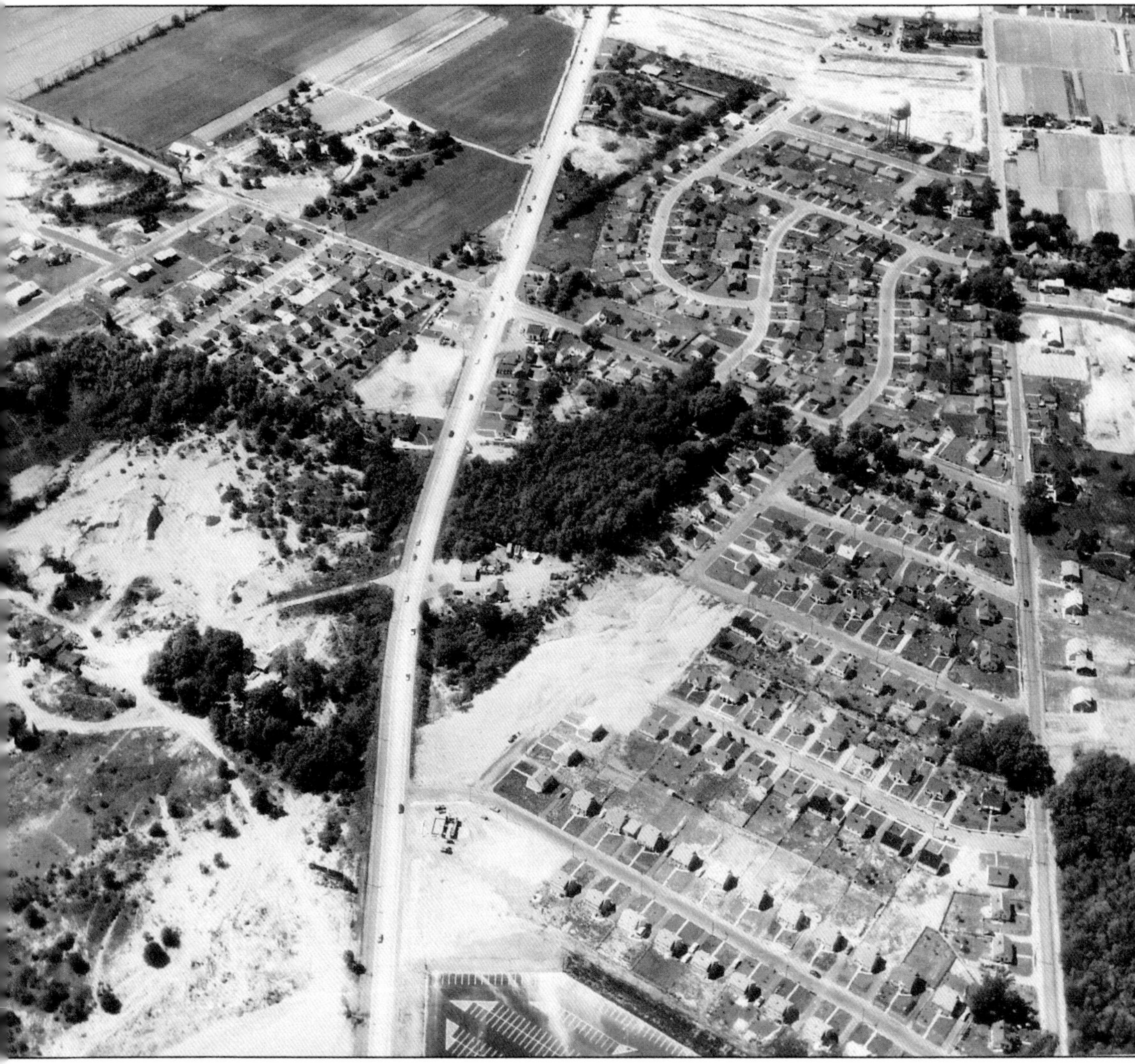

ANOTHER C. 1955 AERIAL PHOTOGRAPH. This view, taken in the same general vicinity as the previous photograph, shows more of the east side of Route 18. The Old Bridge Turnpike runs from the top to the bottom of the photograph, on the immediate right. (Collection of East Brunswick Museum.)

Ten

Yesterday and Today

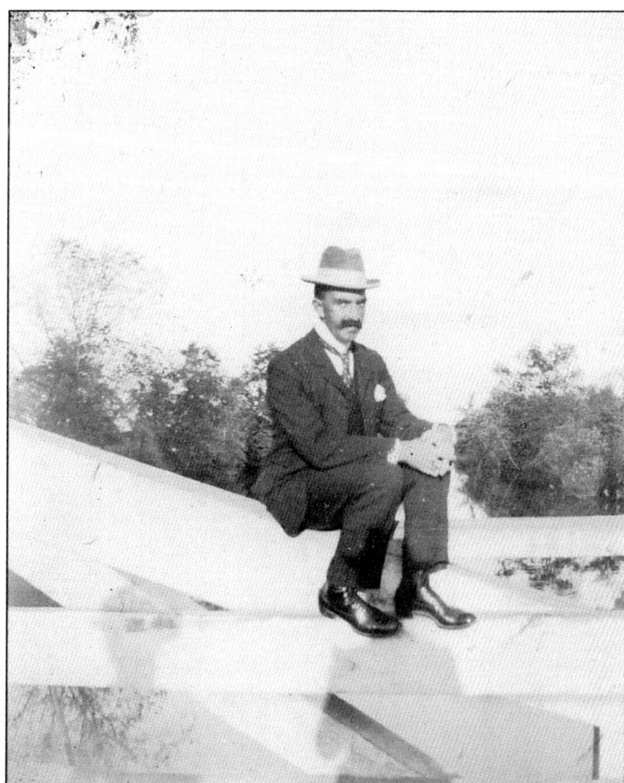

An Unidentified Man Posing on the "Old Bridge." The shadow of the photographer is visible on the bridge. (Collection of Mark Nonestied.)

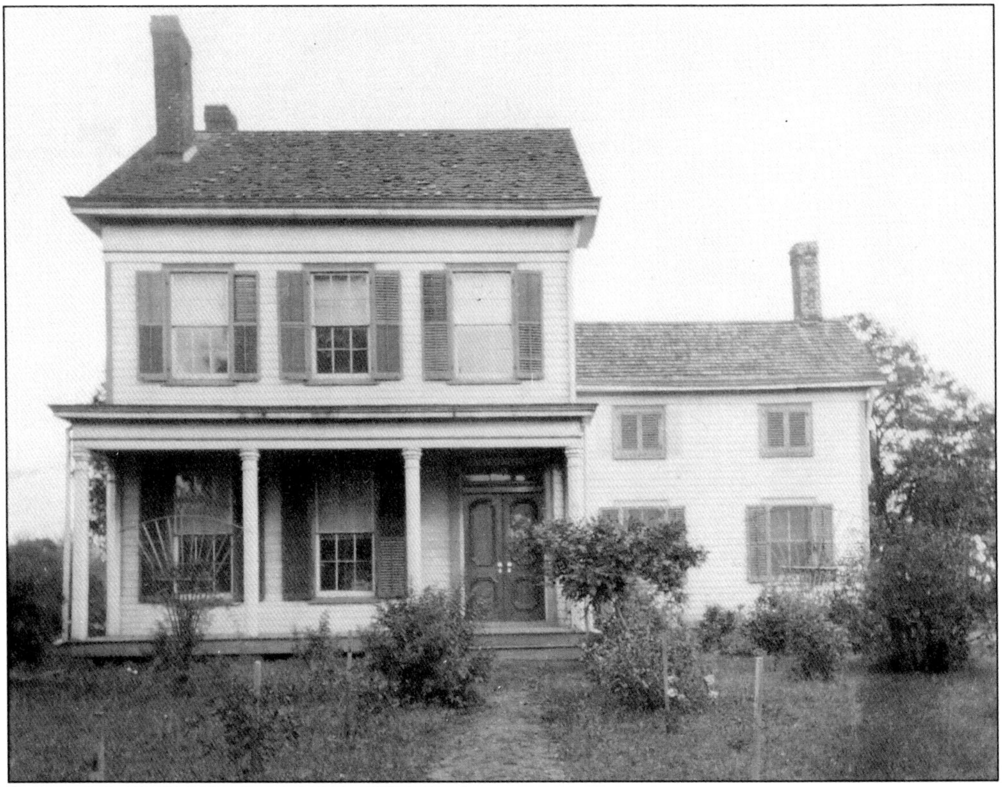

LONE PINE FARM, C. 1900. The farm was located where East Brunswick High School is today. The farmhouse was originally built in the early 1830s. (Collection of East Brunswick Museum.)

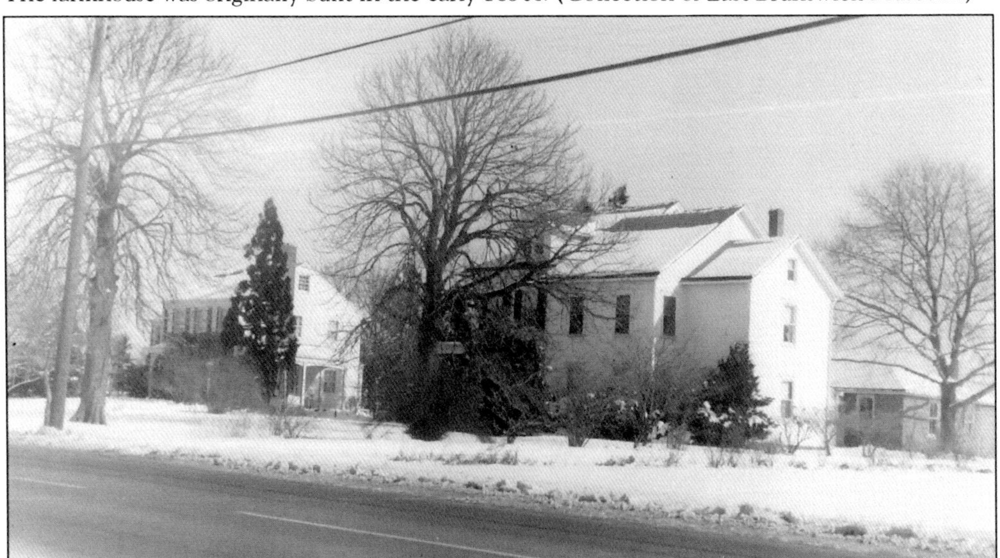

LONE PINE FARM, C. 1960. Today the old farmhouse on 350 Cranbury Road (shown above) looks more like this. The lower section of the house was enlarged. The building to the left of the photograph was built in 1937, and is the home of Grace Auer. (Collection of East Brunswick Museum.)

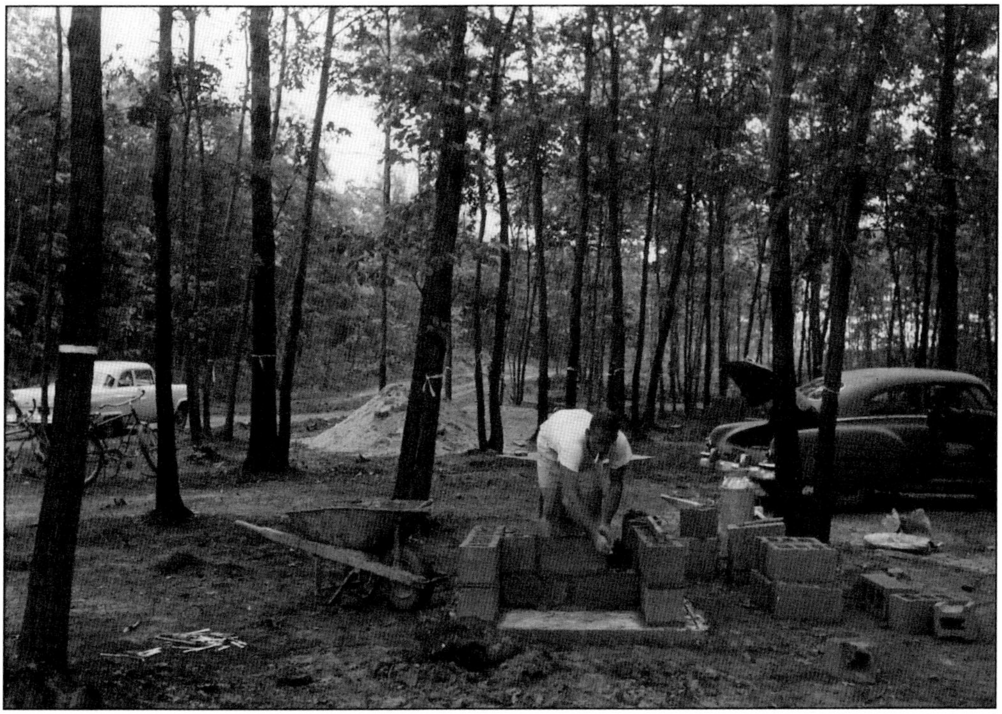

WELSH PARK, C. 1955. A mason is shown here constructing a fire pit. Many volunteers helped with the construction of Birch Hill Park, which was later renamed Welsh Park. (Collection of East Brunswick Museum.)

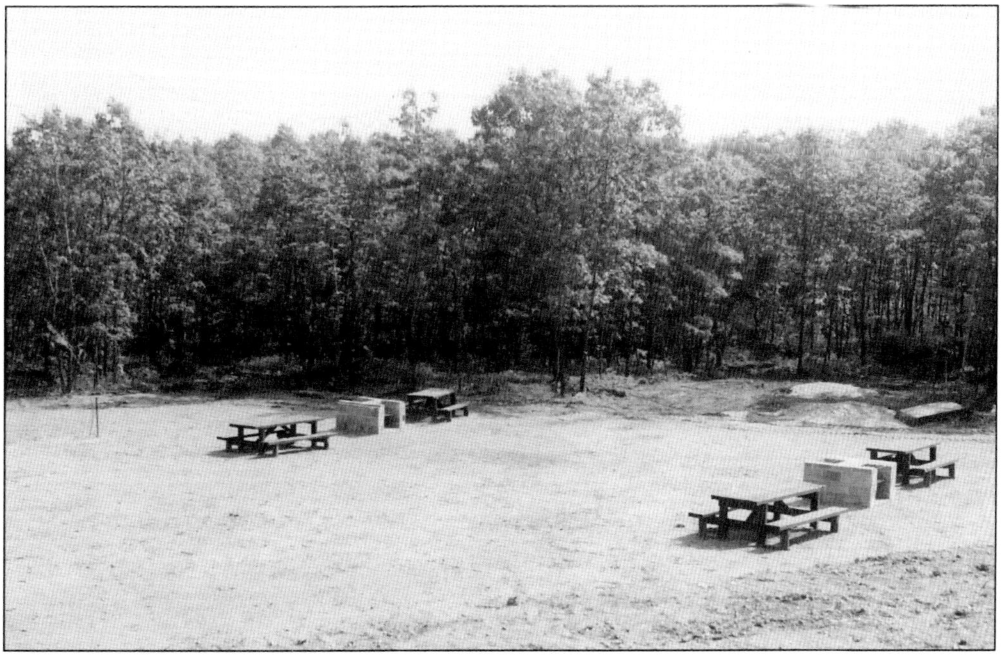

WELSH PARK, C. 1955. With the facilities nearing completion, the park was almost ready for the masses of people that were moving to East Brunswick in the 1950s and 1960s. (Collection of East Brunswick Museum.)

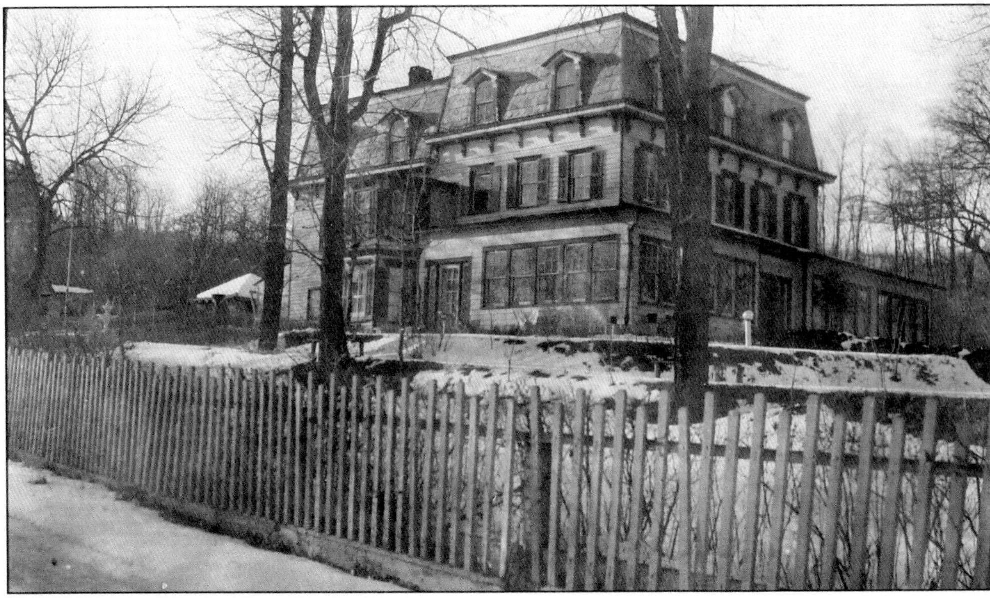

Villa Eugenie, c. 1950. This photograph shows the old Home Boarding School as a resort hotel, prior to a devastating fire in 1954. (Collection of Alberta Yuhas.)

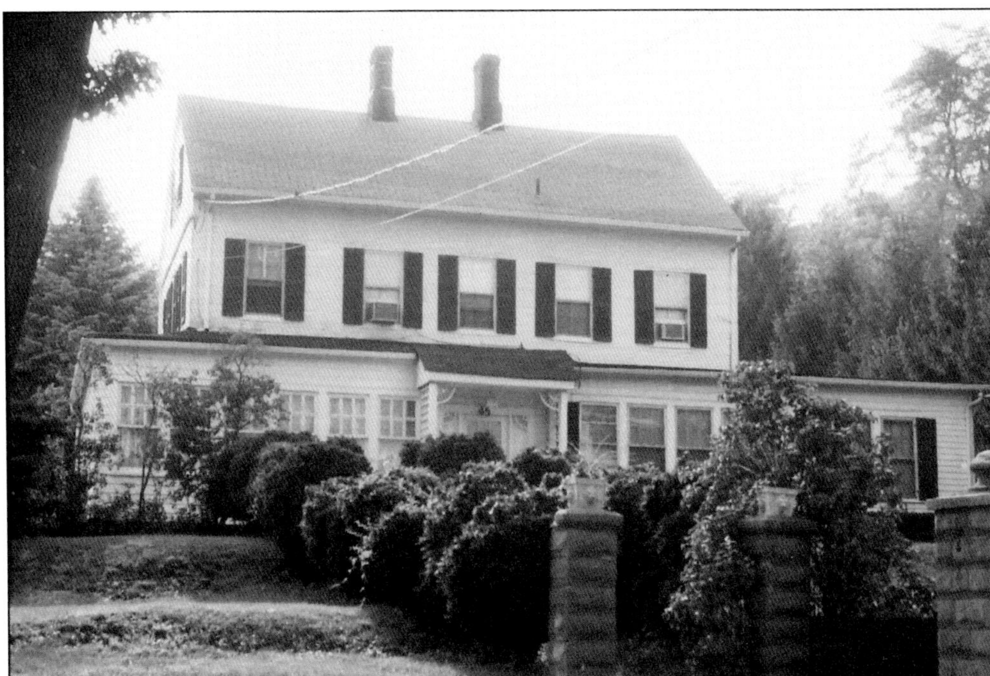

A Modern View of the Old Home Boarding School, Located on River Road in the Township's Historic District. The Mansard roof was removed after a fire destroyed the upper level in 1954. (Photograph by Christine Arciszewski.)

THE OLD PORCH COMES DOWN, C. 1955. John Yuhas took down the old porch on his 27 Kossman Street home. (Collection of Alberta Yuhas.)

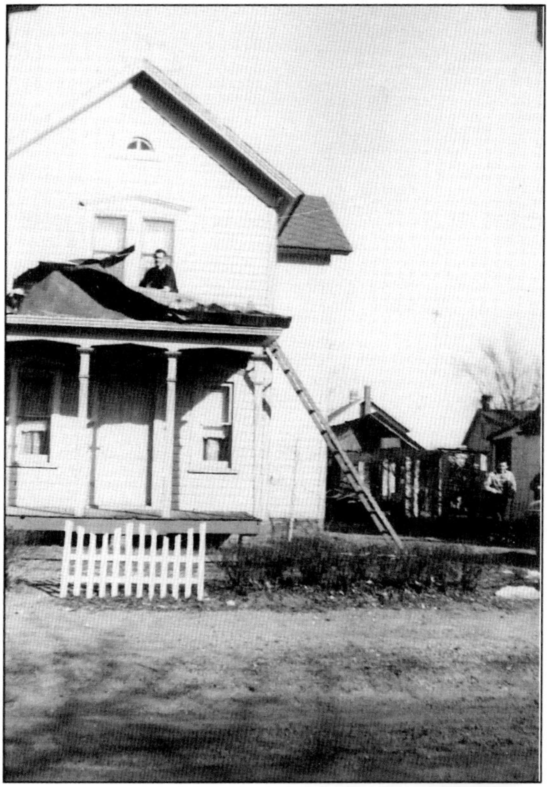

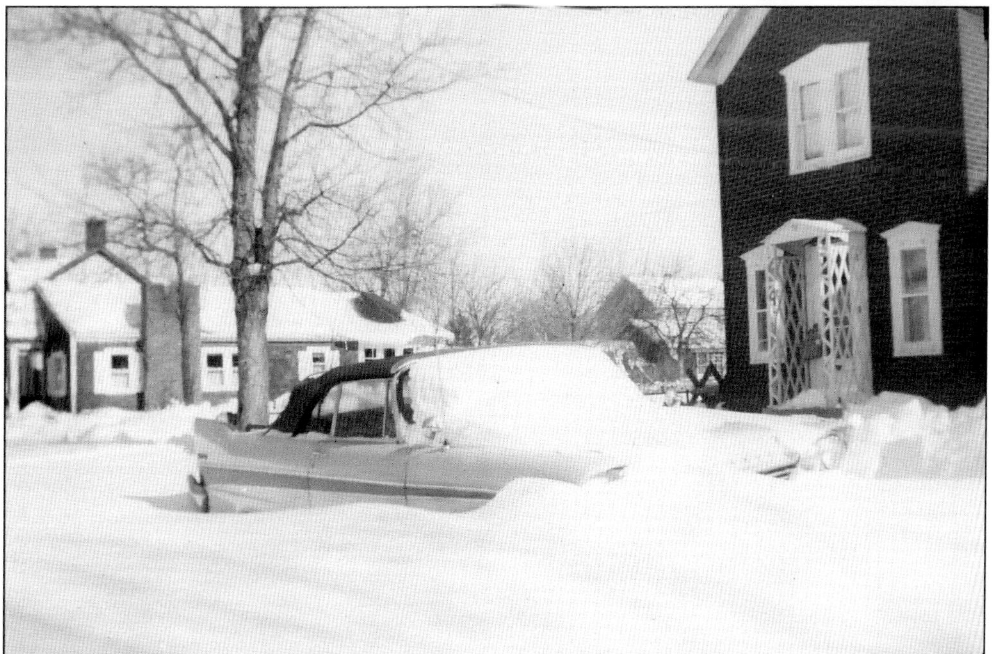

THE YUHAS HOME, SHORTLY AFTER NEW SIDING WAS INSTALLED. The home looks remarkably similar today to the way it does in this photograph. A large window has since replaced the door. (Collection of Alberta Yuhas.)

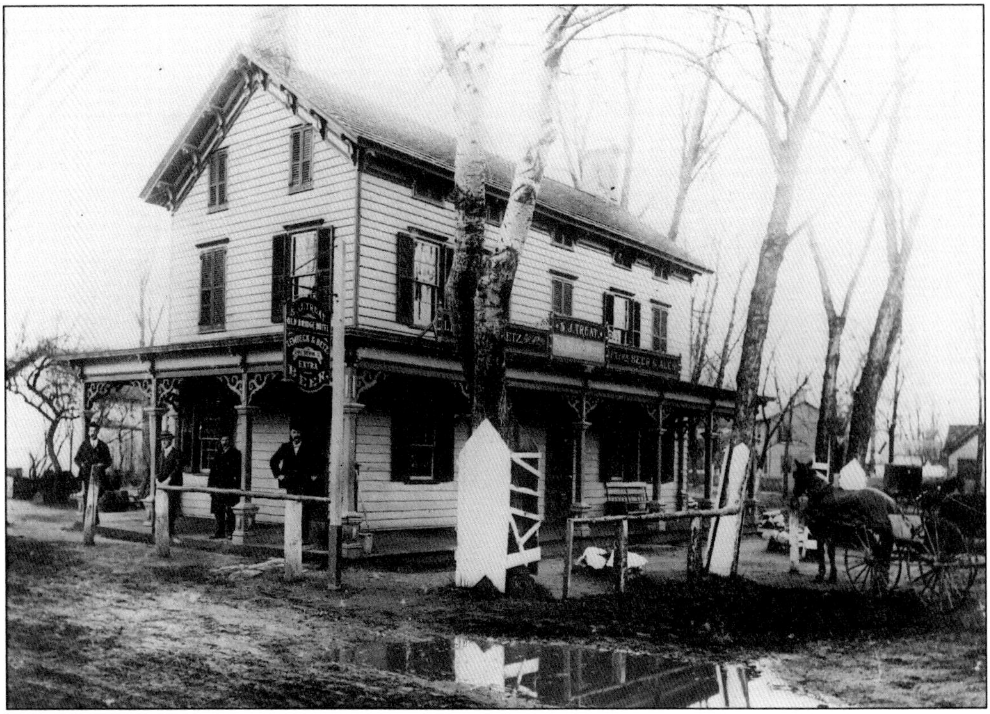

THE OLD BRIDGE HOTEL, C. 1910. The Treat family operated this hotel around 1910. Boards were placed around the trees to prevent the trees from being killed by horses pulling the bark off with their teeth. (Collection of East Brunswick Museum.)

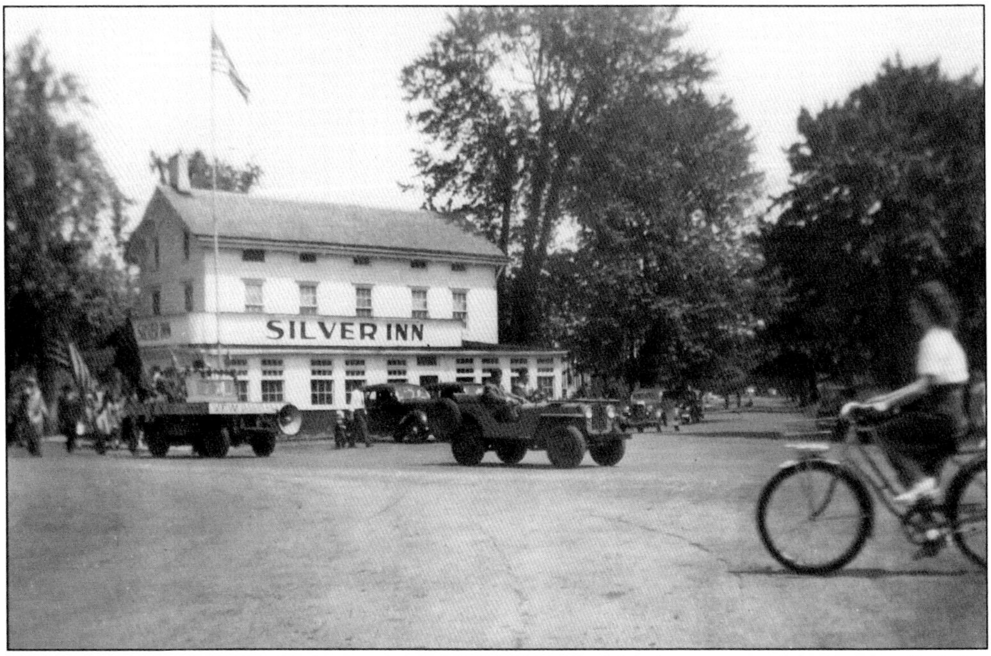

THE SILVER INN, 1937. In later years, the Old Bridge Hotel was remodeled and called the Silver Inn. It was finally burned down in the 1950s as a practice drill by the local fire company. (Collection of East Brunswick Museum.)

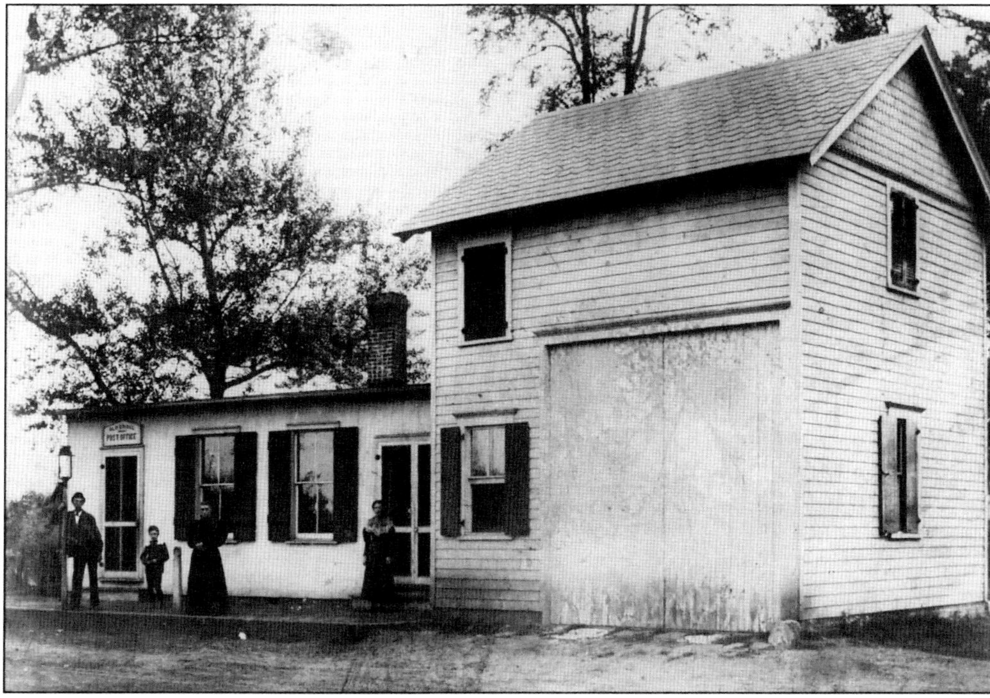

THE WEIGH STATION, C. 1880. The weigh station was located on the corner of the Old Bridge Turnpike and Main Street. The large door would open up to allow wagons with produce inside. Once inside, a scale would weigh the wagon and produce prior to shipment by boat or train. (Collection of East Brunswick Museum.)

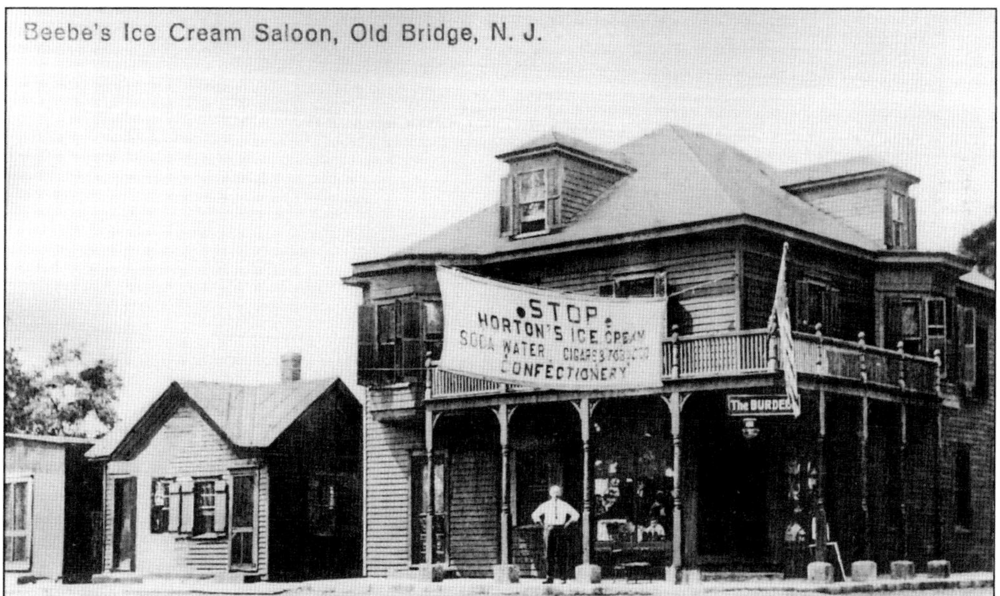

BEEBE'S ICE CREAM SALOON. Around 1900 the old weigh station became Beebe's Ice Cream Saloon. Ice cream was shipped to the store by train. The building still stands today on the corner of the Old Bridge Turnpike and Main Street. Today it is used as a barbershop. (Collection of East Brunswick Museum.)

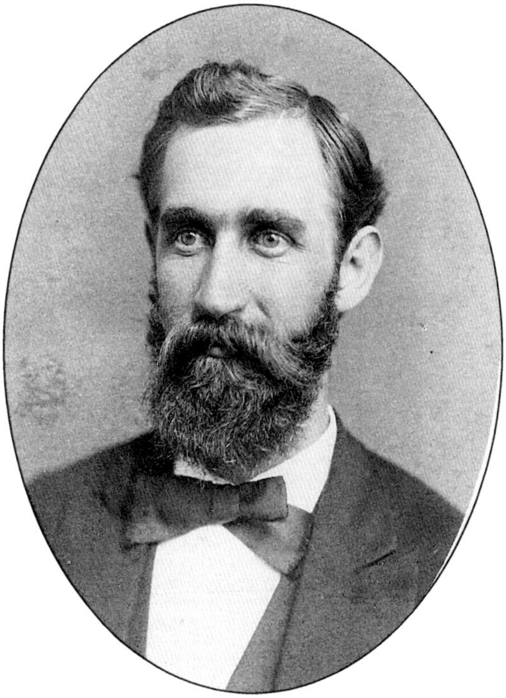 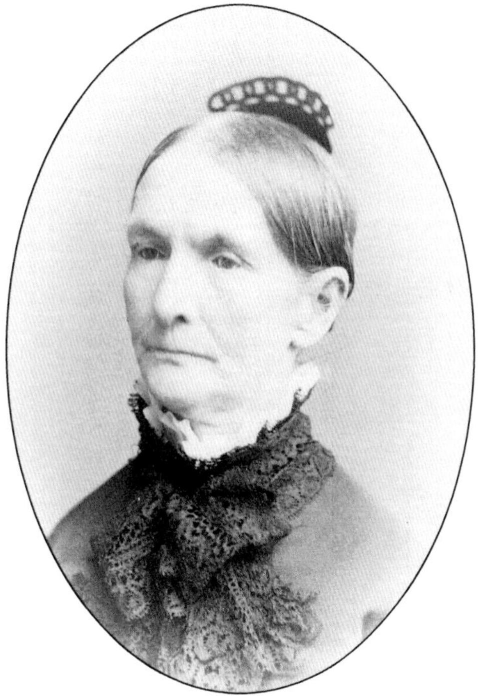

WILLIAM ROGERS AND ADALINE SHOWERS, C. 1880. William Rogers was a local sea captain who lived in the Old Bridge Section of East Brunswick. He sailed between docks along the South River to markets in New York City. He married Adaline in 1834. They both lived long, somewhat hard lives and died in the 1890s. They are buried on the top of Chestnut Hill Cemetery in a grave the overlooks the section of town where they lived and worked for so many years. (Collection of Mark Nonestied.)

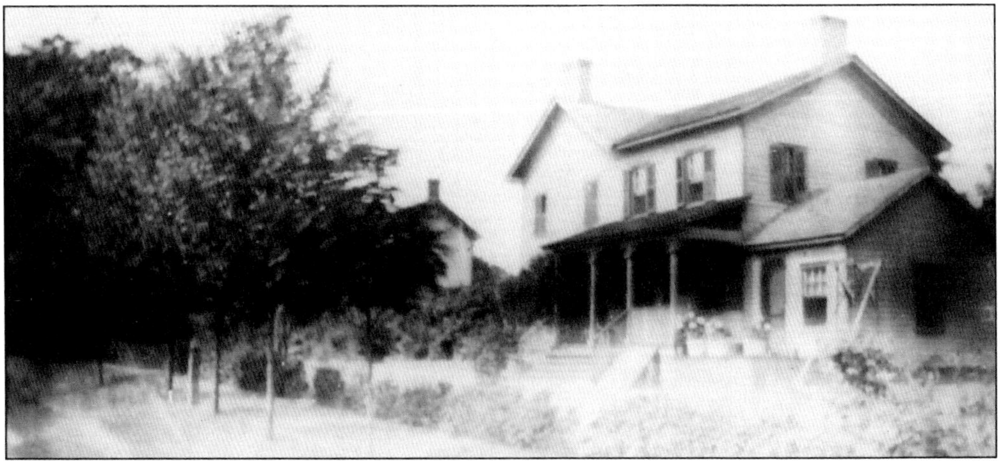

THE ROGERS HOUSE AT 26 MAPLE STREET IN THE OLD BRIDGE SECTION, NOW THE TOWNSHIP'S HISTORIC DISTRICT, C. 1900. Today this home is undergoing an extensive restoration project by its new owners. In our fast-paced society it is important for us not to forget our past. The foundations of our current society were built by previous generations. Some reminders of these generations, like the Rogers house, have survived through the years. We must preserve these testaments to the "glory of the good old days" as a gift for future generations. (Collection of Mark Nonestied.)